RENAISSANCE

PAINTING

IN

MANUSCRIPTS

Edited by Thomas Kren

Catalogue and Essays by

JANET BACKHOUSE

MARK EVANS

THOMAS KREN

MYRA ORTH

with an Introduction by
D. H. Turner

Copublished by
THE J. PAUL GETTY MUSEUM
in Association with
THE BRITISH LIBRARY

RENAISSANCE

PAINTING

IN

MANUSCRIPTS

TREASURES FROM
THE BRITISH LIBRARY

Hudson Hills Press

NEW YORK

First Edition
© 1983 THE J. PAUL GETTY MUSEUM.
ILLUSTRATIONS © 1983 THE BRITISH LIBRARY BOARD.

*Published in the United States by Hudson Hills Press, Inc., Suite 301,
220 Fifth Avenue, New York, NY 10001.*
*Published in the United Kingdom by The British Library, Reference Division
Publications, Great Russell Street, London WC1B 3DG.*
Distributed in the United States by Viking Penguin Inc.
*Distributed in Eire, Europe, Israel, the Middle East, and South Africa
by Phaidon Press Limited.*
*Distributed in Australia, New Zealand, Papua New Guinea, and Fiji by
Australia and New Zealand Book Co. Pty. Limited.*

Renaissance Painting in Manuscripts: Treasures from the British Library is published in
conjunction with an exhibition held at

THE J. PAUL GETTY MUSEUM   OCTOBER 6, 1983–JANUARY 8, 1984
THE PIERPONT MORGAN LIBRARY   JANUARY 20–APRIL 29, 1984
THE BRITISH LIBRARY   MAY 25–SEPTEMBER 30, 1984

This exhibition is supported by an indemnity from the Federal Council on the Arts
and the Humanities.

EDITOR AND PUBLISHER: *Paul Anbinder*
COPY EDITORS: *Sheila Schwartz, Irene Gordon*
DESIGNER: *Betty Binns Graphics*
COMPOSITION: *A & S Graphics, Inc.*
Manufactured in Japan by Toppan Printing Co.

Library of Congress Cataloguing in Publication Data
Main entry under title:
Renaissance painting in manuscripts.

   Catalogue of the British Library loan exhibition
of Renaissance illuminated manuscripts, at the Getty
Museum and the Pierpont Morgan Library in 1983–1984.
   Bibliography: p.
   Includes index.
   1. Illumination of books and manuscripts, Renaissance
—Exhibitions. 2. British Library—Exhibitions.
I. Kren, Thomas, 1950–   . II. Backhouse, Janet.
III. British Library. IV. J. Paul Getty Museum.
V. Pierpont Morgan Library.
ND2990.R46 1983   745.6'7'09407401471   83-12591

ISBN 0-933920-51-2

British Library Cataloguing in Publication Data
Renaissance painting in manuscripts.

   1. Illumination of books and manuscripts, European
   —Catalogues
   I. Kren, Thomas
   745.6'7'094   ND3125

ISBN 0-7123-0024-4

Contents

FRENCH MANUSCRIPT ILLUMINATION   1450–1530
by Janet Backhouse

Foreword

THE British Library is one of the great national collections of manuscript illumination. For more than two centuries the British Museum, from which the British Library was created a decade ago, has collected manuscripts that cover the history of European illumination. While its vast number of important illuminated manuscripts is kept in the Department of Manuscripts, its splendid Grenville Library gallery, noted for the range and quality of its exhibits, offers visitors examples from major areas and from diverse epochs.

The selection focuses on a single period in the history of manuscript illumination, 1450 to 1560, and its three major schools, Flemish, Italian, and French. The British Library has extraordinary strength in this period and its trustees have been magnanimous with their loans. Most of the leading illuminators of the era are represented: Jean Fouquet, Jean Perréal, Simon Marmion, Simon Bening, Attavante degli Attavanti, Matteo da Milano, Amico Aspertini, and Giovan Pietro Birago. A unique signed miniature by the Italian painter Pietro Perugino is included, as well as some of the finest examples of the rare miniatures attributed to the Bruges painter Gerard David. As a result, we have before us a history of the three major schools of illumination as represented by a number of their greatest monuments. The quality and importance of these manuscripts reveal the perspicacity of the British bibliophiles whose extraordinary achievement in collecting we are glad to honor.

The J. Paul Getty Museum and the Pierpont Morgan Library thank the trustees and staff of the British Library and especially Derek H. Turner, Deputy Keeper and Head of Exhibitions in the Department of Manuscripts at the British Library, for sharing their treasures with the American public. They extend their gratitude to the Federal Council on the Arts and the Humanities for the indemnity that has supported the exhibition. Special thanks are owed Thomas Kren, Associate Curator of Paintings at the Getty Museum, for organizing the exhibition and supervising the catalogue, as well as the other contributors, Janet Backhouse, Mark Evans, and Myra Orth.

JOHN WALSH, JR.
Director
The J. Paul Getty Museum

CHARLES RYSKAMP
Director
The Pierpont Morgan Library

London • • Bruges • Ghent
• Antwerp
Tournai • • Malines
Brussels •

• Rouen Valenciennes

Paris •

SEINE RIVER

Fontainebleau •

Orléans •

LOIRE RIVER

Tours •

Bourges •

• Lyons

• Budapest

Milan • • Padua • Venice

Mantua •

Bologna • • Ferrara

Florence • • Pesaro
• Urbino

Perugia •

• Valladolid

• Rome

• Toledo

• Naples

Lisbon •

N

0 100 200 300 400 500 km

Centers of Illumination
and Patronage

0 100 200 300 400 500 miles

Introduction

In the spring of 1981 the J. Paul Getty Museum approached the British Library to see if there might be a possibility of the Library's lending a selection of illuminated manuscripts for exhibition. The idea was for a special demonstration on American soil of the British Library's function as a museum of the book. This seemed very attractive, but it was early realized that it would be more effective if the demonstration took place on the east coast of the United States as well as on the west. The Pierpont Morgan Library was therefore invited to join the discussions as a venue for an eastern showing. Subsequently the British Library decided that the exercise would be best completed by a showing of the exhibition in our own exhibition galleries in the British Museum buildings in London.

The British Library is a young institution in years but a mature one in body. In 1972 an act of Parliament established "a national library for the United Kingdom . . . incorporating the Library of the British Museum." This national library was to be known as "the British Library" and it was to consist of a comprehensive collection of books, manuscripts, periodicals, films, and other recorded matter, whether printed or otherwise. The British Library began to operate on July 1, 1973, when it was constituted by, besides the British Museum Library (including the Science Reference Library), the National Central Library and the National Lending Library for Science and Technology. In August 1974 a private company, British National Bibliography Ltd., was incorporated into the British Library, and on April 1, 1982, the India Office Library and Records became part of the British Library. Exactly a year later the British Institute of Recorded Sound likewise joined the British Library.

The British Library has three main operating divisions. The former British National Bibliography Ltd., together with the former British Museum Copyright Office, provides the nucleus for the Bibliographic Services Division. The former National Lending Library for Science and Technology and the former National Central Library make up the Lending Division. The former British Museum Library, together with the former India Office Library and Records, forms the Reference Division.

The British Museum Library goes back to the foundation of the British Museum in 1753. In that year an act of Parliament created a trust "for purchasing the Museum or Collection of Sir Hans Sloane, and of the Harleian Collection of Manuscripts and for providing one general Repository for the better Reception and more convenient use of the said Collections and of the Cottonian Library, and of the Additions thereto." The nascent British Museum was financed by a public lottery, the first and last ever held in England, and to house it was purchased Montagu House, in Great Russell Street, "in the Parish of Saint George, Bloomsbury." Buckingham House (now Palace) was considered, but rejected as too expensive and not as well situated. In 1757 King George II gave the Museum the Royal Library of the sovereigns of England. In the beginning the British Museum was first a library, secondly a natural history collection, and only slightly a repository of antiquities. The Sloane Library, the Harleian Library, the Cottonian Library, and the Royal Library were the "Foundation collections," and the richness and variety of their contents won for the British Museum, and now for the British Library, a pre-eminent place among the libraries of the world.

Sir Hans Sloane (1660–1753), whose fondness for curiosities was to lead to the foundation of the British Museum, was a fashionable physician largely responsible for popularizing milk chocolate and smallpox inoculation in England. The books he owned, both manuscript and printed, were universal in their subject matter, without any outstanding items among them, although they included a proportion of important scientific and medical material. The Royal Library of England was in effect begun by King Edward IV (1461–83), inspired apparently by the example of the bibliophile Louis of Gruuthuse, a Burgundian statesman who entertained Edward in exile in 1470–71. It is notable for the manuscript books in it, in particular, the Codex Alexandrinus and the Queen Mary Psalter. This fifth-century codex in Greek, one of the three earliest and most important manuscripts of the Bible as a whole, was presented to King Charles I of England in 1627 by Cyril Lucaris, Patriarch of Constantinople, who had previously been Patriarch of Alexandria. The fourteenth-century Queen Mary Psalter, of English origin, is one of the finest illuminated manuscripts in existence. It was seized at the customs when about to be exported from England in 1553 and sent to Queen Mary I. There are two Royal manuscripts in the present exhibition, one of them, Royal Ms. 12 C VIII (Cat. 17), being a volume commissioned in Italy for presentation to Henry VIII of England by Geoffrey Chamber, one of his gentlemen.

The Cottonian and Harleian libraries comprised almost entirely manuscripts. The Cottonian collection was formed by the antiquary Sir Robert Cotton (1571–1631), who set himself the task of gathering and preserving the records of English literature and history dispersed at the dissolution of the monasteries in England at the Reformation. He managed to secure some exceptional examples of manuscript illumination, such as the Lindisfarne Gospels, which was made in the northeast of England toward the end of the seventh century, and—for he did not confine his interests to things English—the Cotton Genesis, made probably in Egypt, at Alexandria, in the sixth century. The Cotton Genesis was badly damaged by fire in 1731.

The Harley manuscripts are so-called after the father and son, Robert and Edward Harley, earls of Oxford, who collected them. Robert, the father (1661–1724), was some-time First Minister of England. Of his son, Edward (1689–1741), it has been said "habitual indolence, rather than incapacity, prevented him from taking part in public affairs." The Harleys were the first English collectors of books to seek systematically for material from outside England, and they were omnivorous in their interests. Of illuminated manuscripts they acquired such treasures as, of English origin, the Ramsey Psalter, probably executed for St. Oswald, bishop of Worcester and archbishop of York (d. 992), and, of continental origin, the Harley Golden Gospels, made at the court of Emperor Charlemagne circa 800. The present exhibition shows four Harley manuscripts. They include Harley Ms. 6205 (Cat. 24), *Les Commentaires de la guerre gallique*, with miniatures by Godefroy le Batave, which was made for presentation to King Francis I of France in 1519, and Harley Ms. 4425 (Cat. 6), a splendid example of the *Roman de la Rose,* which belonged to Count Engelbert II of Nassau (d. 1504), some-time governor of the Netherlands.

The British Museum Act of 1753 envisaged additions to the original collections. The position of the British Museum Library, and now of the British Library, as the leading library in the British Isles was secured by its privilege of copyright deposit, and the Library has always been conscientious and far-seeking in the purchase of foreign books. Manuscripts, British and foreign, have come to the Library from British and foreign sources, by gift and purchase, to the extent that the British Library's holdings now number some 121,000 manuscript volumes, of which some 38,000 are classed as Oriental and some 83,000 as Western. The most important body of manuscripts bequeathed to the Library has been the forty-six splendid illuminated manuscripts from the incomparable collection of Henry Yates Thompson, which the executors of his widow gave in 1941, in furtherance of her wishes. Together with five other manuscripts which had been in Yates Thompson's possession, they have been named after him, and two of them are going to Malibu and New York. One of these, Yates Thompson Ms. 29 (Cat. 16), contains a miniature signed by Perugino himself. The volume, a book of hours, apparently intended for Bonaparte Ghislieri of Bologna (d. 1541), was written by Pierantonio Sallando and also has illuminations by Matteo da Milano and Amico Aspertini.

Most manuscripts that have entered the British Museum Library since 1753 have been cloaked under the anonymous appellation of "Additional." Theoretically they are additions to the Sloane collection. There are other generic names in use, however, applied to specific collections which the Library has acquired. Among these are the Lansdowne Manuscripts, which include vital papers of Queen Elizabeth I's minister William Cecil; the Egerton Manuscripts, bequeathed with funds for addition to their number—and the British Library still purchases manuscripts which it calls "Egerton," although the monies available for this purpose are not worth so much as they were originally, in the early nineteenth century—the Arundel Manuscripts, the jewel of which is a notebook of Leonardo da Vinci; and the Stowe Manuscripts, one of which is in the present exhibition. It is Stowe Ms. 955 (Cat. 22), a charming volume of love poems addressed by Pierre Sala to Marguerite Bullioud. Additional Manuscripts are by no means poor relations of the others in the British Library. The fourth-century manuscript of the Bible in Greek, the Codex Sinaiticus, and the magnificently illuminated Benedictional of St. Ethelwold, made for the bishop of Winchester of that name who died in 984, are numbered as Additional Manuscripts, and a glance at the list of items in the present exhibition reveals that over half of them are Additional Manuscripts.

The British Museum before 1973 was a unique hybrid in being both a national museum and a national library. This could and did cause tensions, but the British Library has its own schizophrenia. We have to remember that we are still a museum. While all writings convey information, a proportion of them are as much, if not more, works of art and/or historical relics as they are works of reference. The high regard in which knowledge was held in less literate ages, the sacred character with which it was often invested as the utterance of a divine being and his servants, the mystique of the word, all this led to the embellishment and illustration of texts, to the art known as illumination. Already during the Middle Kingdom of Egypt (c. 2150–1775 B.C.) the existence of finely written and illustrated copies of the Book of the Dead can be inferred, and Chinese culture has ever been associated with calligraphy. There are those who regard painting as but a branch of calligraphy. In medieval Western Europe manuscript illumination was the chief expression of painting.

The proliferation of printing caused books to become more utilitarian and resulted in the decline of illumination. It is now an unfamiliar form of art, regarded as "medieval" and "specialist." Those of us who are responsible for museums of the book have always to bear in mind that our public requires an introduction to illumination, not least because it does particularly belong to medieval Europe, when art was abstract rather than representational and primarily religious. Future generations, freed from the straitjacket of classicism, may be able to appreciate medieval art more readily, but in the 1980s there is still, in Western civilization, lingering preference for representational art. Despite Einstein and nuclear physics, we are still the children of the Renaissance, which exalted naturalism, exalted it indeed to the point of denaturalizing it.

Manuscript illumination had important manifestations during the period of the Renaissance, the fifteenth and sixteenth centuries, and it is Renaissance illumination which provides the best introduction to manuscript illumination and upon which it was accordingly decided to concentrate for the present exhibition. The fifteenth and sixteenth centuries are the limit of Western man's folk memory. He finds them attractive as being a time of youth and color, of freshness, even of innocence. They were a time of expansion and exploration for Europe, of recovery of ancient knowledge and criticism of established order. In 1492 Columbus sighted San Salvador. In 1517 Luther nailed his theses to the church door in Wittenberg.

Illuminated manuscripts of the Renaissance are a suit in which the British Library has the good fortune to be strong. However, illumination did not flourish in England after 1450, so the exhibition before us has developed into one of treasures from the British Library which includes nothing of British origin. Nevertheless, the advantages of a display of Renaissance illumination seemed such that this should be proceeded with even if Britain herself could not be represented. In the Romanesque period (c. 1080–1220) English painting had been as good as any, and in the early Gothic period (c. 1220–1280) it was second to none. Renaissance illumination has three main avatars, Flemish, French, and Italian. The present exhibition has been divided into these three "nations," and the period being covered is from the middle of the fifteenth century to the middle of the sixteenth. In 1453 Constantinople fell to the Turks, and in 1558 the Holy Roman Emperor Charles V abdicated. These dates, and the events between them, mark the end of the medieval ideal of a Christian civilization, an empire of Christ on earth.

Charles V himself appears in our exhibition as the subject of one of its items, Additional Ms. 33733, the *Triumphs of Charles V* (Cat. 18), which may well have been executed for his son King Philip II of Spain. Charles' Spanish mother and grandmother are both represented. There is a book of hours, Additional Ms. 18852 (Cat. 7), made in Flanders for his mother, Joanna the Mad, Queen of Castile (1504–1555), while the breviary, Additional Ms. 18851 (Cat. 5), was a present to Joanna's mother, Isabella the Catholic, Queen of Castile (1474–1504), from her ambassador Francisco de Rojas, who negotiated the marriage of Joanna to Philip I (the Handsome), the heir to the Netherlands. From this marriage resulted the Hapsburg empire which embraced Germany-Austria, the Netherlands, Spain, and parts of Italy and had at its disposal the riches of Spanish America. It was the greatest power in Renaissance Europe. Philip the Handsome's sister, Margaret of Austria, had married Joanna's brother Juan. Later, twice widowed, she was to be the guardian of her nephew, the future Charles V, and Regent of the Netherlands from 1507 to 1530. Into her hands came an incomplete book of hours, Additional Ms. 34294 (Cat. 15), which the priest Giovan Pietro Birago had illuminated circa 1490 for Bona Sforza, dowager duchess of Milan. Margaret had sixteen minia-

tures added to the manuscript by her Flemish painter Gerard Horenbout. There are four of the Italian miniatures from the Sforza Hours in the exhibition and four of the Flemish. One of the Flemish miniatures shows the *Visitation* (Fig. 15g), in which St. Elizabeth is a probable likeness of Margaret of Austria.

Flanders, with its twin capital cities of Bruges and Ghent, where so much of the best Renaissance manuscript illumination was done, had belonged to the dukes of Burgundy, who had created in their domains a brilliant, late medieval culture which can be described in celluloid terms by the word *Camelot*. The last duke of Burgundy was Charles the Bold (killed in battle in 1477), who was the grandfather of Philip the Handsome and Margaret of Austria. An item in the exhibition, Additional Ms. 36619 (Cat. 1), *Ordonnance pour les gens de guerre* (Ordinance of Charles the Bold), was made for him for promulgation at Trier in 1473, where he was hoping to be made king of Burgundy by Emperor Frederick III. His ambitions were balked, because the emperor left Trier secretly during the night before the day fixed for the investiture of regality.

The greatest of the Flemish book painters was Simon Bening. He was born at Ghent in the last third of the fifteenth century, his father, Alexander, being also an illuminator and his mother being a relative of Hugo van der Goes. Simon was made a freeman of the guild of illuminators and booksellers at Bruges in 1508. He was dean of the guild in 1524, 1536, and 1546, and was established at Bruges from 1516 until his death in 1561. Simon Bening was twice married, and among his five daughters by his first wife, Katharine Stroo, was Lievine, who was also distinguished as a miniaturist. She was invited to England by King Henry VIII and afterward was much esteemed by his daughters Queen Mary I and Queen Elizabeth I. Of Simon Bening, the Portuguese artist Francisco de Hollanda said that he was a most excellent colorist and expert at trees and distances.

Two items in the present exhibition are connected with Simon Bening. There are two leaves with representations on either side of seasonal scenes, Additional Ms. 18855, fols. 108–109v (Cat. 10), and there is the Portuguese Genealogy, Additional Ms. 12531 (Cat. 9). This consists of thirteen leaves intended to comprise an illustrated descent of the kings of Portugal from Magog, grandson of Noah. It was undertaken for the Infante Dom Fernando, the third son of King Manuel I of Portugal and Maria, a sister of Joanna of Castile and daughter of Isabella of Castile. It is unfinished, apparently because of the Infante Dom Fernando's death in 1534. The genealogy was designed by Antonio de Hollanda, the father of Francisco, in Portugal, and the cartoons were to be sent to Simon Bening in Flanders for illumination. The whole work was expected to be complete in two years. Unfortunately things did not go according to schedule. The Infante Dom Fernando, who was an impatient person, tried to hurry the work along too much and it became unsystematic. The Infante seems to have been less hasty with his payments, for five years after the Infante's death Antonio de Hollanda was trying to get money for his share in illustrating the leaves, including both illuminating and drawing.

The thirteen leaves of the Portuguese Genealogy are kept separately, so all can be displayed in the present exhibition. Presumably all their designs are by Antonio de Hollanda, and he may be credited with all the illumination of the first leaf and of the borders of the others, except for the second and the third. The thirteenth is uncolored. The painting on the second and third leaves seems to be entirely by Bening.

On them and in the central panels of the fourth to twelfth leaves and in the calendar miniatures from Additional Ms. 18855 can be seen Renaissance illumination at its best. In Simon Bening's hands representational miniature painting is not self-consciously miniature. When we look at his scenes and figures we do not immediately regard them as a reduction of larger-scale work. They exist as representations in their own right. Simon Bening was the last illuminator to achieve this.

D. H. TURNER
Deputy Keeper
Head of Exhibitions
Department of Manuscripts
The British Library

Preface

THE twenty-four manuscripts and one printed book discussed in this catalogue belong to the glorious era of European illumination that extended from circa 1450 until 1560. The British Library's extraordinary holdings from this period give an overview of the development of manuscript illumination and indicate in broad terms the heights of artistic achievement in three major geographical regions where Renaissance illumination flourished: the Flemish territories (present-day Belgium), France, and Italy.

The British Library's manuscripts from the last great epoch of Flemish illumination, circa 1475–1550, are justifiably renowned. The British Library owns superb examples of most of the major illuminators active after 1470, including probably the world's largest holdings of the work of Simon Bening (Cats. 9, 10), and nearly all are represented here. The manuscripts include such treasures as the famous *Roman de la Rose* owned by Engelbert of Nassau (Cat. 6), the Breviary of Queen Isabella of Castile (Cat. 5), and the Genealogy of the Infante Dom Fernando of Portugal (commonly called the "Portuguese Genealogy," Cat. 9).

For Italian illumination, where regional schools show divergent trends, the selection represents the most important artistic styles and centers represented in the British Library, including Milan, Florence, Naples, and Bologna. Brilliant examples by Giovan Pietro Birago (Cats. 14, 15), Amico Aspertini (Cat. 16), and Attavante degli Attavanti (Cat. 17) are represented, along with beautiful examples of humanist calligraphy by Bartolommeo Sanvito (Cat. 13) and Pier Antonio Sallando (Cat. 16). Unfortunately, owing to the fragility of the binding, the beautiful De Rothesay Hours by Giulio Clovio could not be lent. As the manuscripts represented in this exhibition were all executed after the invention of movable type—Gutenberg published his first Bible in Mainz in 1455—an example of a deluxe illuminated printed book, Giovanni Simonetta's *Sforziada*, with a frontispiece illuminated by Birago, has been lent through the good offices of the British Library's Department of Printed Books (Cat. 14). The *Sforziada* shows how early book publishers sought to imitate the luxurious effects of fine illuminated manuscripts.

For French illumination, fine examples connected with such leading figures as Fouquet (Cat. 19), Colombe (Cat. 20), Bourdichon (Cat. 21), and Perréal (Cat. 22) have been included. Here the selection represents as far as possible the major artists from about 1450 until 1530. These include a leaf from the Hours of Etienne Chevalier (Cat. 19) and several leaves from the so-called "Hours of Henry VII" (Cat. 21).

Recent scholarship has opened up many new approaches to the study of illuminated manuscripts. The renewed interest in the period under review here is reflected in the work of the contributors to this project, each of whom was encouraged to apply his or her own methodology. The twofold intent of the catalogue—to discuss the literature on the manuscripts and, where possible, include new material—has been designed to introduce a wide audience to the delights of manuscript illumination and to inspire further study. Many of the miniatures published here have not previously been reproduced in color; some have never been reproduced at all.

The organization of the present exhibition has required the support, patience, and active participation of many. We are beholden above all to the British Library, to its trustees, to its Director, Alexander Wilson, and to Daniel Whalley, Keeper of Manuscripts. It was Derek H. Turner, Deputy Keeper and Head of Exhibitions, Department of Manuscripts, who first listened sympathetically to the suggestion of a loan exhibition of British Library manuscripts and who has been responsible for making it a reality. We are grateful to him for his unflagging interest in this project and for writing an introduction to the catalogue. Janet Backhouse, who contributed an essay and six catalogue entries (Cats. 18–23), generously shared information about the manuscripts, waded through complicated photographic orders, and saw to it that illustrations and research materials were available on time. To Shelley Jones, Exhibitions Officer, for helping to organize the installation on this side of the Atlantic, and to Mirjam Foot, for the description of bindings contained here, go our sincere thanks. To Robert Fulford, Keeper of the Department of Printed Books, and John Barr, Assistant Keeper, we are indebted for the loan of the *Sforziada* (Cat. 14).

At the J. Paul Getty Trust, the support of Harold Williams. President, made the entire project possible. At the Museum, Otto Wittmann, Chief Curator, encouraged our efforts from the inception of the project; Stephen Rountree, Deputy Director, provided effective counsel and eased our ship through rocky shoals. I am indebted to Burton Fredericksen, Curator of Paintings, for his patience during my absences. The staff of the J. Paul Getty Museum devoted long hours to the realization of this exhibition and its catalogue. Sally Hibbard, Registrar, with the assistance of John Caswell, sorted out matters of insurance, indemnification, and logistics. Throughout the planning and execution of the installation, Bruce Metro, Head of Preparation, advised and assisted us, as did John Ronayne, the designer for the installation at the Getty. In addition, we

xiv Preface

have benefited from the advice of Andrea Rothe, Jeanne McKee, and Barbara Roberts on matters of conservation, of Andrew Blakely on security, and of Jean Keefe and Barbara Brink on matters of publicity.

Sally Bourrie has been the ideal assistant for the organizer of an exhibition. Her limitless energy, resourcefulness, skillful editing, and dogged optimism have helped to get the job done and added an element of fun. Walter O'Neill, Ann Morrissey, and Cathryn LaScola have contributed to the realization of the didactic exhibition. Patrick Dooley designed the brochure and poster, Patricia Inglis assisted with design matters, and Karen Schmidt coordinated production schedules. To all of them go our sincere thanks. George R. Goldner has provided valuable advice; he and his staff in the photo archive, especially Sandra Terner and Rose Lachmann, acquired hundreds of photographs to support our research.

When the plans for the present exhibition were conceived, manuscript illumination lay outside the scope of the museum's collections, and the Getty library contained only a handful of books on the subject. Through the dedication of Anne-Mieke Halbrook, Librarian, and her staff, above all Jennifer Rose and Christine Smith, the foundations for a research library in this area have been established. I am moreover grateful to Ann Morrissey, Jennifer Rose, Barbara Anderson, Hallie Kaymen, and Ellen Konowitz for assistance in obtaining photocopies and loans of urgently required publications.

Director Charles Ryskamp, Curator of Manuscripts John Plummer, Associate Curator William Voelkle, and Registrar David Wright at the Pierpont Morgan Library have enthusiastically supported our efforts and provided welcome assistance and advice.

I would like to offer a special word of thanks to Janet Backhouse, Mark Evans, and Myra Orth for their contributions to this catalogue and the British Library, Walker Art Gallery, and University of Virginia for providing them with the time to complete their work. My colleagues and I want to acknowledge the help of James Marrow, Mary

Robertson, Consuelo Dutschke, Joyce Ludmer, John Rogers, Roger S. Wieck, and William Voelkle in checking references and/or providing research materials. B. H. Breslauer, New York City, has kindly lent four additional leaves that belong to the Hours of Henry VII (Cat. 21).

Many scholars have offered inspiration and contributed to the formulation of our ideas. We remember especially discussions with Otto Pächt, James Marrow, Paola Tosetti-Grandi, Jonathan Alexander, Giulia Bartram, Peter Dreyer, and Michael Kauffmann. For reading drafts of various entries and essays we are indebted to James Marrow, Maryann Ainsworth, Roger Wieck, Gregory Clark, Consuelo Dutschke, Jeffrey Munger, Reinhild Weiss, Shelley Jones, and Derek Turner. Barbara Anderson has provided timely and invaluable service as research assistant, proofreader, and author of the descriptions of the miniatures in catalogue entries 6 and 9. She, Cynthia Hoyt, and Irene Gordon have doggedly pursued the problem of accurate citations in bibliography and footnotes.

George Zarnecki, Eva Irblich, Janet Backhouse, Joanna Cannon, William Voelkle, Charles Parsella, Reinhild Weiss, and especially François Avril deserve thanks for helping us obtain illustrations for this catalogue. For additional photography I am indebted to Donald Hull.

The contributors and I would like to acknowledge the efforts of our typists Kathleen Thorsen, Tory Wilson, Edward Mickle, Lynda Strachen, Nancy King, Diane Biehl, and Sherrie McConnell.

Our publisher Paul Anbinder, our editors Sheila Schwartz and Irene Gordon, and Sandra Knudsen Morgan, Editor at the Getty Museum, valiantly assumed responsibility for a transcontinental production of extraordinary complexity. We are grateful to them for maintaining high standards against continuing pressures to compromise.

Finally, for their personal support of the contributors' work on this project over many months, we thank Jeffrey Munger, Steve Moore, Felipe Cervera, Dennis Dunn, Reinhild Weiss, and Shelley Jones.

THOMAS KREN
Associate Curator of Paintings
The J. Paul Getty Museum

FLEMISH

MANUSCRIPT

ILLUMINATION

1475–1550

THE British Library owns one of the world's finest collections of late Flemish illuminated manuscripts. Acquired mostly by purchase in the mid-nineteenth century, the collection includes some of the most important, rare, and well-documented manuscripts of the late period of Flemish illumination, from circa 1475 to the middle of the sixteenth century.[1] Works by nearly all the leading illuminators or members of their immediate circles are represented. Accordingly, the manuscripts in this section of the exhibition have been chosen to illustrate the major trends and the course of development of these last seventy-five years of Flemish illumination.

The late period commences toward the end of the reign of Duke Charles the Bold of Burgundy (1467–77), son of the brilliant bibliophile and art patron Duke Philip the Good of Burgundy (1396–1467),[2] and extends into the mid-sixteenth century, when Emperor Charles V (1520–58) was sovereign of much of Europe, including the Flemish territories he had inherited from his father in 1506. The leading artists were Simon Marmion, Simon Bening, and the illuminator still known only as the Master of Mary of Burgundy; these three figures rank among the most distinguished illuminators of all time. Circa 1475, a new artistic language, which distinguishes late Flemish illumination from earlier styles, emerged almost simultaneously in both miniature and border (Pls. I, II, III). The miniatures were often inspired directly by the tradition of Flemish panel painting that extends from Jan van Eyck to Hugo van der Goes, and among the main features of the decorated borders are the flowers, acanthus leaves, insects, figures, and other objects set on brightly colored grounds. In particular, the lustrous color and meticulous representation of precious materials in both miniature and border derive from the Flemish panel painters. However the strong influence of panel painting by no means diminished the creativity of the illuminators; on the contrary, manuscript painters were asked to treat a wider variety of subject matter than Flemish painters on panel, and the decoration of a manuscript presented unique artistic problems. As a result the illuminators made a number of original contributions to the development of Flemish naturalism, for example, in the illusionism of the decorative border, in the depiction of landscape, and in narrative. Most of these developments can be found in the private devotional book known as the book of hours (Cats. 3, 4, 7, 8, 15). Small in size, the book of hours was an intimate object easily held in the supplicant's hands.[3]

By 1475 Bruges, an international trading center attracting visitors from throughout Europe, already enjoyed a Europe-wide market for the production of books of hours. Relatively few of the countless books of hours produced there prior to 1475, however, compare in pictorial invention with the manuscripts to be considered here.[4] The borders of the earlier Bruges manuscripts contain acanthus, small flowers with wire-thin stems, birds, and many other small motifs, but they are rendered in matte colors with restrained modeling and the effect is largely two-dimensional. In the miniatures, too, the figures are relatively flat, while the depiction of pictorial space often seems awkward.

After 1475 most of the major illuminators and scribes seem to have worked in Ghent or Bruges, and late Flemish illumination is often ascribed simply to the "Ghent-Bruges School."[5] In the 1470s Ghent was the home of the painters Hugo van der Goes and Joos van Ghent. Jan van Eyck had been active at Bruges, and Hans Memling and Gerard David settled there in the 1460s and 1480s, respectively. Not all the major illuminators were from Ghent or Bruges, however. Simon Marmion was active at Valenciennes and was a member of the guild at Tournai.[6]

The Burgundian dukes, who were the major patrons of Flemish illumination for much of the fifteenth century, frequently held court in Ghent and Bruges. Duke Charles the Bold himself and his third wife, Margaret of York (d. 1504), played an active role in supporting the illuminators responsible for introducing the new style.[7] The Ordinance of Charles the Bold, with a beautiful frontispiece depicting the duke enthroned at court (Fig. 1a), may have been commissioned by Charles. Following the ducal example, members of Charles' court commissioned some of the finest manuscripts of the day. William Lord Hastings, chamberlain to the household of Edward IV of England, received a pension from the duke and commissioned a magnificent book of hours (Cat. 3) illuminated by the Master of the First Prayer Book of Maximilian, who was active at the Burgundian court. Engelbert of Nassau, a lieutenant to Charles the Bold, commissioned the famous *Roman de la Rose* (Cat. 6) and owned a beautiful book of hours illuminated by the Master of Mary of Burgundy.[8]

The manuscripts commissioned by Charles and Margaret exemplify the transition from the old style to the new. In representing the beautiful costumes of the court in brilliant colors and vivid detail (Figs. 1b, 1c), the miniatures in these works display some of the qualities of the late period. But the borders belong to the old style, with a spray of thin vines, some fruit and flowers, and an occasional animal or figure on an uncolored ground. The flatness and restrained coloration of the border contrast with the generally richer, more lustrous coloration of the miniature, although in the 1470s some of the finest miniatures executed for Margaret of York are in grisaille plus one or two other colors (Figs. 3h, 3i).

Hugo van der Goes and other Ghent painters of the 1470s were particularly influential on the artists of the first generation of the new tradition, including the Master of Mary of Burgundy, the Master of the First Prayer Book of Maximilian (Cat. 3), and Simon Marmion (Cat. 4).[9] The influence of Hugo appears first in works by the Master of Mary of Burgundy and is apparent not only in figure types and spatial conception, but also in the depth of feeling conveyed. Active about 1475–85, probably at Ghent, the Master of Mary of Burgundy is the first major exponent of the new style and one of the great Flemish illuminators of the fifteenth century.[10] Hugo's half-length compositions and his figure types were also a source of inspiration for Simon Marmion (Ill. 6, p. 10; Figs. 4c, 4l).[11] Marmion (d. 1489), who had been active for nearly three decades by 1475, was both a painter and an illuminator and received important commissions in both domains. The figure types and compositions of the Master of the First Prayer Book of Maximilian (Figs. 3a, 3b, 3c) also show the influence of Hugo.[12] The Maximilian master may be identical with the illuminator Alexander Bening, who entered the Ghent guild of painters in 1469 under the sponsorship of Hugo and Joos van Ghent.

The second generation of late Flemish painters is dominated by the Bruges illuminator Simon Bening (d. 1561) and the Master of James IV of Scotland. Bening, who entered the Bruges illuminators' guild in 1508, was strongly influenced by the work of Gerard David, and both illuminators were influenced by Hugo.[13] Although primarily an illuminator, the Master of James IV of Scotland was also a painter. He may be identical with the Gerard Horenbout who entered the guild at Ghent in 1487.[14]

The leading illuminators of both generations maintained close connections with panel painters throughout this era. Except for Marmion, whose painted oeuvre still merits a careful study, most of them were strictly involved in manuscript illumination. The city of Bruges had separate guilds for painters and for illuminators; an artist could belong to both, but the painters' guild eventually established regulations which restricted certain commercial practices of the illuminators.[15] Few of the best-known painters were prominent illuminators. The Bruges painter Gerard David may have executed some miniatures (Pl. VI, Figs. 5e, 5f), but they would have constituted a very small portion of his large oeuvre and drawn their inspiration largely from his paintings.

One of the most striking and decisive events for the development of Flemish manuscript illumination is the revolution in the decorated border, which began to convey a spatial illusion independent of other decoration on the page. From the time of Jan van Eyck, Flemish painters had brought an extraordinary veracity to their work, especially in the execution of such details as a flower, a pearl, or an expensive material. In the mid-1470s Flemish illuminators introduced this verisimilitude to the decorated borders of manuscripts.[16] A hallmark of late Flemish illumination is a border decorated with flowers, acanthus, and insects, where each motif casts a shadow on a colored ground (Pls. I–III, V–IX). Although occasionally a Flemish painter fooled the eye by painting a portrait frame to simulate marble, or by depicting surfaces in the foreground with such truth as to appear tangible, nowhere in Flemish art is the illusionism as persistent as in late Flemish illumination.[17] The illuminators gave an independent spatial character to the border and to the miniature. While the decorated borders provide the illusion of an intimate, accessible reality, the miniature offers an illusion of vast space. In addition, the illuminators developed the independent spatial character in another way by including narrative scenes in the border (Figs. 3e, 7a, 7b). It is both this persistent illusionism of the decorated border and the tension between the independent spatial realms of border and miniature that make the manuscripts so fascinating to behold.

The decorated border in the Ordinance of Charles the Bold (Fig. 1a) strongly anticipates the new type of border. The shields suspended at slight angles from the thick acanthus provide a distinctive spatial illusion. But the finest examples of the new type of border are found most often in a smaller format, especially in devotional books, an area in which the collections of the British Library have particular strength.

The death of Mary of Burgundy in 1482 marked the end of the extraordinary Burgundian tradition of patronage for Flemish illuminators. However a change in the kinds of books commissioned had already begun to occur during the last years of her father Charles's reign. From the era of Philip the Good, the Burgundian dukes and their courtiers had engaged the services of the finest artists to illuminate large folio volumes—histories, theological writings, philosophy texts, and romances. Under Philip the Good and Charles the Bold, Simon Marmion's most important commissions, for example, were often large volumes.[18] But with the passing of Burgundian rule shortly after the advent of the new decorative style, the finest illuminators focused their activity increasingly on luxurious devotional books. Accordingly, during the 1470s Marmion's energies shifted to the decoration of such books. Most of the rulers of Europe wanted to own sumptuous Flemish manuscripts with illusionistic borders, and books of hours were among the most popular. Queen Isabella of Castile, her daughter, Joanna of Castile, Margaret of Austria, Regent of the Netherlands, and the Infante Dom Fernando of Portugal commissioned or acquired some of the luxury manuscripts in the present exhibition (Cats. 5, 7, 9, 15).

The special limitations imposed by the book format opened up artistic possibilities not available to painters of altarpieces and devotional paintings on panel. For example, the discovery of each new scene in a narrative sequence as one turns the pages of a devotional book is an aesthetic experience not available to the beholder of even the most elaborate multi-winged altarpiece. To understand some of the possibilities and limitations faced by the illuminator, the character of the book of hours, the most popular type of illuminated manuscript in the late Flemish period, merits discussion.[19] The present exhibition contains four

Ill. 1. Master of Mary of Burgundy. *Christ Nailed to the Cross*, Hours of Mary of
Burgundy. Vienna, Österreichische Nationalbibliothek, Cod. 1857, fol. 43v.

intact Flemish examples (Cats. 3, 4, 7, 8) and a fifth in the miniatures added to an Italian book of hours (Cat. 15), as well as several Italian and French productions (Cats. 15, 16, 23, 25).

A book of hours is a collection of prayers organized around the Little Office of the Virgin, a set of daily devotions to be read at the canonical hours or at established times throughout the day. These devotions are generally referred to as the Hours of the Virgin, from which the generic term book of hours derives. The book of hours contains other texts as well, including a calendar, which identifies the feast days of important saints, a Litany of Saints, the Penitential Psalms, and an Office of the Dead. Most Flemish books of hours of this period have a larger variety of texts, including Gospel extracts, the Hours of the Cross or the Holy Spirit among others, special short prayers or "suffrages" of the saints, and special prayers to the Virgin.

The major texts had their own decorative programs. For example, the Hours of the Virgin was generally decorated by a Life of the Virgin cycle, a sequence of eight miniatures usually beginning with the *Annunciation* and ending with the *Massacre of the Innocents*, the *Flight into Egypt*, or the *Coronation of the Virgin*, each one inserted at the beginning of the new set of devotions for each of the canonical hours. In Flemish illumination a miniature with David praying generally precedes the Penitential Psalms, and a scene depicting a Mass of the Dead often prefaces the Office of the Dead. The most richly illuminated Flemish books of hours contain some sixty or more miniatures (Cats. 4, 7, 8), many of them full page. Scenes in books of hours being largely devotional, they were similar to those depicted in contemporary paintings; the Life of the Virgin, the Passion of Christ (which often illustrates the Hours of the Cross), and the lives of the saints were among the subjects common to both.

The calendar was the only section of the manuscript where the narrative decoration was largely secular. It is often illustrated by the occupations of the months, a visual tradition associated since the early medieval period with the iconography of the times of the year. This allowed illuminators opportunities to develop both secular subjects and landscape settings in ways not available to painters.

The breviary, a liturgical manuscript intended for clerical use (Cats. 2, 5), contained even more numerous and varied texts. Although richly illuminated examples are rare, they could be more sumptuous than an elaborately decorated book of hours. The Breviary of Queen Isabella of Castile (Cat. 5) contains more than 150 miniatures, and represents the workshops of three important artists: Gerard David (Pl. VI, Fig. 5e), the Master of James IV of Scotland (Fig. 5d), and the Master of the Dresden Prayer Book (Pl. VII, Figs. 5a, 5c).

Three main areas in which late Flemish illuminators made a significant contribution to the development of pictorial realism in Flemish art are landscape, border decoration, and narrative. The field of manuscript illumination seems to have attracted artists especially resourceful in the

depiction of landscape. The Master of Mary of Burgundy, Simon Marmion, the Master of James IV of Scotland, and Simon Bening all made important contributions to the history of landscape painting. Otto Pächt has credited the Master of Mary of Burgundy with the introduction of aerial perspective in Northern European art.[20] In the magnificent miniature *Christ Nailed to the Cross* in a book of hours presumably executed for Mary of Burgundy circa 1480 (Ill. 1), the dense atmosphere dissolves contours, especially in the far distance, where the hilly landscape gradually disappears into the mist. The Master of Mary of Burgundy captures the substance of the atmosphere by the subtlest nuances of light and color.

The earliest examples in Flemish art of pure landscape—a scene which is non-narrative with an encompassing view of nature rendered by convincing spatial recession—are found in illuminated manuscripts. Such is the depiction of Flanders in a *Trésor des histoires* in the British Library, datable to about 1470–80 and attributed by Pächt to Simon Marmion (Ill. 2).[21] Figures are purely incidental in this picturesque view of a well-kept countryside. The contemporaneous paintings of Hugo van der Goes and Joos van Ghent also contain convincing vistas of surpassing beauty, but the panel painters never come as close to representing landscape as an independent subject. In fifteenth-century Flemish painting, landscape was primarily a backdrop for large devotional scenes or figures in the foreground. Marmion's experiment with landscape seems to have no parallel in the art of panel painting. He was also particularly concerned with the viewer's perception of near and middle distances. In the Huth Hours he depicts the penitent St. Jerome praying in the thick of a woods (Pl. IV). The eye is led through the trees past the saint, to a clearing, and to more of the forest beyond. Marmion's lush foreground landscape that nearly swallows up the figures foreshadows the early paintings of Albrecht Altdorfer, especially the *St. George* of 1510 (Munich, Alte Pinakothek).

The Master of James IV of Scotland had access to the calendar illuminations of the Très Riches Heures of the duc de Berry when he created the magnificent calendar cycle of the Grimani Breviary, one of the monuments of Flemish illumination.[22] In the *November* miniature (Ill. 3) he presents a landscape that suggests a continuity with the viewer's space that is not apparent in his source. He moves the trees into the foreground and uses them as a device to draw the viewer into a continuous landscape of rolling hills, with the finest details—the blades of grass, the leaves in the boughs of trees, the contours of a church on the distant horizon—beautifully observed. It was only around this time, circa 1515, that painters began to develop landscape settings as fully as illuminators. The first important Flemish landscape painter was Joachim Patinir, whose visionary landscapes are frequently panoramic.[23] However, the Flemish calendar landscapes, which depict primarily the occupations of the months, are closer to the everyday experience of nature.

Simon Bening, also an illuminator of the Grimani Breviary, and the last important master of Flemish illumina-

Ill. 2. Attributed to Simon Marmion. *Flanders,* in the TRÉSOR DES HISTOIRES. London, British Library, Cotton Ms. Augustus A V, fol. 345v.

tion, was the greatest of the landscape illuminators. His calendar cycles contain spacious landscapes that provide a vivid sense of the changing character of the seasons and of daily life. The *December* miniature, a late work of circa 1540, ranks among his finest (Pl. XIII). The autumnal hues, the fallen leaves, and the barren thicket that envelops the equestrian hunter convey the chilly quality of a late fall day. The aerial perspective is a worthy forerunner of the vistas of Pieter Bruegel, and the palpable, tinted atmosphere and grand scale look forward to the art of Claude Lorrain. Francisco de Hollanda, writing in the sixteenth century, called Bening "among Flemish artists the most pleasing colorist who best painted trees and far distances."[24] Thus, illuminators were in many respects the artistic leaders in the treatment of Flemish landscape. Their achievements anticipate aspects of Flemish painting of the sixteenth and seventeenth centuries, especially the emergence of landscape as an independent category of painting.

The decorated borders are perhaps the most inventive and influential features of late Flemish illumination The illusionistically rendered borders with flowers and insects on solid-colored grounds that appear throughout Flemish manuscripts of the late period were widely imitated in French and Italian illumination (Ills. 17, 18, p. 149; Figs. 16b, 16c). The development of illusionism and pictorial space in the borders resulted in numerous variations, such as the simulated damask and the relief-like border of thick, braided branches in the Breviary of Isabella of Castile (Figs. 5a, 5e), or the border with an anagram for the Psalter of St. Jerome in the Huth Hours (Pl. IV). One of the most remarkable is the border by Simon Bening with the *Genealogical Tree of Magog* in which the descendants of Noah are represented (Pl. XI, Fig. 9b). This border is conceived as a deep relief brought to life through the liveliness of movement, characterization, and the play of shadows against the violet ground. It constitutes one of the most beautiful and original examples of Flemish illumination around 1530.

The articulation of the relationship between the distinct spatial worlds of the border and the miniature resulted in some of the most pictorially compelling leaves in Renaissance illumination. In *Christ Nailed to the Cross* (Ill. 1), the

Master of Mary of Burgundy has fashioned an elegant interior setting where the border normally appears. Still a framing device, it is, however, no longer spatially distinct from the miniature. The architecture belongs to the world of the beholder and, spatially, to the miniature in order to draw the beholder into the event. The precious objects adorning the window and ledge immediately catch the eye. In their execution the illuminator shows himself a rival to Van Eyck and Hugo.

Around 1500 one Flemish workshop widely employed architectural settings as border decorations. In the Hours of Joanna of Castile (Cat. 7) the illustration of the *Temptation of Adam and Eve* is set into the wall of the border architecture (Fig. 7a). The illuminator, known as the Master of the David Scenes in the Grimani Breviary, links the distinct spatial realms of the miniature and border by placing the

Expulsion from Paradise in a "stage door" in the border. Adam and Eve seem to have exited from one spatial realm into another.

Some years later, in the Spinola Hours of circa 1515, the Master of James IV of Scotland interrelated the pictorial space of miniature and border by representing an interior in the miniature and the exterior of the same building in the border (Ill. 4).[25] Yet, because the leaves still function as text pages, he retains the moldings that traditionally demarcate areas for border, miniature, and text on the illuminated page. To make the continuity between interior and exterior clear, he offers the suggestion of a figure (barely visible in the reproduction) entering the house in the upper left border, while other figures appear to have just passed from the outdoors into the bedchamber of the house. Flemish illuminated manuscripts occasionally contain iconographi-

Ill. 3. Master of James IV of Scotland. *November*, Grimani Breviary. Venice, Biblioteca Marciana, Ms. Lat. XI 67 (7531), fol. 11v.

Ill. 4. Master of James IV of
Scotland. *Vigil of the Dead*
and *Mass of the Dead*,
Spinola Hours. Malibu,
Calif., The J. Paul Getty
Museum, Ms. Ludwig IX
18, fols. 184v–185.

cally related subjects in the borders, but here they are inte-
grated into a setting shared with the miniature. The miniature on the left folio represents a *Vigil for the Dead*; below,
Death is attacking gallant figures on horseback. The limitless range of possibilities offered by the decorated borders
as pictorial fields is probably the most delightful feature of
late Flemish illumination. Although borderless full-page
miniatures were also common by the 1480s (Figs. 4a, 4d,
4f, 4g, 4i, Pl. IV), illuminators continued to display a fasci-
nation with the relationship between the spatial domains of
the border and the miniature.

In the treatment of both landscape and the decorative
border in the late Flemish period, artists sought to make
the viewer's experience of the image more direct (Pl. IV,
Fig. 7a). A desire for greater involvement on the part of the
viewer is apparent throughout Northern European art in
the fifteenth and sixteenth centuries. The use of the half-
length figure, for example, a device popular in painting,
was adopted with great success by illuminators (Cats. 4,
8).[26] Yet another means they exploited to engage the viewer
was the multiplication of scenes in a pictorial cycle, especially in the Passion cycle, which was depicted in graphic
detail.[27] These subjects challenged the best artists of the era
to depict an emotionally wrenching narrative.

In their treatment of narrative, the Master of Mary of
Burgundy and Simon Bening rivaled such masters as Hugo
van der Goes and Gerard David. The skill of the Master of
Mary of Burgundy in conveying profound feelings is affirmed by the faces of St. John the Evangelist and the Virgin and in her collapsing posture before the suffering

Christ in the miniature of *Christ Nailed to the Cross* (Ill. 1).
The self-absorption and idle curiosity expressed in the
densely packed crowd heightens the sense of isolation of
the three main figures. Simon Bening, in his numerous
Passion cycles, notably those in the Prayer Book of Cardinal Albrecht of Brandenburg (c. 1525–30) and the Stein
Quadriptych, evokes the viewer's sympathy for Christ's
suffering through a dense sequence of narrative events. In
the prayer book, a soft lighting on the face and body of the
passive Christ sets him apart visually from the dark events
that engulf him. He is hauled and dragged from his capture
to the crowning with thorns and the flagellation, to the
appearances before his judges and to the Crucifixion.[28] As
one turns the pages of the Passion cycle of twenty miniatures in this prayer book, it is difficult not to be profoundly
moved. The Stein Quadriptych, an altarpiece of four
panels, is the most elaborate of all late Flemish narrative
cycles. Each panel contains sixteen small half-length miniatures on vellum mounted in a frame, in which Bening tells
the stories of the Life of the Virgin and the Passion of
Christ (Ill. 5). It is not known whether the miniatures were
originally intended for a manuscript or not; they were
probably intended to be displayed in a frame.[29] The quadriptych creates a nearly cinematic effect in its use of the
close-up view, multiple vantage points, and dramatic ac-
tion. The Stein Quadriptych represents a culmination both
in the development of the half-length figure and in the
multiplication of scenes in the narrative cycle. Its power
lies in Bening's exploitation of these devices in conjunction
with his moving portrayal of Christ.

The half-length pictorial type seen in the Stein Quadriptych, a popular format with panel painters, played an important role in late Flemish illumination largely through the influence of a Life of the Virgin cycle conceived by Simon Marmion and incorporated into the "Flora" Hours (Ill. 6, Figs. 4c, 4l).[30] As the Stein Quadriptych demonstrates, this convention heightens the viewer's awareness of characterization. It is, moreover, particularly apt for the intimate scale of the book of hours. The monumentality of the figures in such scenes as the *Visitation* or *St. James the Major Preaching* (Fig. 4l) reflects Marmion's activity as a painter, but the vibrancy of the flesh tones and the vividness of other textures, such as the velvet of the Virgin's dress in the *Visitation,* confirm that his finest achievements

lie in manuscript illumination. Similar half-lengths from his workshop appear in the Huth Hours (Figs. 4i, 4k), and Bening adopted several of the compositions from "La Flora" in the Stein Quadriptych. The half-lengths of Marmion and Bening constitute the final impressive chapter in the development of this format in Flemish art.

The Master of the Dresden Prayer Book is one of the finest illuminators who produced illuminated secular manuscripts in addition to prayer books in the late Flemish period. Active in Bruges by 1480, he seems to have received major commissions into the first two decades of the sixteenth century. The Breviary of Queen Isabella of Castile contains some of his finest miniatures (Pl. VII, Figs. 5a, 5c). An illuminator who loved ordinary types as much as

Ill. 5 [LEFT]. Simon Bening. *Scenes from the Passion of Christ*, Stein Quadriptych. Baltimore, Walters Art Gallery.

Ill. 6 [RIGHT]. Simon Marmion. *Visitation*, "Flora" Hours. Naples, Biblioteca Nazionale, Ms. I B 51, fol. 103v.

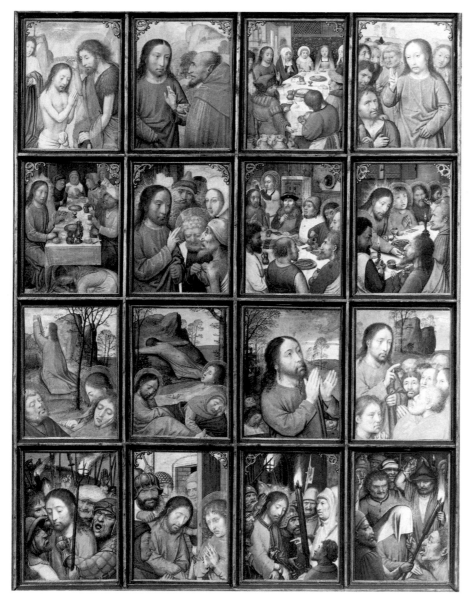

Ill. 7. Master of the Dresden Prayer Book. *The Temperate and the Intemperate*, in Valerius
Maximus, Facta et dicta memorabilia. Leipzig, Bibliothek der Karl-Marx-
Universität, Ms. Rep. I 11b, fol. 2.

Hugo did, he belongs to an older tradition of illumination that is less faithful to nature in drawing and coloring. Winkler hailed the artist as a forerunner of Pieter Bruegel, and in these miniatures and especially the illuminator's large miniatures in the Valerius Maximus in Leipzig it is easy to understand why (Ill. 7).[31] A wry and sympathetic observer of human behavior, the vitality and humor of his characterizations give him a unique position in the Flemish art of his era. He was one of a small number of late-fifteenth-century Flemish illuminators who stood securely outside the mainstream of illuminators inspired by the naturalism of Flemish paintings.

One illuminator who specialized in devotional books was the Master of the Prayer Books of c. 1500, a follower of the Master of the Dresden Prayer Book. Yet he was also responsible for a *Roman de la Rose* (Cat. 6) which is the most distinguished of more than a hundred surviving illuminated copies of this text from the fourteenth and fifteenth centuries. Few miniatures of the late fifteenth century give a more vivid sense of the pageantry and courtly tradition of the era than the *Roman* in the British Library

(Pl. VIII). Contemporaneous treatments of the subject of the Garden of Love such as fifteenth-century engravings seem dull by comparison.[32]

Finally, another important secular manuscript in the exhibition is the magnificent Genealogy of the Infante Dom Fernando of Portugal (Cat. 9) of 1530–34, designed by Antonio de Hollanda and illuminated by Simon Bening. It is the only known illuminated genealogy in Flemish art and is an outstanding example of Bening's mature style.

In late Flemish illumination the pictorial realism found in Flemish painting underwent its own evolution, determined by the requirements and limitations of the decorated book, especially the private devotional book. The illuminated manuscript offered opportunities for artists to develop pictorial realism in landscape and secular subjects, in narrative, and in the illusionism of the border. In many instances these developments were more advanced than the work of contemporaneous painters. This period is not only one of the main chapters in the history of Flemish illumination, but it is also an important chapter in the history of Flemish painting.

NOTES

1. Still the best reference work on the late Flemish period as defined here is Winkler 1925. A new study by Georges Dogaer is in preparation.

2. Two excellent studies of the manuscript patronage of Philip the Good are Brussels 1959 and Brussels 1967a.

3. A number of excellent facsimiles of the major Flemish illuminated manuscripts have been published, including one of Cat. 3 (Turner [1983]). See also de Schryver 1969a; Alexander 1970; Salmi 1974; Trenkler 1979.

4. The leading Bruges illuminator during the third quarter of the century was probably Willem Vrelant, a Dutchman settled in Bruges by 1454. On the controversial issue of his oeuvre, see the summary of the literature provided in Euw/Plotzek 1979–82, II, pp. 151–57. An example of a book of hours in the Vrelant style in the British Library is Harley Ms. 2900 (Winkler 1925, p. 179).

5. The term "Ghent-Bruges School" emerges almost simultaneously in the literature in the writings of Durrieu 1891, p. 69, and Destrée 1892, p. 263. Recently Dogaer 1979, while acknowledging the dominant role played by Ghent and Bruges in late Flemish illumination, has argued that the term is too restrictive, since the distinctive decorative style of the period was also current in other cities. The Flemish manuscripts in this exhibition appear for the most part to have been executed in Ghent or Bruges, but the particular town of origin can rarely be established conclusively.

6. On Marmion, see Cat. 4.

7. On the patronage of Margaret of York, see Brussels 1959, pp. 150–51, nos. 191–198, and Brussels 1967b.

8. On the Hours of Engelbert of Nassau (Oxford, Bodleian Library, Mss. Douce 219–220), see Pächt 1948, pp. 33–34, 38, 67; Lieftinck 1969, I, chap. VI; and Alexander 1970.

9. On the influence of Hugo, see Cat. 3, and especially Pächt 1948, pp. 21, 30–31; de Winter 1981, pp. 377–86.

10. The best studies on the Master of Mary of Burgundy are Pächt 1948 and Lieftinck 1969.

11. Ringbom 1965, pp. 134–38.

12. On the Master of the First Prayer Book of Maximilian, see Cat. 3, and de Winter 1981, pp. 353–417.

13. For the literature on Simon Bening, see Cats. 9 and 10, and Euw/Plotzek 1979–82, II, no. IX, 19.

14. For the literature on this artist, see Cat. 15, and Euw/Plotzek 1979–82, II, no. IX 18.

15. On regulations governing the illuminators' guild in Bruges, see Farquhar 1980, pp. 371–83.

16. The basic study is Hulin de Loo 1939b, pp. 169–80; see also Cat. 1. Winkler 1915, p. 336, identified a number of manuscripts of lesser artistic quality which also were likely executed during the reign of Charles the Bold and exhibit the new style of border.

17. See, for example, Jan van Eyck's *Portrait of Timotheus* (London, National Gallery); Petrus Christus' *St. Eligius* (New York, The Metropolitan Museum of Art, Robert Lehman Collection); or the reverse of Memling's *St. Veronica* (Washington, D.C., National Gallery).

18. For examples of his work, see Brussels 1959, nos. 58–62.

19. On this subject, see especially Harthan 1977.

20. Pächt 1948, pp. 25–26.

21. Cotton Ms. Augustus A V, fol. 345v; see Pächt 1978, colorplate I, p. 5.

22. See Cat. 15; Coggiola 1908–10; Gasparrini Leporace 1954; Salmi 1974.

23. Friedländer 1967–76, IXb, and Koch 1968.

24. Quoted by Durrieu 1910, p. 166.

25. Euw/Plotzek 1979–82, II, no. IX, 18, esp. figs. 407, 417, 430, 432.

26. Ringbom 1965 is the basic study of the development of the half-length figure in this period.

27. See especially Marrow 1979, and Cat. 8.

28. Euw/Plotzek 1979–82, II, no. IX, 19, figs. 469–542.

29. See especially Ringbom 1965, pp. 204–09, figs. 191–194; Kupfer-Tarasulo 1979a; Marrow 1979, pp. 79, 106, nn. 316, 448, figs. 49, 75.

30. The "Flora" Hours has long been accepted in the literature as by Marmion (Winkler 1925, p. 189; Courcelle-Ladmirant 1939, pp. 225–33; and Ringbom 1965, chap. VI). Its quality and importance, as well as Marmion's responsibility for it, have recently been called into question by Hoffmann (1969, p. 245, n. 8; 1973, p. 273, n. 50) and de Winter (1981, p. 365). De Schryver (1969a, pp. 149–57) and Hindman (1977, p. 204) ignored the "Flora" Hours in their studies of books of hours from the Marmion group. See also the discussion in Cat. 4. A remarkable antecedent for the overly large heads in these miniatures, their pronounced cheekbones, and the modeling in long, closely placed brush strokes is found in the *Grandes chroniques de France,* illuminated by Marmion (Leningrad, State M.E. Saltykov-Shchedrine Public Library); see Reinach 1904, pp. 7–79, pl. 1, and Voronova 1980.

31. Winkler 1921, p. 7.

32. Compare, for instance, the engravings of the Master of the Garden of Love, in Hollstein 1949–, XII, pp. 179–80.

1 Ordinance of Charles the Bold

Brussels (?), circa 1474–76. Additional Ms. 36619

MANUSCRIPT *Vellum, 41 leaves; 30.5 × 21.6 cm. 1 full-page miniature and 1 illuminated border (fol. 5), decorated initials. On the inside back flap, a bookplate with a coat of arms with the motto "Benigno numine";*[1] *on the blank leaves, records by Martin de Choisey of the births of his children (1649–74) and other family events. Burgundian* bâtarde *script.*

BINDING *Modern crimson velvet binding on oak boards with gilt bosses and clasps.*

PROVENANCE *Probably Charles the Bold, Duke of Burgundy, and his wife, Margaret of York; Marc Antoine Martin de Choisey, Seigneur de Barjon Anot and Panthenay, seventeenth century; Jean Bouhier, Dijon, by 1721; William Beckford, Fonthill Abbey, Wiltshire; sale, Phillips, Fonthill Abbey, September 9, 1823, lot 606, as "quarto, highly illuminated"; Paul Barrois; Earl of Ashburnham, 1849, Ms. 2; Ashburnham-Barrois sale, Sotheby's, London, June 10–14, 1901, lot 434; purchased by the book dealer Bernard Quaritch and sold to the British Museum in the same year.*

THIS manuscript contains an ordinance concerning the regulation of the military levies of Duke Charles the Bold of Burgundy, a ruler whose great enthusiasm for battle resulted only in numerous defeats and an early death. In it Charles set down the procedure for the appointment and installation of his military captains, who served a one-year term from the beginning of each new year, surrendering the baton and regulations of their office at the end of the year. Charles wrote military ordinances to establish "the organization and discipline of the armies in their minutest detail," and his own copies were often illuminated.[2] The half-dozen ordinances dating from between 1468 and 1476, and enjoying a wide influence in the following century, constitute Charles' most significant contribution to European military organization.[3]

The duke issued the present ordinance in the autumn of 1473 while at the Abbey of Saint-Maximin in Trier, where he resided from September 30 to November 25, 1473.[4] At Trier he met regularly with Emperor Frederick III, trying to persuade the emperor to grant him a royal crown; but Charles' attempts failed and they probably explain the reticent Frederick's quiet departure from the city in the early morning of November 25.[5] The text of the British Library ordinance is dated *"lan de grace mil quatrecent soixante et treize,"* but the present copy was not necessarily written and illuminated in the same year, because it is not the copy signed by the duke. The British Library manuscript was probably written not long after the issue of the ordinance

and certainly before the death of Charles in the battle at Nancy on January 5, 1477.

The British Library manuscript contains a single miniature with an elaborate illuminated border (Fig. 1a). The miniature shows the duke at court enthroned upon a dais beneath a canopy of honor. The borders of the canopy bear the flint-and-steel device of the Order of the Golden Fleece; the dais is covered with the duke's coat of arms. To Charles' left, one Knight of the Golden Fleece receives a baton while another, in ceremonial robes and apparently wearing the golden chain of the order, receives a bound volume. Other Knights of the Golden Fleece are seated along the left wall of the chamber opposite ecclesiastical dignitaries; in the foreground an audience of courtiers watches the ceremony, their backs to us. The mottoes of Charles and his wife, Margaret of York—*"je lay en prins"* and *"bien en aviengne"*—appear above (barely visible in reproduction), on one of the crossbeams; another motto, *"honeur,"* is on the rear wall left of the door. The monograms of the duke and duchess are represented above the left doorway, and opposite are the devices of the Golden Fleece and the Cross of St. Andrew.[6]

De Schryver suggests plausibly that the miniature represents the inauguration of the captains appointed by Charles at the beginning of each year.[7] In this ceremony, conducted before an audience of Charles' ambassadors, each appointee knelt before the duke to take the oath and to receive a baton and a paper book containing the orders for war.

Winkler attributed the miniature to an imitator of Philippe de Mazerolles, whom he identified erroneously as the Master of the Conquest of the Golden Fleece.[8] Mazerolles was court painter to Charles beginning in 1467; he received payments from the latter in the previous year for decorations for an Hours of the Virgin and other devotional texts; in 1475 he was paid for the decoration of a number of Charles' ordinances.[9] In the view of this compiler, Winkler is correct in suggesting a connection with the miniatures he attributed to Mazerolles, for example, the frontispiece to the Vienna *Ordinance of the First Officer of the Livery* of 1469 (Fig. 1b), representing the duke installing a prominent officer in his court. Although the drawing is crisper and livelier in the Vienna miniature, the proportions and types of figures are similar. It appears likely that the illuminator of the London miniature worked in the orbit of the Vienna master. However, de Schryver has argued persuasively against the attribution of the Vienna miniature to Mazerolles and assigns it to an illuminator in the circle of Lieven van Lathem, who was in the employ of Charles in 1469. In any case, there is no evidence to connect Charles' payments of 1475 to Mazerolles with the London volume.[10]

Fig. 1a. Flemish Master. *Charles the Bold Receiving the Oath of Fidelity from His Military Captains*; borders with the ducal arms and the shields of his territories, fol. 5.

Fig. 1b. Circle of Lieven van Latham. *Charles the Bold Presenting an Ordinance to the First Master of the Livery.* Vienna, Österreichische Nationalbibliothek, Cod. ser. nov. 2616, fol. 1v.

appears in the Breviary of Margaret of York, which was also executed prior to the death of Charles.[14] Such borders are featured throughout the Flemish manuscripts in the present exhibition (Pls. I–III, v–IX). An example executed only a few years after the ordinance appears in the breviary from Rooclooster (Pl. I). The border in the ordinance is, however, not purely decorative. It contains an assemblage of blazons, which constitutes the arms of Charles' six duchies, nine counties, one marquisate, and three other lordships, along with his coat of arms.[15] Its style of execution resembles the new type of border in two ways. First, the blazons are suspended by buckled straps from golden acanthus. The shields hang at slight angles to the page and the acanthus occasionally extends over the edges of the border, thereby giving it a subtle but unmistakable illusionistic character. Second, these decorations are painted on a solid gray ground. The prominent motif of acanthus leaves was already common in the older type of Flemish border on plain ground (e.g., Fig. 1b) and they continued to appear in the new type of border (Pls. I, II). The British Library manuscript was illuminated about the same time as the emergence of the new decorated border.[16]

According to Durrieu, other copies of the same ordinance are to be found in The Hague, Munich, and Copenhagen.[17]

A related manner of illumination appears in a manuscript commissioned about the same time by Charles and Margaret, a life of St. Colette owned by the Convent of the Colettine Poor Clares in Ghent.[11] The types of the figures in the miniature of the *Appearance of St. Anne and Her Kindred to St. Colette and St. Francis* are similar, and this page bears an initial akin to the one beneath the miniature in the British Library ordinance (Fig. 1a).[12] Both initials contain the monogram of Charles and Margaret within them; in the Colettine manuscript a crown rests on it. Delaissé suggests that both the Vienna ordinance and this manuscript may have been produced at Brussels, so it is possible that the London ordinance was also executed there.[13]

The border of this miniature is an early example of the illusionistic border so typical of late Flemish illumination—commonly a naturalistic decoration with flowers, insects, and occasionally birds, animals, and figures that cast shadows against a solid-colored ground. One of the earliest datable examples of a typical Flemish illusionistic border

Fig. 1c. Flemish Master. *A Chapter of the Order of the Golden Fleece under Charles the Bold*, in Guillaume Fillastre, LIVRE DE LA TOISON D'OR. Brussels, Bibliothèque Royale, Ms 9028, fol. 6.

BIBLIOGRAPHY Dorez 1903, pp. 159–60; Warner 1903; London (British Museum) 1907, p. 162; Winkler 1915, p. 302, n. 1; Winkler 1925, pp. 90, 137, 178; Durrieu 1927, pp. 66, 99, pl. XXXIX (fol. 5); Millar 1928, p. 15, pl. XLI (fol. 5); Hulin de Loo 1939b, p. 161; de Schryver 1969b, p. 440, n. 32; Vaughn 1973, p. 205, n. 1; Ettro 1976, col. 369, fig. 3.

NOTES

1. The description in London (British Museum) 1907, p. 162, identifies the bookplate as representing "Carter or Heselden." Fairbairn identifies *"Benigno numine"* ("Under a propitious deity I have prospered") as appearing on the arms of the Barned, Bentley, Copeland, Hicks, Hereford, Meigh, Pitt, Rowland, and Smith families (Fairbairn 1908, I, p. 8) and Berry associates it with the Earl of Chatham (Berry [1828], I, p. 226).

2. Vaughn 1973, p. 205.

3. Ibid., pp. 204–05. The historical background is derived from Vaughn's interpretation.

4. The text is printed in Guillaume 1848, App. H. He states that the ordinance was found in Charles' tent after the battle of Morat, June 16, 1476, but it is not certain that the copy found then is the one under consideration here.

5. Vaughn 1973, pp. 140–55.

6. This description is based on the account by Warner 1903, no. 46.

7. De Schryver 1969b, p. 440; see also Vaughn 1973, pp. 204–05, n. 1.

8. Winkler 1915, p. 302, n. 1, and 1925, p. 178; on the Master of the Conquest of the Golden Fleece, see Winkler 1915, pp. 303–06, and 1925, pp. 89–90. De Schryver 1969a, pp. 23–34 provides a history of scholarship on Mazerolles and its problems.

9. Durrieu 1927, p. 66.

10. De Schryver 1969a, p. 48.

11. Brussels 1959, no. 186, and Corstanje 1982.

12. Corstanje 1982, colorplate 11.

13. Brussels 1959, nos. 184, 186.

14. Cambridge, St. John's College, Ms. H. 13; see Pächt 1948, no. 6, pl. 23a; Brussels 1959, no. 198; Lieftinck 1969, I, chap. I, II, figs. 1–4, 7–11. Winkler 1915, p. 336, identified several other examples, which are artistically inferior, as probably executed before 1477; for an example dated 1477, see Ring 1949b, p. 87, fig. 26; Brussels 1959, no. 265; Ghent 1975, no. 610.

15. Burgundy is at the top center between the duchies of Lothier and Brabant. The duchies of Limbourg and Luxembourg occupy the corners; the duchy of Guelders appears under Limbourg. Reading farther down on the left from the shield of the duchy of Guelders are the shields of Flanders; the counties of Guelders, Hainault, Zeeland; Antwerp, a marquisate of the Empire; and Salines. On the right, in descending order, are Artois, the counties of Brabant, Holland, Namur, Frisia, Malines, and Zutphen (Warner 1903, no. 46). According to Warner, an engraving of the ducal arms executed in 1468 on the occasion of Charles' marriage to Margaret of York provided the model for this arrangement. It is reproduced in Alvin 1859, p. 144, and Ettro 1976, fig. 1. Zutphen and the duchy of Guelders are additional, having been acquired in 1473. A drawing in a sixteenth-century Swiss copy of Charles' military ordinances (Bern, Historisches Museum, no. 36666) represents the same coats of arms (Bern 1969, fig. 228).

16. In this context it bears mentioning that an earlier manuscript which clearly anticipates the new type of Flemish border, with a strong spatial illusion and solid-colored ground, was also executed for Charles the Bold, as early as 1469. This is the prayer book written by Nicholas Spierinc and illuminated by Lieven van Lathem (Paris, Collection de Charnacé); see the borders on fols. 43v and 49v, illustrated in de Schryver 1969a, figs. 3 and 6, and Durrieu 1927, pl. XLII.

17. Durrieu 1927, p. 66. The manuscripts are identified by Ettro 1976, col. 369, fig. 2, who illustrates the example in The Hague (Rijksmuseum Meermanno-Westreenianum, Ms. 242 10 C 3). Another manuscript in The Hague (Rijksmuseum Meermanno-Westreenianum, Ms. 10 C II), which, however, is probably an Ordinance of the Order of the Golden Fleece and not an Ordinance of Charles the Bold (see The Hague 1980, no. 34, ill. p. 59), is of interest here because it resembles the frontispiece miniature in Guillaume Fillastre's *Livre de la toison d'or* (Fig. 1c). According to Dhanens 1980, pp. 168–70, fig. 119, this miniature may derive from a lost work by Jan van Eyck. Its centralized composition with a symmetrical audience chamber and members of the court seated against the lateral walls is followed in the miniature in the British Library Ordinance of Charles the Bold.

2 Breviary

Monastery of St. Paul, the "Rooclooster," near Brussels, circa
1477–80. Additional Ms. 11863

MANUSCRIPT *Vellum, 400 + vii leaves; 8.9 × 12.7 cm 1
small miniature (fol. 23); 4 illusionistic borders on solid-colored
grounds (fols. 23, 140, 234, 336) and others of spray-and-
acanthus on plain ground. Hybrida and rounded Italian gothic.*

BINDING *Original pink-stained calf binding, blind-tooled, probably from Rooclooster.*

PROVENANCE *Monastery of St. Paul, the "Rooclooster," near
Brussels; probably H. J. Van Campenhout; his sale, Bertaot,
Brussels, 1830, no. 164; Samuel Butler, Bishop of Lichfield;
purchased by the British Museum in 1841.*

B Y the end of the medieval era, the best illuminators
were far more often in the employ of princes and
the aristocracy than of monastic orders. This breviary is a
rare example of a manuscript illuminated by an artist in the
immediate circle of the Master of Mary of Burgundy but
not intended for a ruler or member of the court. Rather it
was written and decorated for the use of the canons in the
Windesheim monastery called Rooclooster, near Brussels.
It is further distinguished from manuscripts done in the
master's circle by its sparse decoration, including only a
single small miniature and relatively few decorated borders. It contains both the new type of illusionistic border
and an older type of decorated border generally associated
with Ghent illumination of the 1470s (Fig. 2a).[1]

Two other breviaries are known to have been illuminated for Rooclooster, another in London (Add. Ms.
11864) and one in Brussels (Bibliothèque Royale, Ms. IV
860). Both closely resemble the present one in dimensions,
script, and border decoration, although the former is distinctly inferior in quality of decoration to the manuscript
under consideration, the latter finer.[2] The Brussels manuscript contains a single miniature (Fig. 2b) which represents *King David in Prayer*. It is by the Master of Mary of
Burgundy. There is also a single miniature in Add Ms.
11863 representing the same subject (Pl. 1), but between the
two miniatures subtle differences in execution are apparent. Although the pose of the London David may derive
from the Master of Mary of Burgundy, the modeling of
forms lacks the touches that give the hands and face three-
dimensionality in the Brussels version.[3] Therefore Lieftinck is probably correct in suggesting that this *David*

miniature is not by the Master of Mary of Burgundy himself.[4] It is rather by a gifted follower.

In the Rooclooster breviary in London the pale rose and
gold of King David's robes are set off by the greens and
blues of the landscape. David is isolated from the picturesque view of a wooded grove, a temple, and the rooftops
of distant Jerusalem. The handling of landscape and architecture resembles the setting of *Augustus and the Tiburtine Sibyl* in the Hours of Mary of Burgundy and Maximilian (Fig. 2c), the latter also a fine example from the famous
illuminator's immediate circle.[5] The breviary in London
and the Hours of Mary and Maximilian may be by the
same hand.

Fig. 2a. Flemish Master. Decorated border,
fol. 35.

Fig. 2b. Master of Mary of Burgundy. *King David in Prayer*, Breviary. Brussels, Bibliothèque Royale, Ms. IV 860, fol. 36.

The decorative border is among the most exquisite produced in the decade 1475–85. The gold and brown tonalities of the ground are applied with the freedom of an ink wash. Transparent shadows convey the illusion that the golden acanthus and flowers float above the ground, which changes from transparent to opaque and itself seems immaterial. The border decorations show a sensitivity to the descriptive powers of light and a nuance of modeling which constitute one of the finest achievements of Flemish illumination. In the Madrid Hours of William Lord Hastings (Fig. 2d), an approximately contemporaneous manuscript from the circle of the Master of Mary of Burgundy, the occasional transparency of the ground color, the motifs of acanthus and small flowers on their stems, and their arrangement resemble the borders in the London breviary.[6] The two borders may also be the product of the same illuminator.

Lieftinck argues that the illuminator of a Rooclooster manuscript must have been an inhabitant of the monastery itself, presumably a lay brother, as was another professional artist, the painter Hugo van der Goes.[7] He points out

Fig. 2c [LEFT]. Circle of the Master of Mary of Burgundy. *Augustus and the Tiburtine Sibyl*, Hours of Mary of Burgundy and Maximilian. Berlin, Staatliche Museen Preussischer Kulturbesitz, Kupferstichkabinett, Ms. 78 B 12, fol. 178.

Fig. 2d [RIGHT]. Circle of the Master of Mary of Burgundy. *Mass of St. Gregory*; Hours of William Lord Hastings. Madrid, Museo Lázaro-Galdiano, no. 15503, fol. 21v.

Pl. 1. Circle of the Master of Mary of Burgundy. *King David in Prayer* (enlarged detail below), Breviary from Rooclooster. Add. Ms. 11863, fol. 23.

that monasteries of the Windesheim order did not commission prominent illuminators to decorate manuscripts written within the confines of the monastery. However, in the period of Hugo's association with Rooclooster—the late 1470s, when the present manuscript was executed—those attached to the monastery were treated fairly liberally.[8] Hugo took on important commissions while he lived there, just as the Master of Mary of Burgundy and his followers also earned important commissions during the same period.[9] If Lieftinck is correct, then both the Master of Mary of Burgundy and the illuminator of the London breviary would necessarily have been residents of Rooclooster at approximately the same time as Hugo. Moreover, the close artistic relationship between Hugo and the Master of Mary of Burgundy would seem to strengthen Lieftinck's argument. In the end, however, the only secure evidence for linking either of the illuminators under consideration here with Rooclooster is the single breviary that each illuminated for the monastery.[10] Lieftinck's thesis is plausible, but difficult to substantiate.

Given the similarities in script, contents, decorative styles, and dimensions between the Brussels and London manuscripts, the London breviary was probably executed not long after 1477, the date given in the Brussels manuscript (fol. 304).

BIBLIOGRAPHY London (British Museum) 1850, p. 13; Lieftinck 1969, I, pp. xiii–xiv, xxviii, 14, 20–23, II, figs. 45–46; Dogaer 1972, p. 98; Hilger 1973, p. 40, n. 46; Van Buren 1975, p. 307.

NOTES

1. Lieftinck 1969, I, p. 22.

2. Add. Ms. 11864 entered the British Museum along with Add. Ms. 11863; see London (British Museum) 1850, p. 13; Lieftinck 1969, I, pp. 22–23; Van Buren 1975, p. 293, n. 36. This second London breviary contains fifteen borders and fifteen small initials. On the Rooclooster breviary in Brussels, see Lieftinck 1964a, no. 37a; Lieftinck 1964b, cols. 254–92, figs. 1, 2; Lieftinck 1969, I, pp. xiii–xiv, 13–23, esp. 18–20.

3. For a similar pose, compare the figure of the priest in the *Circumcision* in the Breviary of Margaret of York (Cambridge, St. John's College, Ms. H. 13; Lieftinck 1969, II, fig. 7). See also Lieftinck's remarks on the way in which the illuminator painted the inside of a hand (1969, I, p. xiii, II, figs. 39, 43, 49, 59, etc.). Although this cannot be the only criterion for distinguishing between the master and his imitators, it seems to be a valid one.

4. Lieftinck 1969, I, p. 21; see also Van Buren 1975, p. 307.

5. This manuscript was long attributed to the Master of Mary of Burgundy (Winkler 1925, pp. 158–59; later by Pächt 1948, no. 11). It was Lieftinck who rightly pointed out the distinction in handling between these and the finest works of the master (1969, I, pp. 126–47, II, figs. 202–207, 211–212, 215–234, 236–260). Lieftinck's view has been accepted by Van Buren (1975, p. 307) and de Winter (1981, pp. 353, 358, 362, 374, 423–24, n. 16); de Winter attributes some of the miniatures to the Master of the First Prayer Book of Maximilian.

6. See Cat. 3, n. 8.

7. Lieftinck 1946b, and 1969, I, pp. xiii–xiv.

8. Lieftinck 1969, I, p. 17.

9. Winkler 1964, pp. 1–2.

10. Van Buren 1975, p. 293, discusses whether or not it would be suitable to rechristen the Master of Mary of Burgundy "The Rooclooster Master" on the basis of Lieftinck's argument. Even if he is correct regarding the illuminator's association with Rooclooster, this change seems inadvisable, since most of the patronage of the Master of Mary of Burgundy remained secular.

3 Hours of William Lord Hastings

Use of Sarum; probably Ghent, late 1470s. Additional Ms. 54782

MANUSCRIPT *Vellum, 300 leaves; 16.5 × 12.3 cm. 28 miniatures with ornamental borders around the miniatures and the facing text pages; 4 half-page miniatures with ornamental borders; 7 other ornamental borders (single leaves with miniatures originally facing these 7 borders may have been cut off, fols. 13, 26, 45, 46, 47, 52, 61¹); the arms of Hastings appear four times, on fol. 184v painted over the royal arms of England. Burgundian bâtarde script.*

BINDING *Modern, red morocco, richly tooled.*

PROVENANCE *Bernard Quaritch, London; purchased by C. W. Dyson Perrins, 1910 (Ms. 104); bequeathed by his widow to the British Museum, December 1968.*

THE HOURS of William Lord Hastings is the masterpiece of one of the major artistic figures of late Flemish illumination, the Master of the First Prayer Book of Maximilian. A prolific artist who was probably active mainly at Ghent, his career spans nearly fifty years. The Hastings Hours was executed in his youth, most likely during the first years of the late Flemish period (circa 1475–1550) or shortly thereafter, when he and the Master of Mary of Burgundy, the leading illuminator of his time, were active at the Burgundian court of Duke Charles the Bold and Margaret of York. The Master of Mary of Burgundy was responsible for the development of a new style of decoration which the Master of the First Prayer Book of Maximilian brought to an unusual degree of refinement in the Hastings Hours. This is the style of illusionistic decorative motifs (Pls. II, III), in which the flowers, acanthus leaves, insects, and other motifs cast shadows. Above all, the artistic achievement of the Master of the First Prayer Book of Maximilian in the Hastings Hours resides in the unified decorative treatment of the two-page spread, especially in the harmony of color between miniature and border. It appears, moreover, to have exercised a lasting influence on Flemish illumination.

Several theories have been proposed regarding the patron of this manuscript. Warner identified the Hastings coat of arms as belonging to Sir Edward Hastings, who became a Knight of the Order of the Garter in 1554 and Baron Hastings of Loughborough in January 1557 or 1558.[2] On fols. 13, 74, and 151, the Hastings shield is surrounded by the garter. However, Backhouse has argued convincingly that the arms refer to Sir Edward's ancestor, William Lord Hastings (c. 1430–1483), who was installed as a Knight of the Garter in 1462, the first member

of his family to receive this honor.[3] The main evidence for the association with William, who was chamberlain to the royal household and long an intimate of King Edward IV, lies in a specially inserted miniature of *St. Leonard*, the name saint of William's father.[4] The *St. Leonard* is one of only four half-page miniatures in the manuscript, the others, arranged immediately before and after it, being *St. Paul*, *St. David of Wales*, and *St. Jerome*. As the only miniatures on text pages, they were in all likelihood included at the request of the patron after the overall iconographic program had been established. Like the rest of the illuminations, they were executed by the Master of the First Prayer Book of Maximilian, probably just prior to the completion of the decoration.[5]

In the *Mass of the Dead* miniature the royal arms of England are overpainted with shields bearing Hastings' arms, an alteration which, along with the aforementioned additional miniatures, suggests that Hastings became the patron of the manuscript only after another Englishman withdrew his patronage. However, several original decorative features offer evidence that the manuscript was initially commissioned by a member of the English court. In one decorated border, banners with the royal arms of England hang from long trumpets that sound from the royal barge, and a long streamer flowing from a flagstaff carries the first word of the motto of the Order of the Garter, *"Honi."*[6] It seems as likely, therefore, that Hastings, himself a prominent English courtier, originated the project and the alterations reflect decisions made in the course of the manuscript's execution.

One of the four specially inserted miniatures is a unique representation of *St. David of Wales* (Fig. 3a). Its significance for Hastings is not entirely clear, although several connections with Wales deserve mention. First, Hastings was both chamberlain of North Wales and constable of Harlech Castle. Second, he had sworn fealty to the king's son, the Prince of Wales, and the present miniature depicts the saint dressed as a prince, with the royal coronet and the royal scepter. Turner has pointed out pentimenti which show that the saint was originally drawn with a bishop's miter and crosier; the changes indicate that the patron wanted to emphasize St. David's royal origins.[7]

Hastings merits some attention as a patron because this manuscript and another Flemish book of hours, now in Madrid, which he commissioned slightly earlier, are two of the finest examples of the style introduced by the Master of Mary of Burgundy.[8] Hastings' patronage was thus important in the development of this style. As leader of the Burgundian party at the English court, Hastings had extensive contacts with the Burgundian court, from which he

Fig. 3a. Master of the First Prayer Book of Maximilian. *St. David of Wales*, fol. 40.

illuminated books of hours. One notable volume in his library was a *Mirror of the World,* translated by William Caxton and printed by him in 1481 with a dedication to Hastings. Hugh Bryce, Lord Mayor of London in 1485–86 and Governor of the King's Mint under Hastings, commissioned the publication.[13]

In the matter of book design, the second Hastings Hours is one of the most refined Flemish devotional books to survive. The Master of the First Prayer Book of Maximilian has managed to achieve a unified and harmonious effect in the two-page spreads. Not only are miniatures and border motifs crisply drawn throughout, but the purity of color and the manner in which colors are interrelated between border and miniature give each opening an extraordinary, self-contained vitality. For example, in the spread with the *Martyrdom of St. Thomas à Becket* (Pl. II) the two bright yellow borders decorated with gold-brown acanthus and small white flowers complement Thomas' golden chasuble in the center of the miniature. The composition is wonderfully designed, the brutal subject given a strange beauty by the symmetry of the attackers' movements and the pattern of assaulting weapons. In addition, the gold bands that line both inner and outer edges of the border, casting shadows within the border, further unify the two-page spread and give the border a relief character.

Another example of this illuminator's genius is the two-page opening with a miniature of *St. Catherine of Alexandria* (Pl. III), perhaps the most beautifully drawn figure in the manuscript. The gold of the saint's dress complements the brilliant blue of the border ground, while small accents of a deeper blue appear within the miniature—in the helmet of the emperor and in the cloth backing for Catherine's book—and the border has its own golden inner and outer frames. The pale rose of the canopy is repeated in the flowers of the border in even paler shades. Some of the colors within the miniature are echoed in the facing border. Finally, it bears mentioning that despite the unity in color design of each decorated opening, subtle differences in color values suggest that facing borders were executed independently of each other and perhaps by distinct hands, which would not be surprising in such a richly illuminated manuscript.

The narrative borders that appear on the text pages facing miniatures add a worldly character to the decorations, and they serve as a reminder of the sophisticated, mostly secular patronage for such books. In addition to the picturesque scene of the English royal barge on a river, there are borders with a jousting tournament, one with wild men in a landscape, and, perhaps the most charming of all, a border facing the miniature of the *Adoration of the Magi* which shows several figures, including ladies in courtly costume, receiving largesse in the form of a shower of coins (Fig. 3b). The cumulative effect of successive two-

received a pension. In 1466 and 1467 he was one of the ambassadors who negotiated the marriage between Edward's sister, Margaret of York, and the Count of Charolais, the future Duke Charles the Bold of Burgundy. Hastings was also lieutenant of Calais, only about sixty miles from Bruges, from 1471 on.[9]

The Duke and Duchess of Burgundy, the most sophisticated patrons of illumination of their day, may have been responsible for introducing Hastings to the latest developments in Flemish illumination during the 1470s. Their numerous important commissions included a breviary illuminated by the Master of Mary of Burgundy, probably not long before the death of Charles in 1477.[10] Moreover, it seems probable that the Master of the First Prayer Book of Maximilian was responsible for an important manuscript in Margaret's library, the *Chronicle of the Counts of Flanders,* which was presented by Mary of Burgundy to her stepmother, Margaret, in 1477.[11]

Hastings had the opportunity to become familiar with the finest Flemish painters as well. In Bruges around 1480 his sister Elizabeth, and his brother-in-law, Sir John Donne, commissioned an altarpiece by Hans Memling.[12] Unfortunately, little more is known about Hastings' patronage or the contents of his library than the two superb

page openings is dazzling for quality of execution, richness of color, and variety of decorative motifs.

Little is known of the early activity of the Master of the First Prayer Book of Maximilian, although de Winter has ascribed two well-known books of hours from the circle of the Master of Mary of Burgundy to the early period of the Maximilian Master.[14] These attributions—the Madrid Hastings Hours and the famous Berlin Hours of Mary of Burgundy and Maximilian—seem to me not entirely convincing. I propose instead that the *Chronicle of the Counts of Flanders,* which was illuminated at Ghent in 1477 or the previous year, is more likely to represent his early activity.[15] The visual criteria are the facial types and the manner of execution. In the London Hastings Hours, as in the *Chronicle,* the illuminator modeled faces in gray with pink highlights—usually applied around the eyes, especially to accent cheekbones, on the chin, above the upper lip, and on the tip of the nose (Figs. 3a, 3c). The handling of the bushy hair in these two miniatures and elsewhere also corresponds in both manuscripts. The hairstyle of the

sword-wielding, kneeling figure in the center of the *Revolt of the Citizens of Ghent* (Fig. 3c) and the facial features of his victim directly below him on the ground resemble both St. David of Wales (Fig. 3a) and St. Paul (fol. 38). These types recur throughout the work of the Master of the First Prayer Book of Maximilian, for example, in a book of hours, now in Brussels, executed for Philip of Cleves prior to 1485, and in the portrait of King Louis XI of France in the frontispiece miniature in a *Life of St. Adrian* in Vienna, rightly attributed by Hilger to the Master of the First Prayer Book of Maximilian.[16] Finally, the quality of movement, the poses, and the facial types of the young men reaching for coins in the border opposite the *Adoration of the Magi* (Fig. 3b) reveal further correspondences with the combatants in the *Revolt of the Citizens of Ghent* in the *Chronicle.*

The designs for the miniatures in the London Hours of William Lord Hastings had an immediate and long-term impact. Nearly all are the earliest known examples of figural compositions that were copied repeatedly in

Fig. 3b. Master of the First Prayer Book of Maximilian. *Adoration of the Magi*; decorated border with the *Shower of Gold*, fols. 42v–43.

Pl. II. Master of the First Prayer Book of Maximilian. *Martyrdom of St. Thomas à Becket,*
Hours of William Lord Hastings. Add. Ms. 54782, fols. 55v–56.

Pl. III. Master of the First Prayer Book of Maximilian. *St. Catherine of Alexandria*,
Hours of William Lord Hastings. Add. Ms. 54782, fols. 68v–69.

Fig. 3c. Attributed to the Master of the First Prayer Book of Maximilian. *Revolt of the Citizens of Ghent*, in the CHRONICLE OF THE COUNTS OF FLANDERS. Holkham Hall, Library of Viscount Coke, Ms. 659, fol. 226.

Fig. 3d [LEFT]. Master of the First Prayer Book of Maximilian. *St. Anthony Abbot*, fol. 50v.

Fig. 3e [RIGHT]. Master of Mary of Burgundy. Text page; border with *St. Anthony in the Wilderness*, "Voustre Demeure" Hours. Madrid, Biblioteca Nacional, Ms. Vit. 25–5, fol. 191.

Fig. 3f [LEFT]. Master of the First Prayer Book of Maximilian. *St. Margaret and the Dragon*, fol. 62v.

Fig. 3g [RIGHT]. Circle of the Master of Mary of Burgundy. *Annunciation*, Hours of William Lord Hastings. Madrid, Museo Lázaro-Galdiano, Ms. 15503, fol. 73v.

Flemish illumination for the next fifty years. Such copies appear not merely within the illuminator's own sphere of activity, but in manuscripts illuminated by others as well, including the Grimani Breviary, the Prayer Book of Albrecht of Brandenburg, and the *Hortulus animae*.[17] From this perspective, the London Hastings Hours might well be considered one of the seminal works of the late Flemish tradition.

To my knowledge only two miniatures in this manuscript are derived from miniatures in other Flemish manuscripts. The *St. Anthony Abbot* (Fig. 3d) is based on a design by the Master of Mary of Burgundy. It contains three vignettes from the saint's life in the wilderness which closely follow a historiated border in the "Voustre Demeure" Hours in Madrid (Fig. 3e). The Hastings *St. Margaret and the Dragon* (Fig. 3f) was probably also copied from another illumination. The figure of St. Margaret corresponds in posture and in arrangement of drapery folds to an Annunciate Virgin who appears in several Flemish

manuscripts roughly contemporaneous with or slightly earlier in date than the Hastings Hours, including the Madrid Hastings Hours (Fig. 3g) and the Hours of Philip of Cleves in Brussels. That the St. Margaret derives from an *Annunciation* miniature and not vice versa is apparent from the dove of the Annunciation, which the Master of the First Prayer Book of Maximilian anomalously introduced into St. Margaret's iconography.

It appears likely that the Master of the First Prayer Book of Maximilian was active at the Burgundian court in 1477. This is supported by numerous visual connections with some of the other large illuminated texts commissioned by Margaret of York and executed at Ghent. For example, the scene of *Charles the Bold at Mass* in an undated collection of moral and religious treatises (Fig. 3h) and other, mostly grisaille, scenes from Margaret's manuscripts show similarities in color, setting, and architectural details to the London Hastings miniatures of *St. David of Wales* (Fig. 3a), *St. Margaret and the Dragon* (Fig. 3f), *St. Nicholas*

Fig. 3h. Master of the Moral Treatises. *Charles the Bold at Mass*, in a collection of moral and religious treatises. Brussels, Bibliothèque Royale, Ms. 9272–6, fol. 55.

Fig. 3i [ABOVE]. Circle of the Master of Mary of Burgundy. *St. Peter of Luxembourg and His Sister*, in a collection of moral and religious treatises. Oxford, Bodleian Library, Douce Ms. 365, fol. xvii.

Fig. 3j [RIGHT]. Master of the First Prayer Book of Maximilian. *St. Elizabeth of Hungary Clothing the Poor*, fol. 64v.

(fol. 57v), and *St. Leonard* (fol. 39).[18] The quality of execution is much broader in the treatises, a manuscript ascribed to an illuminator in the circle of the Master of Mary of Burgundy; but the axial central figure, the predominantly gray setting, the role of the monochromatic backdrop as a foil for the areas of bright color, and the drawing of the column bases are features shared with Figs. 3a and 3f.[19] In a miniature of *St. Peter of Luxembourg and His Sister* (Fig. 3i) in another collection of moral and religious treatises, written at Ghent in 1475 by the scribe David Aubert for Margaret of York, the long, loose strokes, the hatchings of the shadows, and the recessional pattern of the floor tiles find correspondences in the *St. David of Wales* and *St. Nicholas* miniatures, while the crisp contours of the nun recall the features of the Hastings *St. Elizabeth of Hungary* (Fig. 3j).[20] Finally, the scale of the figures and their settings in the treatises of 1475 resemble the Hastings miniatures. While these relationships do not argue unequivocally for further attributions to the Master of the First Prayer Book of Maximilian, they clearly indicate the milieu of his visual ideas.

Moreover, as de Winter has shown, this illuminator was strongly influenced by Flemish painters of the day, especially the Ghent artist Hugo van der Goes, whose bearded male figure types are in evidence throughout the London Hastings Hours (Figs. 3a, 3b). Hugo's several versions of the *Nativity* strongly influenced the Hastings *Nativity* miniature.[21] And Dieric Bouts' altarpiece with the *Martyrdom of St. Erasmus* was the inspiration behind the Hastings miniature of this subject.[22]

Several facts allow us to establish an approximate date for the creation of the Hastings Hours. In June 1483 Hastings was executed by Richard of Gloucester, the future King Richard III, in the first of a series of events leading to the usurpation of the throne of Edward IV. Therefore, Hastings' death provides a *terminus ante quem* of 1483. Moreover, since the Hastings Hours cannot readily be separated from the leading currents in Flemish art of the late 1470s, it is probably roughly datable to this period. Among the manuscripts under discussion here it is probably later in date than either the Madrid Hastings Hours or the "Voustre Demeure" Hours from which it seems to have derived miniatures. However, neither of these two is securely datable, except that both were also probably completed by the time of Hastings' death in 1483.[23] In the view of this compiler, the London manuscript was probably executed shortly after the 1477 *Chronicle of the Counts of Flanders*. A date not later than 1480 seems plausible, as Van Buren has suggested.[24] De Winter has proposed a somewhat later dating.[25]

De Winter identifies the Master of the First Prayer Book of Maximilian as very probably—and plausibly—the Ghent illuminator Alexander Bening.[26] Warner localized the manuscript to Bruges, but it seems as likely that the London Hastings Hours was executed within the Ghent artistic milieu discussed here. Van Buren has also proposed a connection with Ghent.[27]

Finally, an unpublished manuscript executed within a few years of the Hastings Hours deserves to be added to the oeuvre of the Master of the First Prayer Book of Maximilian (San Marino, Calif., The Huntington Library, HM. 1148). The color harmonies of the decorative borders exhibit a strong kinship with the London Hastings Hours. It appears to contain the work of the same scribe and similar decorated initials on gold-brown grounds.[28] Turner has pointed out that the scribe of the London Hastings Hours also executed the script in the following manuscripts, all of them datable within the period 1475–85: the Madrid Hastings Hours, the Hours of Philip of Cleves in Brussels, the Hours of Mary of Burgundy and Maximilian, and the second Hours of Philip of Cleves in Vienna.[29]

BIBLIOGRAPHY Warner 1920, I, no. 104, pl. LXXXVIII; Winkler 1925, pp. 113, 169; London (Royal Academy) 1953, no. 598; Backhouse 1973b, p. 684; Van Buren 1975, pp. 306–07; Pächt 1976; Scott 1976, pp. 52–53, n. 194, p. 85; Trenkler 1979, pp. 81–82, 84, figs. 10, 15; de Winter 1981, pp. 347, 362–63, 369, 374, 397, 406, 408, 424, n. 20, 425, n. 26, figs. 26, 52, 72, 78, 92, 150, 160; Turner [1983].

NOTES

1. Warner 1920, I, p. 237.

2. Ibid., p. 240.

3. Backhouse 1973b, p. 684.

4. See the discussion by Derek Turner in the introduction to the forthcoming facsimile edition of the Hastings Hours (Turner [1983]). I am grateful to Mr. Turner for allowing me to study portions of his text.

5. The Master of the First Prayer Book of Maximilian is named after a manuscript of 1486 in Vienna, Österreichische Nationalbibliothek, Cod. 1907 (Hilger 1973); the attribution was first suggested by Pächt in London (Royal Academy) 1953, no. 598.

6. Warner 1920, I, p. 240, suggested that the royal arms might indicate that the manuscript belonged to Henry VII or Henry VIII, but he allowed rightly that these features may merely indicate that the manuscript's destination was England.

7. Turner [1983].

8. The Madrid manuscript (Museo Lázaro-Galdiano, Ms. 15503) is the so-called "First Hours of William Lord Hastings"; see Pächt 1948, no. 17, p. 68; Lieftinck 1969, I, pp. xx, 109–25, 178–81, II, figs. 165–201, 288; Pächt 1976; de Winter 1981, pp. 353, 424, n. 20, figs. 99, 104, 118. Van Buren 1975, p. 307, refers to the British Library manuscript as the second Hastings Hours, as does de Winter 1981, pp. 347, 424, n. 20. Both of them consider the Madrid manuscript to be earlier in date than the London Hours. Pächt, in both studies cited, considered the Madrid manuscript to be by the Master of Mary of Burgundy himself. Lieftinck doubted the attribution; he was followed by Van Buren, who attributed it to a "Ghent Associate," and de Winter, who considered it to be in part from the hand of the Master of the First Prayer

Book of Maximilian. However, this compiler does not find de Winter's attribution entirely convincing.

9. Fotheringham, in *Dictionary*, XXV, pp. 148–49.

10. On this breviary, see Cat. 1, n. 14.

11. Holkham Hall, Library of Viscount Coke, Ms. 659; Dorez 1908, pp. 89ff., pls. LIV–LV; Winkler 1925, p. 113; Pächt 1948, no. 5, figs. 6–9; Brussels 1959, no. 195; Hassall 1970, pp. 13–15, 25–30; Lieftinck 1969, I, pp. viii–ix, who does, however, propose to identify the hand with that in the Berlin Hours of Mary and Maximilian (Berlin, Staatliche Museen, Kupferstichkabinett, Ms. 78 B 12). Although no books of hours in the new manner are known from the library of Margaret of York, she commissioned or received a number of important large historical, religious, and philosophical texts written in Ghent between the years 1474 and 1477 and employed some of the finest illuminators and scribes of the day; see Pächt 1948, nos. 2–6; Brussels 1959, nos. 191–199; Brussels 1967b, p. 4; Dogaer 1975. For Margaret of York's manuscripts now in the British Library, see Dogaer 1975, p. 110, and Cat. 2 above.

12. Now London, National Gallery; McFarlane 1971, pp. 1–15.

13. Scott 1976, pp. 52–53, 85, n. 194.

14. De Winter 1981, pp. 353, 424, n. 20.

15. See n. 11 above.

16. For the Brussels manuscript (Bibliothèque Royale, Ms. IV 40), see Laloire 1905–06; Winkler 1925, p. 168; Hulin de Loo 1939b, pp. 175–76, pl. IIIa; Pächt 1948, no. 30; Brussels 1959, no. 274; Delaissé 1965, pp. 204–07; Lieftinck 1969, I, pp. 168–70; Van Buren 1975, p. 307; de Winter 1981, pp. 362, 424, n. 20, 425, n. 24. For the Vienna *Life of St. Adrian* (Österreichische Nationalbibliothek, Cod. ser. nov. 2619), see Winkler 1925, p. 208; Hulin de Loo 1939b, p. 173, pl. Ia; Pächt 1948, no. 12; Lieftinck 1969, I, pp. 152–56, II, figs. 263–270; Hilger 1973, p. 54, n. 94; Van Buren 1975, p. 307, n. 2. In addition to the similar facial type and modeling of flesh in the frontispiece of the *St. Adrian* and in the London Hastings Hours miniatures, the former has a related color sensibility, especially for the decorative possibilities of blue and gold. The drawing of the figure of Queen Charlotte of Savoy also recalls the features of St. Elizabeth of Hungary (Fig. 3j).

17. Venice (Biblioteca Marciana, Ms. lat. XI [7531]); Malibu, Calif., The J. Paul Getty Museum (Ms. Ludwig IX 19); and Vienna, Österreichische Nationalbibliothek (Cod. 2706), respectively. De Winter 1981, figs. 26–28, 72–76, 78–80, 86, 92–94, 149–152, 160–162, illustrates numerous examples of repetitions of miniatures where the earliest version appears in the London Hastings Hours. Most of these repetitions are attributable to the Master of the First Prayer Book of Maximilian.

18. Brussels 1959, no. 196.

19. A colorplate of fol. 182 of the treatises (ibid., pl. 8), showing Margaret of York in prayer, gives an idea of the similar effect in the use of bright colors on a gray background.

20. Pächt 1948, no. 3; Brussels 1959, no. 192.

21. De Winter 1981, pp. 377, 382–85. However, the central figure group of the Hastings *Nativity* seems to this writer more likely based on a lost *Nativity* by Hugo known through a putative copy in Antwerp, Koninklijk Museum voor Schone Kunsten; see Friedländer 1967–76, IV, pl. 28a, no. 17d.

22. Friedländer 1967–76, III, pl. 15. A miniature of the *Martyrdom*, very similar to the London miniature and also ultimately derived from Bouts, appears in the Madrid Hastings Hours, fol. 36v (Lieftinck 1969, II, fig. 195).

23. Lieftinck 1969, I, p. 88, where the "Voustre Demeure" Hours is dated 1480–83; see also Van Buren 1975, p. 292.

24. Van Buren 1975, p. 307.

25. De Winter's view (1981, p. 425, n. 20) that the manuscript was still not finished when Hastings died in 1483 because the borders are more advanced than the illuminator's eponymous manuscript of 1486 seems implausible. If this were the case, the Hastings Hours would have been completed four or five years after Hastings' death. Since the style of the manuscript is very unified, its decoration would not likely have extended over so many years. Moreover, since the Hastings Hours appears to be the illuminator's finest work, it is not surprising that his best illuminations were produced when he was working in close proximity to the Master of Mary of Burgundy.

26. De Winter 1981, pp. 355–57.

27. Van Buren 1975, p. 307; also Warner 1920, I, p. 237.

28. Consuelo Dutschke will publish a complete description of this manuscript in the forthcoming catalogue of medieval manuscripts in the Huntington Library.

29. I am grateful to Mr. Turner for showing me his notes on liturgical and textual features of the London Hastings Hours. On the Vienna Philip of Cleves (Österreichische Nationalbibliothek, Cod. ser. nov. 13239), see Lieftinck 1969, I, pp. 165–70, II, figs. 284–286.

4 Huth Hours

Use of Rome; probably Valenciennes, late 1480s. Additional Ms. 38126

MANUSCRIPT *Vellum, iii + 252 + iii leaves + 2 detached inserts on paper; 14.8 × 11.6 cm. 24 full-page miniatures, 24 roundels in the bas-de-page of the calendar, and 50 other small miniatures. Full borders in the calendar, on the leaves with small miniatures, and on some of the full-page miniatures; partial borders on all of the text pages. A number of prayers added on the flyleaves in various sixteenth- and seventeenth-century hands, in Latin, French, and Italian. 2 large sheets of paper, 21.6 × 30.5 cm, folded and inserted, with a description of the manuscript in Italian (probably written in the late eighteenth century, it records implausibly that the book of hours once belonged to King Henry VIII and subsequently to a noble Flemish family, and, moreover, that the letters* HOLBE *at the lower left of the decorative border of fol. 228 (Pl. IV) may be read as a partial signature of the illuminator, Hans Holbein the Younger). Rounded gothic script.*

BINDING *Leather, stamped, Ghent or Bruges (?), circa 1500.*

PROVENANCE *Henry Huth, before 1880; Alfred H. Huth; bequeathed to the British Museum, 1912.*

THIS book of hours is one of the most richly illuminated devotional books from the workshop generally identified with Simon Marmion (d. 1489). Largely on the basis of circumstantial evidence, Dehaisnes and Winkler identified Marmion, a painter and illuminator from Valenciennes who enjoyed considerable fame, as the artist of a sizable oeuvre of illuminated manuscripts and a small number of paintings executed over four decades.[1] The oeuvre consists mostly of large secular and religious manuscripts produced during the reigns of Philip the Good and Charles the Bold and shifts to small but richly illuminated devotional books in the mid-1470s.[2] De Schryver recently attributed some of the finest of the later manuscripts, including the Huth Hours, to an illuminator he calls the Louthe Master, after one of the patrons of a book of hours on Winkler's list.[3] The Huth Hours presents some evidence, however, to suggest that the artistic activity of the Louthe Master is too narrowly defined by de Schryver. The Huth miniatures support Winkler's conception of the oeuvre of Marmion, which convincingly encompasses a more diverse body of work. Led by a protean artistic figure, Marmion's shop employed a number of assistants, but it followed a unified development.[4] Although this is not the place to analyze his entire oeuvre, an evaluation of the Huth Hours requires some consideration of the artistic definition that Winkler established for Marmion's work.

The Huth Hours offers a summation of this illuminator's

achievement primarily in the domain of devotional books, but it also reflects the latest trends in Flemish illumination. For example, a number of Marmion's finest illuminated devotional books predate the introduction of the brightly colored, illusionistic borders on solid-colored grounds. The Huth Hours, along with many devotional books from the Marmion shop, belongs to the later period. It adopts the new manner of border decoration throughout, including a variety of illusionistic borders, all derived from the Master of Mary of Burgundy and his circle. These include architectural borders (fols. 12, 46), a border that creates the illusion of a sheet of vellum lying on a decorative brocade and casting its shadow on the actual vellum leaf (fol. 241), a narrative border (fol. 146), and a border of letters seemingly set at random in rows of lozenges (Pl. IV) but probably a reference to the text opening they decorate.[5]

The Huth Hours can be dated and located within Marmion's development in relation to the artist's other books of hours. In my view, they include, in roughly chronological order, the Berlaymont Hours,[6] the so-called "Hours of Henry VIII,"[7] the Salting Hours,[8] the Rolin Hours,[9] the Turin Hours,[10] the Louthe Hours,[11] a book of hours in the Pierpont Morgan Library,[12] a book of hours in the Houghton Library,[13] the "Flora" Hours,[14] and a sequence of four full-page miniatures in Berlin, excised from the famous "Voustre Demeure" Hours.[15] The first three manuscripts show the older style of spray-and-acanthus Flemish borders typical of the 1470s (Fig. 4b), while the Rolin Hours has details of costume that seem datable not later than the 1470s. The remaining five all contain representative examples of the illusionistic strewn-pattern borders of the late Flemish period,[16] so they are not likely to have been produced prior to 1475, but rather closer to 1480 or later.

Coloring, iconography, figure types, and the treatment of landscape are the unifying features of most of the miniatures in these books of hours. Except in the two sets of monochrome miniatures in Turin and Madrid, coloring offers the clearest visual hallmark of this workshop. The palette tends toward pastel tonalities: salmon, peach, lavender, pale blues, as well as soft browns, chocolate browns with golden highlights, light grays, and kelly greens.

The Huth *Annunciation to the Shepherds* (Fig. 4a), viewed in relation to other treatments of this subject in this group of manuscripts, gives an idea of the illuminator's development as a landscape painter which culminated in the Huth Hours. For example, in comparison with the relatively early *Annunciation to the Shepherds* in the Berlaymont Hours (Fig. 4b), the Huth miniature shows a more sophis-

Fig. 4a [ABOVE]. Simon Marmion. *Annunciation to the Shepherds*, fol. 79v.

Fig. 4b [TOP RIGHT]. Simon Marmion Workshop. *Annunciation to the Shepherds*, Berlaymont Hours. San Marino, Calif., The Huntington Library, HM. 1173, fol. 44.

Fig. 4c [RIGHT]. Simon Marmion. *Annunciation to the Shepherds*, "Flora" Hours. Naples, Biblioteca Nazionale, Ms. I B 51, fol. 120v.

Fig. 4d [LEFT]. Simon Marmion. *Nativity*, fol. 75v.

Fig. 4e [RIGHT]. Simon Marmion. *Nativity*, Berlaymont Hours. San Marino, Calif.,
The Huntington Library, HM. 1173, fol. 47.

ticated treatment of the foreshortening of upturned heads,
the gesture of cupped hands to protect the eyes, the path of
the river leading the eye toward the horizon, and the angels
with sweeping, overlong robes and banderoles.[17] Only the
palette, especially the light green of the meadow, and the
stick-legged sheep seem to have changed little during the
artist's development. But in the Huth Hours the illuminator gives the landscape a convincing scale and more
lucid organization. The river has greater breadth and helps
to unify the compositional space. The miniature now fills
the entire page, and the figures show greater variety of
pose and type and more freedom of movement. Indeed,
the Huth miniature is one of the crowning examples of the
conquest of space in late-fifteenth-century Flemish illumination. A comparison between the *Nativity* miniatures in
the Huth Hours and the Berlaymont Hours (Figs. 4d, 4e)
reveals even more clearly that the two manuscripts, although from different periods, issued from the same workshop. Nearly identical in conception are the facial type and
attire of the kneeling Virgins, the type of Joseph, and the

frame structure of the manger. The main distinction lies
once again in the landscape: an elaborate, hilly countryside
is visible through the open walls of the stable in the Huth
Nativity.

The relationship between the Huth Hours and the
Houghton Hours extends beyond the illuminations to such
features as script, arrangement of the decoration, and the
collaboration of other illuminators. As Kenyon has pointed
out, a number of miniatures and borders are nearly identical in the two manuscripts.[18] Hindman has remarked on
the similarities in the size and placement of the small miniatures, the shared script style—rounded gothic—the
number of lines per text page, and aspects of secondary
decoration, including initials and line endings.[19] Both
calendars are decorated with illusionistic acanthus and
flower borders with historiated roundels and, in both,
the roundels are illuminated by the Master of the Dresden Prayer Book. Moreover, it seems possible that a third
illuminator painted some full-page miniatures in the two
manuscripts.[20]

Fig. 4f. Simon Marmion. *St. Jerome in Penitence*, Book of Hours. Cambridge, Harvard University, Houghton Library, Mss. Typ 443 & 433.1, fol. 14v.

In landscape the Houghton miniatures show a level of maturity on a par with the Huth *Annunciation to the Shepherds*. In the beautiful *St. Jerome* in the Houghton manuscript (Fig. 4f), the recession of the rocky, irregular terrain is rendered with perfect clarity. The eye is led easily over the tops of bushes and trees into the woods. The illuminator suggests the density of the forested landscape without sacrificing the individual character of the trees. The same subject is treated in quite a different manner in the Huth Hours. The illuminator represents St. Jerome (Pl. IV) in the thick of the woods rather than on the bare rock. Jerome is glimpsed through dense foliage; the woods continue behind him, and the eye travels to the edge of a meadow and then to more thick growth. The Huth *St. Jerome* is more intimate and less grand than the Houghton illumination. Is the Huth version an inventive imitation by an assistant, or an experiment by the same master? It is difficult to judge without placing the two miniatures side by side, but the high quality of both and the handling of foliage suggest that they are probably from the same hand. The figure types of St. Jerome and the crucified Christ are remarkably similar in them. The Huth version seems a bold experiment, a departure from a successful vocabulary.[21] There is no equivalent treatment of landscape in Flemish panel painting at this time. In the *Temptation of St. Anthony* miniature in the Huth Hours (Fig. 4g), a concern

Fig. 4g [RIGHT]. Simon Marmion. *Temptation of St. Anthony*, fol. 133v.

Fig. 4h [FAR RIGHT]. Simon Marmion. *St. Anthony in the Wilderness*, Louthe Hours. Louvain-la-Neuve, Bibliothèque Universitaire, Ms. A 2, fol. 101v.

Pl. IV. Simon Marmion. *St. Jerome in Penitence*, Huth Hours. Add. Ms. 38126, fols. 227v–228.

Fig. 4i [LEFT]. Simon Marmion Workshop. *Madonna and Child*, fol. 102v.

Fig. 4j [BOTTOM LEFT]. Simon Marmion. *Madonna and Child*. Berlin, Staatliche Museen Preussischer Kulturbesitz, Kupferstich-kabinett, Ms. 78 B 13, no. 1, detached leaf.

with the presentation of dense, lush foliage is again in evidence. In the treatment of the hermit St. Anthony in the Louthe Hours (Fig. 4h), which is probably datable a few years earlier, thick trees are apparent but the development is not carried as far. The Huth miniatures may therefore represent the most sophisticated expressions of the artist's concern with the depiction of near and far distances.

Six miniatures in the Huth Hours have half-length figures: *Pentecost* (fol. 45v), *Coronation of the Virgin* (fol. 97v), *Madonna and Child* (Fig. 4i), *Noli me tangere* (fol. 148v), *St. James the Major Preaching* (Fig. 4k), and a *Pietà* (fol. 240v). Probably earlier in the 1480s, Marmion had executed a series of twenty miniatures with half-length figures on small individual sheets, which are set into larger pages and incorporated into the monumental, but rarely studied, "Flora" Hours (Ill. 6, p. 10; Figs. 4c, 4l).[22] Two similar sheets are included among four he supplied to "Voustre Demeure," the elaborate book of hours which is mostly illuminated by the Master of Mary of Burgundy (Fig. 4j).[23]

Although Ringbom has suggested that the Huth half-lengths predate the "Flora" Hours, they seem rather to derive from both this manuscript and the leaves from the "Voustre Demeure" Hours in Berlin.[24] Intimately linked in pictorial conception, the Huth half-lengths may be distinguished from the "Flora" and Berlin miniatures by their method of execution. For example, the lovely *Madonna and Child* in the Huth Hours (Fig. 4i) is a reverse variant of the *Madonna and Child* in Berlin (Fig. 4j).[25] The facial types of the Virgin and the Child are quite similar, although the proportions of the Virgin in Berlin are slightly taller. In both, the Christ Child holds a rosary and the Virgin wears a transparent veil with frosty highlights. In the Berlin *Madonna and Child,* the flesh tones have an extraordinary vibrancy and the velvet bodice, a lively tactile quality. Extremely fine, closely placed strokes give relief to the surface and create vivid textural effects. The brushwork is similar in the Huth *Madonna,* but less controlled and more schematic. The illuminator relies more on a grid of extremely fine hatching and cross-hatching in red, and the effect is a bit hard.[26] The distinction between the two miniatures is a fine one, but sufficient to reveal the hand of the master in the one and a workshop hand in the other.

Four of the other half-lengths in the Huth Hours also seem to derive from the "Flora" Hours. In the *Pieta,* for example, the quality of modeling in the "Flora" version is more refined and convincing and, much as in the Berlin leaves, long thin strokes are built up for rich textural effects and profound nuances of color. The quality of the Huth miniature is once again extremely high, but the execution less painstaking.[27] Likewise, the *Noli me tangere* and *St. James the Major Preaching* (Fig. 4k) are probably based upon the "Flora" miniatures, and they are by a lesser hand than the other half-length miniatures in that manuscript (Fig. 4l).[28] The Huth *Pentecost* miniature may also derive ultimately from two miniatures in the "Flora" Hours—the *Pentecost* (fol. 67v) and the *Ascension of Christ* (fol. 253v).[29]

The innovative miniatures of the "Flora" Hours show stylistic links with more than the half-length miniatures of the Huth Hours. The *Annunciation to the Shepherds* (Fig. 4c), despite the difference between half-length and full-length formats, recalls the Huth miniature (Fig. 4a) in iconographic details, the treatment of landscape, the conception of the figures, and the concern with the problem of foreshortening from the back. Also similar in both is the long sweeping drapery of the angel holding a wisp of a banderole, and the contrast of the angel to the background —in the "Flora," a dark figure against a light sky, in the Huth miniature, light against dark. Even the minute daubs that give shape to the foliage suggest not merely a like conception but perhaps the same hand. The facial types in the half-length "Flora" miniatures have a more pronounced bone structure, which distinguishes them from otherwise similar types in the full-length miniatures in the other books of hours, but the distinction is probably a result of the dissimilar formats; the same hand is most likely responsible for the best work in both.

It appears, therefore, that at least two hands may be isolated in the execution of Marmion-style miniatures in devotional books of the 1470s and 1480s. This is not surprising. Given the requirements of the large cycles of illumination in many of these projects, it is rare that one finds a manuscript where as many as twenty miniatures appear to be entirely from the master's hand. Despite fundamental similarities in coloring, composition, and figural type, there may be more than one hand in the Marmion style among the manuscripts, such as in the Huth Hours and Morgan M.6; and there is evidence of workshop collaboration in the Huth Hours.

If Marmion is indeed rightly identified as the main illuminator of these books of hours, then the Huth Hours probably dates from a period not long before his death in 1489. Even if Marmion is not the illuminator, such a dating may not be far off. The "Flora" Hours has generally been dated to the mid-1480s and was probably not executed before 1486.[30] It seems unlikely that the Huth and Houghton Hours were executed more than a couple of years later.

Finally, two important full-page miniatures in the Huth Hours are apparently not from the Marmion workshop:

Fig. 4k [TOP RIGHT]. Simon Marmion Workshop. *St. James the Major Preaching*, fol. 135v.

Fig. 4l [RIGHT]. Simon Marmion. *St. James the Major Preaching*, "Flora" Hours. Naples, Biblioteca Nazionale, Ms. I B 51, fol. 318v.

the *Visitation* and the *Disputation of St. Barbara,* both probably by the same hand.[31] The palette of pale, subtly modulated tonalities in gray and brown in both recalls to some degree the Marmion miniatures; but the brushwork, especially in the *Visitation,* is wetter and more transparent, more like modern watercolor. In both miniatures there is a technique of fleck-like brushwork in the landscape and architecture reminiscent of the *St. Anthony Abbot* (fol. 99v) in the Houghton Hours, a miniature from the following of the Master of Mary of Burgundy.[32] Winkler initially suggested that the two miniatures in the Huth Hours might be by Bening, and Turner has accepted this.[33] If they are Bening's work, which seems unlikely, they would necessarily have been inserted several decades after the manuscript was completed. Winkler subsequently revised his opinion and attributed the miniatures to Horenbout, which is also unconvincing.[34] Most distinctive is the facial type of St. Barbara, whose dark round pupils resemble most the Virgin of the *Visitation.* The figure type of St. Barbara appears to be unique in Flemish illumination of the period.

On the basis of a decorative border displaying the letters MY/YM (or perhaps MV/VM), Winkler suggested that the manuscript may have been commissioned for Margaret of York, but there is no additional internal evidence to support this view and it has not gained wide acceptance.[35]

BIBLIOGRAPHY *Huth Library* 1880, II, pp. 723–24; Kenyon 1912, no. XIII, pp. 16–19, pls. 13–16; London (British Museum) 1925, pp. 26–28; Millar 1914–20, pp. 96–97, 103, 105, 106, 107, pls. XXXV–XXXVII; Winkler 1925, pp. 40, 170, pl. 10; Winkler in Thieme/Becker 1907–50, XXIV, p. 123; Winkler 1943, p. 60, figs. 6, 7; Ring 1949a, no. 174, pls. 101–102; Ringbom 1965, pp. 196–98, 200, 202, figs. 171, 172; Turner 1967, pp. 50–51, pl. IV; Hoffmann 1969, pp. 245, 268–70, pl. 96b; de Schryver 1969a, p. 152, n. 263; Hoffmann 1973, pp. 273, 274; Hindman 1977, pp. 188–90, 204; Sterling 1981, pp. 10–11, 13–14, 17, fig. 4.

NOTES

1. Dehaisnes 1892; Winkler 1925, pp. 40, 178. See also Winkler 1913c, pp. 264–65, figs. 17–20.

2. For some of the former, see Brussels 1959, nos. 57–62.

3. De Schryver 1969a, pp. 149–55, on the Huth Hours, p. 152, n. 263. Hoffmann 1973, p. 247, and Hindman 1977, pp. 188–91, also support de Schryver's attribution of the Huth Hours to the Louthe Master. On the Louthe Hours (Louvain-la-Neuve, Bibliothèque Universitaire, Ms. A 2), see Casier/Bergmans 1914–22, II, pp. 67–75; Winkler 1925, p. 182; de Schryver 1969a, pp. 149–55; Hoffmann 1973, pp. 274–75; and Demuynck 1979. I am grateful to Mr. Demuynck for providing me with a copy of his thesis.

4. Pächt 1978, p. 8, n. 11, and 1979, p. 14, and Sterling 1981, pp. 4–8, publish further circumstantial and visual evidence in support of the integrity of Winkler's original grouping and the identification with Marmion. Sterling furthermore demonstrates a relationship between a miniature of the *Mass of St. Gregory* in the Huth Hours (fol. 125v) and a recently discovered panel attributed

to Marmion and now in the Art Gallery of Ontario, Toronto (1981, figs. 1, 4, 6, 8–10, 19).

5. Some of the letters at the bottom of the border, P, S, A, and I, H, E, R, O, may be taken to allude to the *Psalterium Iheronimi.*

6. San Marino, Calif., The Huntington Library, HM. 1173; Destrée 1918; Hoffmann 1973, pp. 273, 275; Hindman 1977, p. 203, n. 45; Thorpe [1977]. The manuscript will receive a complete catalogue description in the forthcoming catalogue of medieval manuscripts in the Huntington Library by Consuelo Dutschke.

7. Tournai, Bibliothèque de la Ville, Ms. 122; see Ghent 1975, under no. 596.

8. London, Victoria and Albert Museum, Salting Ms. 1221; see Winkler 1925, p. 180; Brussels 1959, no. 263; de Schryver 1969a, p. 152; Hoffmann 1973, p. 273; Harthan 1977, pp. 148–49, pls. 146–147; Hindman 1977, pp. 193, 201, figs. 12–14, 26–29.

9. Madrid, Biblioteca Nacional, Ms. res. 149; see Ghent 1975, under no. 596; Dominguez Rodríguez 1979, no. 2, pl. p. 16.

10. Turin, Museo Civico, Ms. 558; see Ghent 1975, under no. 596.

11. See n. 3 above.

12. New York, The Pierpont Morgan Library, M.6; see Brussels 1959, no. 205; Hoffmann 1973, p. 273, n. 50; Hindman 1977, pp. 188–89, figs. 3–6; Voelkle 1980, pp. 1–2. The *Annunciation* (fol. 21) and the *Mass of St. Gregory* (fol. 153v) miniatures seem to be painted (or repainted?) by other hands (Voelkle, figs. IB3 and IC2).

13. Cambridge, Harvard University, Houghton Library, Mss. Typ 443 & 443.1; Quaritch 1892, pp. 14ff.; Coggiola 1908–10, pp. 149, 156; Kenyon 1912, pp. 17, 18 (where it is referred to as Mr. White's manuscript); Hoffmann 1973, p. 273; Hindman 1977, pp. 189–91; Cambridge 1983, no. 24.

14. Naples, Biblioteca Nazionale, Ms. I B 51; Coggiola 1908–10, pp. 145, 148; Winkler 1925, p. 189; Courcelle-Ladmirant 1939; Ringbom 1965, pp. 199–205; Hoffmann 1973, p. 273, n. 50.

15. Berlin, Kupferstichkabinett, Ms. 78 B 13, nos. 1, 9, 11, 20. For the "Voustre Demeure" Hours (Madrid, Biblioteca Nacional, Ms. Vit. 25–5), see Winkler 1913c, pp. 264–65, figs. 17–20; Winkler 1925, p. 159; de Schryver 1969a, p. 155; Lieftinck 1969, I, pp. 81, 86, 104, II, figs. 128, 161; Hoffmann 1973, p. 273.

16. In the Morgan Library manuscript, however, the illusionistic decorations are not properly borders, but panels below the miniatures. The modeling and scale of these borders are, respectively, more refined and larger than in the other examples and are almost certainly not by Marmion or his workshop.

17. A figure very similar to the Huth angel appears in the miniature of this subject in the Tournai, Madrid, and Louvain manuscripts.

18. These include the miniatures of *St. Christopher* and *St. Jerome,* the borders with the *Martyrdom of St. Barbara,* and the

architectural columns draped with a banderole (Kenyon 1912, pp. 17–18).

19. Hindman 1977, pp. 189–91.

20. See discussion below.

21. Hoffmann 1969, pp. 268–70, discusses the importance of landscape in this miniature.

22. There may have been twenty-two originally; the additional two—*Sacrifice of Isaac* (fol. 117v) and *Christ Taking Leave of His Mother* (fol. 230)—are inserted in a Flemish book of hours of a later date (Munich, Bayerische Staatsbibliothek, Clm. 28345); see Ringbom 1965, fig. 184. The *Sacrifice of Isaac* in Munich is, moreover, a variant of the composition with full-length figures of this subject in the Huth Hours (fol. 14v).

23. Lieftinck 1969, I, pp. 77–108, II, figs. 115–164.

24. Ringbom 1965, pp. 198, 209.

25. See also Winkler's discussion (1913c, p. 265) of this miniature in relation to other examples of Marmion's illuminations. The *Ascension of Christ* miniature in the Huth Hours (fol. 209v) is probably also derived from one by Marmion in Berlin, Ms. 78 B 13, no. 11.

26. Winkler 1925, p. 178, calls the miniatures with half-length figures in the Huth Hours "typical for his workshop."

27. A related *Pietà*, probably from the Marmion workshop, is in the Philadelphia Museum of Art; see Cleveland 1967, no. VII, 7. Related figure types appear in companion panels forming a *Pietà* in the Groeningemuseum, Bruges. They are catalogued by Dirk de Vos as "after Marmion(?)" in de Vos 1979, pp. 136–37. A drawing of a *Pietà* with full-length figures in the Fogg Art Museum, Harvard University, has also been attributed to Marmion; see Mongan 1942.

28. The distinction of hands was already noted by Kenyon 1912, p. 17.

29. Ringbom 1965, figs. 166, 172. A closely related version of the Huth *Pentecost* miniature is a single leaf in the Fitzwilliam Museum, Cambridge, Ms. 304. It is known to me only in a photograph.

30. There are few indications to date the "Flora" Hours precisely, but the miniatures by the Master of the First Prayer Book of Maximilian in the "Flora" are not datable prior to 1486, when he executed the First Prayer Book of Maximilian (Vienna, Österreichische Nationalbibliothek, Cod. 1907). The Vienna work is the last dated example of the early style of the Master of the First Prayer Book of Maximilian. His "Flora" miniatures represent a second manner, where he is strongly influenced by Marmion. This style seems to have emerged shortly after 1486, for example, in a breviary for Namur (Berlin, Staatsbibliothek, Ms. theol. lat. 2°285, fol. 7v) that is dated 1488 and 1489; see Berlin 1975, no. 158. Courcelle-Ladmirant 1939, p. 224, identifies a *terminus ante quem* of 1483 for the text of the "Flora" Hours. De Winter 1981, p. 424, n. 20, on the other hand, dates the "Flora" a bit later, circa 1489–91. Since Marmion died in 1489, de Winter's dating is only possible if his miniatures, which are inserted, were executed before the decoration of the rest of the book was begun. Likewise, Wieck, in Cambridge 1983, no. 24, dates the Houghton Hours circa 1485–90.

31. Fols. 66v and 145v; see Winkler 1925, figs. 6, 7; Turner 1967, pl. IV.

32. Pächt 1948, no. 31, pp. 71–72 under "Doubtful Attributions."

33. Winkler 1925, p. 178, and Turner 1967, p. 51, who suggests the miniatures were added to the manuscript circa 1520–30.

34. Winkler 1943, p. 60.

35. Winkler 1925, p. 123; see also Turner 1967, p. 51. A similar architectural border with the same initials on the banderole appears in a Flemish book of hours in the Beinecke Rare Book and Manuscript Library, Yale University (Ms. 287, fol. 38); see Cahn/Marrow 1978, no. 78, pp. 261–62; and in another Flemish book of hours in the Vatican Library, Ms. Vat. lat. 10293, fol. 13v; see Vatican City 1979, no. 63, pl. XI. Six miniatures from the Huth Hours were copied in a minor Flemish book of hours of the early sixteenth century now in Sir John Soane's Museum in London (Ms. 4); see Millar 1914–20, pp. 96–97, 103, 105–07; Harthan 1977, pp. 150–53.

5 Breviary of Queen Isabella of Castile

Use of the Spanish Dominicans; Bruges, before 1497. Additional
Ms. 18851

MANUSCRIPT *Vellum; 523 leaves; 23.2 × 15.9 cm. 45 half-page and 105 smaller miniatures; hundreds of border decorations and initials; arms of Francisco de Rojas added at the bottom of fol. 437; arms of Queen Isabella of Castile, her children, Joanna and Juan, and their spouses as full-page decoration on fol. 436v. Rounded gothic script.*

BINDING *Early-nineteenth-century dark brown morocco with fifteenth-century panels in dark brown morocco, blind-tooled, Spanish Mudéjar style.*

PROVENANCE *Francisco de Rojas, presented to Queen Isabella of Castile probably in 1497; John Dent, by 1817; Philip A. Hanrott; Sir John Tobin, Liverpool; Rev. John Tobin, Liscard, Cheshire; British Museum purchase from the book dealer William Boone, 1852.*

ALONG with the Grimani Breviary and the Mayer van den Bergh Breviary, this is one of the most important illuminated breviaries of the late Flemish period.[1] Unlike the popular books of hours and prayer books, which were produced for the devotions of the laity, the breviary is a liturgical manuscript produced for the use of the clergy. Many fewer richly illuminated breviaries than books of hours are known from this later period. However, breviaries contain a larger and more varied body of texts than the devotional books. As demonstrated by the Breviary of Isabella of Castile—a veritable treasure house of Flemish illumination—breviaries also afforded the artist a wider range of subject matter and more extensive opportunities for decoration.

This breviary contains two leaves with coats of arms. One full page (fol. 436v) bears the arms of Queen Isabella of Castile and León in the center above two smaller coats of arms: at the left, those of her daughter, the Infanta Joanna of Castile, impaling the arms of her husband, Philip the Handsome, Governor of the Netherlands; at the right the arms of Isabella's son, the Infante Don Juan, impaling those of his wife, Margaret of Austria. At the bottom of the leaf opposite (Fig. 5d) is another coat of arms, that of Francisco de Rojas, an ambassador of Isabella and King Ferdinand of Aragon; in 1496 and 1497 he negotiated the marriages of their children to the children of Emperor Maximilian I.[2] Rojas appears to have been in Flanders on a fairly regular basis from 1492 on; in Bruges he commissioned an altarpiece from Hans Memling.[3] Since the time of its acquisition by the British Museum in 1852, the breviary has generally been thought to have been presented by Rojas to

Queen Isabella on the occasion of her son's marriage in 1497.[4] A dedicatory inscription added to the lower half of the right border of fol. 437 states that Rojas presented the manuscript to Isabella "Queen of Spain and Sicily."[5]

Lázaro, however, has observed that Isabella was Queen of neither Spain nor Sicily.[6] She was Queen of Castile and León, and her husband was King of Aragon. His domains, not hers, included Sicily; and only their grandchild Charles V actually assumed the title of king of a united Spain in 1516.[7] Lázaro therefore concluded that the inscription is likely a forgery and was probably added after the death of Isabella.[8] Both Rojas' and the royal family's arms must have been added just after the completion of the breviary, so it still seems certain that Rojas owned and perhaps even commissioned it. Its usage was conceived for a Spanish patron, and Rojas may originally have intended to present it to Isabella. The similarity of the full-page decoration, with three sets of arms placed in a shallow, illusionistic space, to the depiction of the arms of Isabella in a beautiful Flemish book of hours executed within a decade of her breviary, confirms the authenticity of the breviary's coat of arms.[9]

Queen Isabella was one of the first Spanish rulers who showed a strong interest in Flemish art, and the sumptuous London breviary must have assumed a place of honor in her collection. In addition to the aforementioned hours, she owned another Flemish book of hours (Madrid, Biblioteca del Palacio Real), some Flemish tapestries, and paintings by Juan de Flandes and Michel Sittow, her court painters.[10] It is therefore not surprising that at least one Flemish book of hours may also be securely identified as executed for her daughter, Joanna (Cat. 7).[11]

The monumental task of decorating the breviary, which contains more than 150 miniatures, a third of them a half-page or larger, was divided mainly between two important workshops; and four other of the finest miniatures appear to be the products of a third and fourth master. The main illuminators are the Master of the Dresden Prayer Book, who was probably in charge of the decoration of Isabella's breviary,[12] and an illuminator known as the Master of James IV of Scotland, whom Winkler identified with Gerard Horenbout (see Cat. 15). The other four miniatures—the finest in the manuscript—are related to the paintings of Gerard David.

The Master of the Dresden Prayer Book seems to have been responsible for nearly two-thirds of the miniatures located between fols. 8v and 358 and for the one on fol. 499. The three different types of borders found on these pages are typical of his manuscripts. The blue-and-gold borders of acanthus and flowers on a plain ground (e.g.,

Fig. 5a. Master of the Dresden Prayer Book.
Christ and the Adulteress, fol. 86.

panel painters. His colors call to mind the palette of the later Marmion, but they are often brighter and more decorative.[16]

The reputation of the Master of the Dresden Prayer Book in later Flemish illumination rests largely upon his *bas-de-page* miniatures, delightful landscapes with figures, in the calendars of books of hours illuminated with other artists, including Marmion and the Master of Mary of Burgundy.[17] For example, the Huth Hours contains some of his finest small calendar miniatures (Fig. 5b), while the Isabella breviary has more ambitious full-border calendar miniatures in his style; but, curiously for such an important commission, they are here no more than workshop productions.

The achievement of the Master of the Dresden Prayer Book extends beyond the domain of landscape. Winkler has proclaimed his gifts as a narrative artist both in the Isabella breviary and in a large Valerius Maximus (see Ill. 7, p. 11).[18] His narrative style shows a particular sympathy for ordinary men and a concern for the function of secondary characters in a scene. For example, in *Christ and the Adulteress* the two men flanking the adulteress look at the

fol. 49v) appear in the artist's eponymous work, the Dresden Prayer Book.[13] A second type of border with black and gray acanthus on a plain ground (fols. 37v, 41v) appears in a book of hours by this illuminator in The Hague.[14] These two kinds of borders are also similar to the borders of mid-century Bruges illuminators, especially in the manuscripts grouped around Willem Vrelant.[15] Finally, a third type of border in the Isabella breviary is the more fashionable illusionistic type with flowers and insects scattered across brightly colored fields. Here the Master of the Dresden Prayer Book offers his own distinctive variation on the tradition. In the border of fol. 86, with the miniature of *Christ and the Adulteress* (Fig. 5a), thick branches are braided into a sculptural frame. The matte colors and widely spaced hatching in this border are representative of his technique, which eschews the lustrous surfaces and tight brushwork so typical of Flemish art of this period. Of all the illuminators in the late Flemish tradition, the Master of the Dresden Prayer Book was the most independent of the general trend to adapt the pictorial realism of Flemish

Fig. 5b. Master of the Dresden Prayer Book.
April, Huth Hours, fol. 4v (Cat. 4).

ground to draw attention to where Christ appears to be writing before he tells them, "He that is without sin among you, let him first cast a stone at her" (John 8:7). In the *Consecration of David* (Fig. 5c) the spirit of the event is conveyed vividly by the engagement of the audience. In the *Parable of Dives and Lazarus* (Pl. VII) the indulgence of the rich Dives' luxurious world is highlighted by the idle postures of the pages blowing their horns, while the dog who would lick the poor Lazarus' wounds leaps up when he smells the bones in the hand of the hungry Lazarus. At the right the illuminator shows the rich man's fate in hell and, in the sky above, Lazarus in the bosom of Abraham. The miniatures of the Master of the Dresden Prayer Book are rich in narrative detail, and his scenes are often dramatic, with elements of irony and humor.

An examination of this illuminator's larger oeuvre is much needed. Especially unusual and important in the Isabella breviary is his sequence of mostly Old Testament subjects from fols. 111v to 194v, a group that has not been the subject of careful study. Although his work stands outside the mainstream of later Flemish illumination, the Master of the Dresden Prayer Book is a consistently inventive artist. A number of good examples of his illuminations have come to light since Winkler's publications.[19]

The second major decorative campaign in the Isabella breviary was carried out by the Master of James IV of Scotland and his workshop.[20] His sequence of miniatures, which includes a beautiful *Coronation of the Virgin* (Fig. 5d), consists mainly of depictions of saints and extends from fols. 404v to 481v. The miniatures are important for our understanding of his development because they are among the relatively few works by him that are at least roughly datable, that is, they were executed not long before 1497.[21]

Ever since Dibdin first published the Isabella breviary, four miniatures that recall the paintings of Gerard David have usually been singled out as its finest illuminations: a *Nativity* (fol. 29), an *Adoration of the Magi* (Pl. VI), a *St. Barbara* (Fig. 5e), and *St. John on Patmos* (Pl. V). Dibdin called the *St. John on Patmos* "the choicest illumination in the volume," and he considered it to be by the same hand as the *Adoration* and *Nativity*.[22] Waagen agreed that the *St. John* was the finest, and in a publication of the Palaeographical Society, this miniature, along with the *Adoration*, is illustrated, while the latter was illustrated again in another British Museum publication of 1903.[23] Warner subsequently selected the *St. Barbara* and the *Parable of Dives and Lazarus* (Pl. VII) to illustrate the manuscript, and Herbert in 1911 singled out the group of four Davidian miniatures as the most beautiful.[24] Two years later, Winkler

Fig. 5c [TOP LEFT]. Master of the Dresden Prayer Book. *Consecration of David*, fol. 124.

Fig. 5d [LEFT]. Master of James IV of Scotland. *Coronation of the Virgin*, fol. 437.

Pl. v. Flemish Master. *St. John on Patmos*, Breviary of Queen Isabella of Castile. Add.
Ms. 18851, fol. 309.

Pl. VI. Gerard David or Workshop. *Adoration of the Magi*, Breviary of Queen Isabella of
Castile. Add. Ms. 18851, fol. 41.

Pl. VII. Master of the Dresden Prayer Book. *Parable of Dives and Lazarus,* Breviary of
Queen Isabella of Castile. Add. Ms. 18851, fol. 252.

agreed that they were all by the same hand, and probably by Gerard David.[25]

Links to the paintings of David, especially for the first three miniatures, are inescapable. The central figure grouping of the *Nativity* is nearly a mirror image of that in David's Friedsam *Nativity* in the Metropolitan Museum, New York.[26] The miniature differs only in the insertion of an additional angel and in the facial type of the Virgin, which resembles more closely the Virgin in David's *Nativity* in the Cleveland Museum of Art, a variant of the Metropolitan Museum composition.[27] The *Adoration of the Magi* has long been recognized as a modified copy of David's *Adoration* in Munich (Alte Pinakothek), itself a copy after a lost painting by Hugo van der Goes.[28] The illuminator has made the composition more compact to fit the format of the miniature, a solution that works well. Although *St. Barbara* does not correspond precisely with a known David painting, her facial type and expression, her seated pose, and compactness of form call to mind a familiar Davidian female type, as in the *Virgin Enthroned with Angels* in the Louvre.[29] Moreover, even the *St. John on Patmos*, while handled in a broader, more painterly fashion, betrays a Davidian facial type.

There are no signed or documented miniatures by David, nor is he known to have been a member of the

illuminators' guild in Bruges. David was known to have supplied patterns for illuminators, and the evidence of his influence on late Flemish illumination, especially on the art of Simon Bening, is well established. Moreover, upon his death in 1523, the illuminators' guild held a service in his honor, so he was very likely in close contact with illuminators throughout his career. If he painted any miniatures at all, the practice was not an important part of his activity. On the other hand, the historical circumstances support his having illuminated a few miniatures over the course of a long career, especially those in a luxurious book produced in Bruges. Many authorities, notably Winkler, Pächt, and Veronée-Verhaegen, are inclined to accept the *Nativity*, the *Adoration of the Magi*, and the *St. Barbara* as by, or very probably by, David.[30]

Their extreme refinement and rare stylistic character as illuminations—especially in the resonance of color and handling of light in the drapery, as in the robe of the Virgin in the *Adoration of the Magi*—may be counted as evidence that they are the odd illuminations by David himself or his assistants. However, lacking documentation of any activity for David as an illuminator, the attributions must be qualified. A number of other miniatures have been attributed to David, but none of those known to this compiler approaches these three in quality, except the single leaf of a *Virgin among Virgins* in the Pierpont Morgan Library (Fig. 5f).[31]

The *St. John on Patmos* is conceivably the most beautiful miniature in Flemish illumination. The drawing of St. John, especially in the drapery folds and in the hands, and their modeling, display a refinement that is rare even in the illumination of this period. The handling of the water with its shimmering reflections, the low vantage point, the dewy freshness of the foliage, and the sublime aerial perspective, all contribute to its poetic appeal. Winkler eventually had doubts about ascribing the *St. John* to David, and only Scillia has argued to retain the attribution, on the theory that it was begun by David and completed by another hand.[32] There are characteristics in it that call to mind miniatures attributed to the Master of James IV of Scotland in the Spinola Hours of the early sixteenth century. The latter's *St. Julian* shares with the *St. John* the treatment of the shallow, cupped waves, their translucence and white highlights, and, with his *Crucifixion*, the vibrant atmospheric quality.[33] However, in the *St. John* the nuances of light and color are more refined, the anatomy more convincing, the contours crisper and sharper. The modeling of the hands and feet especially betrays the sensitivity of David's touch, but the handling of the landscape finds no equivalent in his work. The *St. John on Patmos* is the work of a great artist—or is it two? The visual evidence seems insufficient to support an unqualified attribution.[34]

An inferior late-fifteenth-century hand was responsible

Fig. 5e. Gerard David or Workshop. *St. Barbara*, fol. 297.

Fig. 5f. Gerard David or Workshop. *Virgin among Virgins*. New York, The Pierpont Morgan Library, M.659, detached leaf.

for the miniatures on fols. 365, 372, 374, 386, 390, 392, and 399. Still further miniatures, such as the *St. Catherine* on fol. 368v, appear to have been executed only after 1814, when Dibdin remarked on the absence of a miniature on that folio.[35] His call to provide one was probably soon heeded. Less than forty years later Waagen praised the *St. Catherine* as one of the finest in the manuscript; he was unaware of its recent vintage.[36] Other miniatures by this nineteenth-century hand are found on fols. 363v, 364, and 367.

BIBLIOGRAPHY Dibdin 1817, I, pp. clxiii–clxviii; Waagen 1854, I, p. 131; London (British Museum) 1868, pp. 159–60; London (Palaeographical Society) 1873–83, III, nos. 258, 259, pls. 174, 175; London (Palaeographical Society) 1903; Warner 1910, III, pp. 15, 16, pls. XLV, XLVI; Coggiola 1908–10, p. 149; Herbert 1911, pp. 318–19; Winkler 1913a, pp. 276–77, figs. 15, 16, 19–22; Destrée 1914, pp. 145–46, ill. opp. p. 156; Winkler 1914, pp. 232–38, 243; Lázaro 1924, pp. 138–39; Winkler 1925, pp. 95, 98, 176, 177, pl. 55; Durrieu 1927, pp. 40, 84, pl. LXXX; Lázaro 1928; Winkler 1943, pp. 59–61, 63, fig. 15; Wescher 1946, p. 198; London (Royal Academy) 1953, no. 606; Winkler 1964, p. 189, fig. 154; Turner 1967, no. 65, pl. 16; Delaissé 1968, p. 73; Biermann 1968–69, p. 63, n. 77; Friedländer 1967–76, VIb, pp. 91–92, 103, no. 181, pl. 192; Scillia 1975, pp. 182–84, 190–94, 212–13, 282, 288–89; Limentani Virdis 1981, pp. 90, 91; de Winter 1981, pp. 344–47, n. 4, fig. 3; Cleveland 1982, p. 153.

NOTES

1. Venice, Biblioteca Marciana, Ms. lat. XI 67 (7531), and Antwerp, Mayer van den Bergh Museum. For the former see Salmi 1974; on the latter, see Gaspar 1932.

2. Rodríguez Villa 1896, pp. 183–84.

3. Friedländer 1967–76, VIb, supp. 228, p. 109, pl. 232.

4. London (British Museum) 1868, p. 160; London (Palaeographical Society) 1873–83, III, nos. 258, 259; Warner 1910, p. 15; Winkler 1914, p. 232, n. 1; Durrieu 1927, p. 84; Turner 1967, no. 65.

5. "*Dive Elisabeth / Hispaniar[um] et Siscilie Regine ze / xpianissi[m]e pontent / tissi[m]e Semp[er] augus / te, supreme Dñe / sue clementissime / Franciscus de Roias eiusde[m] ma / iestatis hu[m]i / limus servus ac / creatura, optime / de se merite H[ic] / marin . . . hi . . . ex / obsequio obtulit*" ("To the blessed Elizabeth, queen of the Spaniards and of Sicily etc., his most Christian, most powerful, ever august, and most clement supreme lady, Franciscus de Roias, the most humble servant and creature of that same Majesty, offered this . . . in homage"). I am grateful to Richard Rouse and Gino Corti for their assistance with this translation.

6. Lázaro 1928, especially p. 19.

7. Joanna, who became Queen of Castile upon her mother's death in 1504, would have become Queen of Spain upon her father's death in 1516 had she been mentally competent; Elliott 1977, pp. 134–38.

8. Lázaro 1928, p. 17, also believed that the Rojas arms were forged. It is clear that they were not part of the original decoration of the page, but they were likely added very soon after the book's completion.

9. Cleveland Museum of Art, no. 63.256, fol. 1v; de Winter 1981, pl. II, pp. 343–46.

10. Ibid., pp. 346–47, nn. 8, 9, p. 422, for the literature on her patronage.

11. Several other books of hours have been thought to have belonged to Joanna, among them the Houghton Hours at Harvard and a manuscript in Munich, Bayerische Staatsbibliothek, Clm. 28345. On the former, see Cat. 4, n. 13; on the latter, Winkler 1925, p. 187. See also Cat. 8.

12. Winkler 1914 is still the basic work on this artist; see also Winkler 1925, pp. 95–98, pls. 51–56.

13. Winkler 1914, p. 232, figs. 2–5; see also Bruck 1906, no. 138, figs. 216–232. The Dresden Prayer Book unfortunately suffered extensive water damage during World War II.

14. The Hague, Museum Meermanno-Westreenianum, Ms. 10 F 1; see Byvanck 1924, no. 46, pp. 133–34.

15. On the Vrelant style of border, see Brussels 1959, pp. 100–01.

16. Otto Pächt has discovered evidence that suggests that the Master of the Dresden Prayer Book may have been active at

Amiens, where Marmion had also worked (referred to by Sterling 1981, pp. 10–11 and n. 22). The master collaborated with Marmion in the Louthe Hours, the Huth Hours (Cat. 4), and the "Flora" Hours.

17. Winkler 1925, pp. 178, 183, 189.

18. Winkler 1914, pp. 232–38; and 1925.

19. Some of the historiated borders and miniatures in the Spinola Hours (Malibu, Calif., The J. Paul Getty Museum, Ms. Ludwig IX 8), especially fols. 109v, 110, 119v, and 120, are by the Master of the Dresden Prayer Book, or very close to his style; see Euw/Plotzek 1979–82, II, p. 256, figs. 421–424. A fine miniature of the *Raising of Lazarus,* almost certainly contemporaneous with the Isabella breviary, appears in a book of hours recently sold at Sotheby's, London, June 21, 1982, lot 20, fol. 156v. Closer to the Dresden Prayer Book and the earlier period are fifteen full-page miniatures in a tiny book of hours sold from the Arthur Houghton Library and now in the collection of H. P. Kraus, New York. A superb Valerius Maximus once owned by the prominent Burgundian bibliophile Jan Crabbe has been attributed by Delaissé to the Master of the Dresden Prayer Book (see Bruges 1981, no. 97, pl. 17); and Pächt/Alexander (1966–73, I, p. 28, no. 369) have identified illuminations by him in Oxford, Bodleian Library, Douce Ms. 381.

20. Winkler 1925, p. 177, originally attributed the most important of these miniatures (fols. 437, 477v, 481) to the Master of the Croy Prayer Book, and only later (1943, pp. 59–61) did he attribute the entire sequence to the Master of James IV of Scotland.

21. On the chronology of the Master of James IV of Scotland, see Cat. 8.

22. Dibdin 1817, I, p. clxv.

23. Waagen 1854, I, p. 131; London (Palaeographical Society) 1873–83, III, pls. 174, 175; Warner 1903.

24. Warner 1910, pls. XLV, XLVI; Herbert 1911, p. 318.

25. Winkler 1913a, pp. 276–77.

26. Friedländer 1967–76, VIb, no. 159, pl. 161, and p. 92.

27. Cleveland 1982, no. 53, pl. XXVI. In this catalogue Stechow lists the breviary miniature as fifth in a chronological sequence of six representations of the subject after David, which includes a miniature in a prayer book of 1486 in the Escorial. Schöne 1937, p. 170, who first attributed the latter miniature to David, also attributed fourteen miniatures in this prayer book to David. I know them only through a few poor reproductions.

28. Winkler 1913a, p. 276. A more faithful copy of the David painting appears much later in a large, superb miniature (c. 16.5 × 22.9 cm) ostensibly from the circle of Simon Bening; it is now in the collection of Ian Woodner, New York; see Malibu 1983, no. 45. Winkler 1964, p. 189, points out that Bening also copied the Munich David in the Grimani Breviary.

29. Friedländer 1967–76, VIb, no. 165, pl. 176.

30. Winkler 1925, pp. 134, 176–77; Pächt in London (Royal Academy) 1953, no. 606; Veronée-Verhaegen in Friedländer 1967–76, VIa, pp. 91–92. Scillia 1975, pp. 190–94, considers the *St. Barbara* and *St. John on Patmos* to have figures by David and the other two as the work of assistants. Turner 1967, no. 65, considers all four as "probably by Gerard David."
    Weale 1863, pp. 223–34, was the first to try to prove that David executed some miniatures; see also Weale 1866, p. 500, and Weale 1895, pp. 47–70; and the more recent studies of Van de Walle de Ghelcke 1949, pp. 65–75, and 1952; Schöne 1937, pp. 170–74; Scillia 1975. I have not had access to the studies of Van de Walle de Ghelcke.

31. Detroit 1960, p. 399, no. 212, ill.

32. Winkler 1925, pp. 176–77; Scillia 1975, pp. 193–94.

33. Euw/Plotzek 1979–82, II, colorplate p. 283 and fig. 405.

34. The design for the *St. John* miniature must have received some exposure in the North, however, because a miniature derived from it was executed not long afterward, probably in the first decade of the sixteenth century, in a book of hours (Vienna, Österreichische Nationalbibliothek, Cod. 1862, fol. 10v); see Winkler 1915, ill. opp. p. 336.

35. Dibdin 1817, I, p. clxvi.

36. Waagen 1854, I, p. 131.

6 *Roman de la Rose*

Bruges (?), circa 1490–1500. Harley Ms. 4425

MANUSCRIPT *Vellum, ii + 186 + ii leaves; 39.4 × 29.2 cm. 4 half-page miniatures (fols. 7, 12, 14v, 39) and 88 smaller miniatures (one column in width), 4 decorated borders and numerous initials. On fol. 7 a coat of arms, repainted, of a Knight of the Golden Fleece; originally the arms of Engelbert of Nassau. Burgundian* bâtarde *script.*

BINDING *Green morocco with gold tooling, circa 1900.*

PROVENANCE *Engelbert II of Nassau (d. 1504);*[1] *Jean Antoine II Mesmes (d. 1723); Valentin Esprit Fléchier (d. 1710); probably his sale, Woodman and Lyon, London, January 25, 1726, lot 67.*[2]

THE Harley *Roman de la Rose* is the greatest illuminated codex of the immensely popular allegorical poem of chivalric love. In medieval literature the *Roman de la Rose* is eclipsed only by Dante's *Divine Comedy* in the number of surviving manuscript copies. Approximately 250 are known, mostly dating from the fourteenth and fifteenth centuries, and sixteen are in the British Library.[3] At least two-thirds of the manuscripts have miniatures, often extensive cycles, and the poem inspired imagery on tapestries, ivories, and other decorative objects.[4] By circa 1500 eight printed editions had appeared, many with woodcut illustrations.[5] The third printed edition, dated circa 1487, from Lyons, is the source for the text of the present volume.[6]

The Harley *Roman de la Rose* is brilliantly and extensively illuminated. The enchanting settings, courtly costumes, and young, romantic characters account for its wide popular appeal. The pageantry of the large miniatures and the exotic dress (Pl. VIII) reflect the lavish taste of the Burgundian court under Philip the Good and Charles the Bold. Both men enjoyed wardrobes of the most expensive materials and sponsored magnificent court festivities that lasted for days. Not surprisingly, the poem was very popular at the Burgundian court, and the miniatures of the Harley *Roman de la Rose* capture some of the flavor of this era. Despite the popularity of the *Roman,* the present volume is one of only three illuminated Flemish examples from the fifteenth and sixteenth centuries listed by Winkler.[7]

Engelbert of Nassau, the probable patron of the *Roman de la Rose*, was a prominent lieutenant of both Charles the Bold and Philip the Handsome. A knight of the Burgundian chivalric Order of the Golden Fleece from the age of twenty-two, Engelbert is best known today as the owner of the famous book of hours illuminated by the Master of

Mary of Burgundy in the Bodleian Library.[8] Even in his personal book of devotions, the worldly taste of the Burgundian court is apparent. Engelbert's hours contains a delightful sequence of hawking scenes in the margins, themselves a rarity for a book of hours. Significantly for the present context, the scenes show ladies and pages attired in the most stylish costumes of the fashion-conscious era.[9] On the basis of costume the Harley *Roman de la Rose* has been dated to circa 1490.[10] It was certainly executed after circa 1487 and before the death of Engelbert in 1504.

The poem itself, begun about 1220 by Guillaume de Lorris, who wrote 4,000 of its 22,000 lines, and completed by Jean de Meun later in the century, tells the story of the Lover and his quest for the Rose that symbolizes romantic love. The allegorical tale is recounted as though revealed in a dream. The Lover rises early on a fragrant May morning, dresses himself, and strolls along a river bank to admire the fruits of the new spring. Arriving at a high, crenelated wall, he examines ten painted niche figures, personifications of the Seven Vices, and Poverty, Old Age, and Sorrow. The large miniature on fol. 7 (Fig. 6a) combines the principal elements of this introductory passage from the author's dreaming in bed to his first sighting of the wall. Several small illuminations are devoted to the individual personifications, for example *Poverty* on fol. 11v (Fig. 6b).

Eager to explore a lush orchard behind the wall, the young man knocks on a door, which is opened by the beautiful maiden Idleness. She leads him through the orchard to a lawn where graceful couples carol amid musicians and jongleurs. In the large illumination of fol. 14v (Pl. VIII) the young man (now in different dress) is depicted at the left as he is approached by a woman who invites him to dance. Sir Mirth and Gladness lead the procession of carolers, followed by the winged God of Love with his Beauty, Lady Wealth with her squire, Lady Largesse with a knight descended from King Arthur, and Candor with her young knight.

Leaving the revelers to their dancing, the young man ambles through the orchard, eventually coming upon a rose hedge. Although seized with a desire to pluck a rosebud, he is prevented by its protective thorns as well as his wish not to offend the owner. Suddenly, the God of Love pursues (fol. 18v) and shoots him with arrows that make the young man, now the Lover, long even more ardently for the Rose. Proclaiming his victory, the God warns of the trials awaiting the eager but inexperienced Lover in his amorous quest.

The Lover is then left to ponder his dilemma between desire and fear. Fair Welcome, a handsome and charming young man, entices the Lover to approach the Rose. The

Fig. 6a. Master of the Prayer Books of c. 1500. *The Lover Asleep, Rising, and Going for a Walk*, fol. 7.

Fig. 6b. Master of the Prayer Books of c. 1500.
Poverty, fol. 11v.

abstractions who try to discourage him. In sharp contrast to the delicate, courtly tone of Guillaume de Lorris, who sees Love as the root of all virtue, Jean de Meun's approach is more somberly erudite, heavily laden with classical and biblical references illustrating the dark premise that Love is the source of the world's evils. Several of the illuminations accompanying this second section in Harley 4425 are literary scenes, among them Delilah cutting a swooning Samson's hair in fol. 83v (Fig. 6c), in which the misogynous point is dramatically made.

Until recently the Harley *Roman de la Rose* seemed an anomaly in an era whose greatest artistic achievements fell in the domain of devotional books. Winkler identified the illuminator as "The Master of the Prayer Books of c. 1500," who, as the name suggests, seems to have specialized in executing routine prayer books for the open market.[13] The secular *Roman* is both his greatest achievement and artistically one of the most original manuscripts of the age. The illuminations have still not been studied systematically either in the context of their own time or in relation to the pictorial tradition connected with the text.[14]

When Winkler named the master in 1915, the Harley *Roman de la Rose* seemed a moment of brilliance in an otherwise routine oeuvre. However, several recent discoveries allow us to view the *Roman de la Rose* as more than an isolated achievement by this artist. These manuscripts suggest that when engaged with secular themes he worked

Lover accepts the invitation but is thwarted by Danger, who banishes the Lover from both the Rose and Fair Welcome. After much advice, the Lover returns to beg forgiveness of Danger, who is persuaded to allow him to see Fair Welcome once more. On fol. 36 a small illumination depicts the Lover being led by Fair Welcome into the fenced area of the hedge, where the coveted bud has enlarged and begun to open. Just as the emboldened Lover has kissed the Rose, an outraged Jealousy decides to end such indiscretion by immuring the rose hedge and Fair Welcome, imprisoning the latter in a tower. Fol. 39 (Pl. IX) summarizes the end of Lorris' section of the *Roman*, showing the crenelated fortress wall watched over by the turbaned chaperone with the keys in his hand;[11] beyond, the tower is guarded at the front gate by Danger and at the side gates, by Shame and Fear. The tower itself is crammed with soldier-friends of Jealousy. Standing in the distance, the Lover forlornly contemplates the loss of Fair Welcome and the Rose. It bears mentioning in the context of this illumination that throughout the miniatures in this and other fifteenth-century examples, Fair Welcome is depicted not as the young man described by Lorris but as a fair young woman who seems to assume the role of the Beloved.[12]

In Jean de Meun's additions to the *Roman*, the Lover is subjected not only to physical obstacles but also to a series of exhausting philosophical debates with Reason and other

Fig. 6c. Master of the Prayer Books of c. 1500.
Samson and Delilah, fol. 83v.

Pl. VIII. Master of the Prayer Books of c. 1500. *Dance of Mirth* (reduced—actual size detail on p. 54), in Guillaume de Lorris and Jean de Meun, ROMAN DE LA ROSE. Harley Ms. 4425, fol. 14v.

Pl. IX. Master of the Prayer Books of c. 1500. *Fair Welcome Imprisoned by Jealousy*
(reduced—actual size detail on p. 55), in Guillaume de Lorris and Jean de Meun, ROMAN
DE LA ROSE. Harley Ms. 4425, fol. 39.

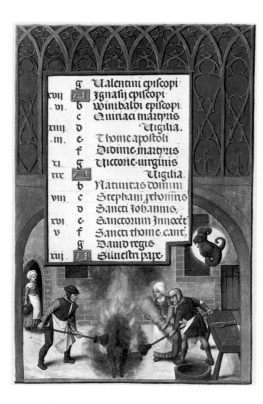

Fig. 6d. Master of the Prayer Books of c. 1500.
December, Book of Hours. Munich, Bayerische
Staatsbibliothek, Clm. 28345, fol. 13.

calendar decoration. Its bustling activity and finely observed farmyard animals constitute one of the most beautiful secular illuminations of the late period. Gagnebin and Pächt have convincingly attributed illuminations in several other secular manuscripts, including another in the British Library, to this master.[19] Although less impressive than the examples given above, they confirm that this illuminator was more than just a specialist in prayer books.

When Winkler wrote in 1915, the patron of the Harley *Roman* had not been identified with much certainty and none of the patrons of the master's other manuscripts was known at all. At that time it seemed that this master had not attracted the attention of the finest patrons, but such a notion can no longer be sustained. Engelbert of Nassau was an important bibliophile and connoisseur of illumination in the late fifteenth century, as demonstrated by his book of hours in the Bodleian Library and the present manuscript, among others.[20] Engelbert, moreover, seems to have particularly enjoyed the art of the Master of the Prayer Books of c. 1500. He owned the Xenophon *Cyropaedia* now in Geneva, also illuminated by this master.[21]

The Master of the Prayer Books of c. 1500 also had other prominent patrons. He painted a number of miniatures in a book of hours executed for Queen Isabella of Castile.[22] And Pächt has identified his hand in yet another secular manuscript, a volume of poems by Charles d'Orléans, probably illuminated for a member of the English royal family.[23] So the Master of the Prayer Books of c. 1500 seems to have enjoyed a period of prominence and success within his lifetime.

Winkler considered the Master of the Dresden Prayer Book to be the teacher of the present artist,[24] and the Munich calendar miniatures demonstrate his artistic debt in figure types and iconography to the older Bruges illuminator. The younger master may well have been a Bruges resident himself, as the same work seems to form a bridge between his presumed mentor and the young Simon Bening, who joined the Bruges guild in 1507 (Cats. 9, 10). Moreover, the Vergil manuscript to which the Master of the Prayer Books of c. 1500 added two important miniatures was originally owned by the prominent bibliophile, Jan Crabbe (1457/59–1488), the abbot of Duinen, not far from Bruges, and the city was, of course, a major center for the production of books of hours.[25] Therefore the *Roman de la Rose* may have been executed in Bruges. In light of recent additions to the master's oeuvre, the Harley *Roman de la Rose* may be ascribed to an illuminator with a strong affinity for secular themes at a time when important commissions for profane manuscripts were relatively few. Both the miniatures of the Harley *Roman de la Rose* and the activity of the Master of the Prayer Books of c. 1500 merit closer study.

with a freedom that inspired his finest illuminations. The number of secular commissions available was probably not great. But even within the many attractive prayer books that he illuminated, the occupations of the months in the calendar section excited his imagination in a way that religious iconography did not.[15] The secular narratives of the calendar miniatures of a book of hours in Munich (Fig. 6d) are among his most appealing illuminations.[16] The hallmarks of his miniatures in the *Roman de la Rose* are in evidence here: opaque arboreal foliage and courtly costumes, slightly stiff figural movement, crisply delineated brickwork, and a palette dominated by matte blues, reds, and greens. His gifts as a colorist are revealed in the *December* miniature in the crackling, transparent flames that roast the boar.

The Master of the Prayer Books of c. 1500 also received one other important commission to illuminate a secular manuscript. Second only to the *Roman de la Rose* in quality and invention are the magnificent large illustrations to a Vergil (Fig. 6e), rightly attributed by Pächt to this master.[17] Here the illuminator uses the landscape as a panoramic stage for an ambitious narrative sequence. Like the Lover in the opening miniature of the *Roman* (Fig. 6a), Aeneas is depicted at four different moments, and he wears a similar elaborate hat. The bright orange and yellow flames leaping from the houses of Troy recall vividly the flames in the *December* calendar miniature in Munich. Equally novel and exciting is the illustration to Vergil's *Georgics* (fol. 41v), where the figures and animals are derived from calendar iconography.[18] However, the Master of the Prayer Books of c. 1500 has conceived the scene on a grander scale than that found in late-fifteenth-century

Fig. 6e. Master of the Prayer Books of c. 1500. Scenes from the AENEID, in Vergil, WORKS. Holkham Hall, Library of Viscount Coke, Ms. 311, fol. 122v.

BIBLIOGRAPHY London (British Museum) 1808–12, III, p. 143; Shaw 1843, pls. 56–58; Ward 1883–1910, I, pp. 892–94; Blomfield/Thomas 1892, pp. 22–25, figs. 2, 3; Sieveking 1903; Bourdillon 1906, p. 12; Langlois 1910, pp. 144–45; Warner 1910, III, pl. XLVII; Herbert 1911, p. 318; Kuhn 1913–14, pp. 40, 65, pl. 14; Winkler 1915, pp. 338–41, figs. 53, 54; Winkler 1925, pp. 128, 179; Cartellieri 1926, pl. 13; Durrieu 1927, pp. 80–81, pl. 72; Loomis/Loomis 1938, p. 129; Pächt 1948, p. 56, n. 27; London (Royal Academy) 1953, no. 609; Knaus 1960, cols. 577–78; Tuve 1966, p. 257, n. 15, p. 324, figs. 94, 107; Wright/Wright 1966, II, p. 403, n. 7; Fleming 1969, pp. 28, 42, 71, 208; Hassall 1970, p. 33; Wright 1972, pp. 145–46, 152, 238, 358–59, 444; Gagnebin 1976, under no. 74, p. 171; Scott 1980, pp. 196, 197, figs. 135–137; Bruges 1981, under no. 87.

NOTES

1. Durrieu recognized that the coat of arms does not correspond with those of any of the Knights of the Golden Fleece, and that it had been altered. On the basis of the arms in the *Monstrelet* in Leiden (Universiteits Bibliotheek, Cod. Vossianus Gallicus, 2), he believed the *Roman* arms originally were identical with those of Count Henri of Nassau, who became a Knight of the Golden Fleece in 1505. Winkler 1925, p. 179, accepted this view, but Pächt 1948, p. 59, suggested that the arms are those of Engelbert II of Nassau, because the crest of his coat of arms was decorated with peacock feathers. This view has been generally accepted. See also Knaus 1960, cols. 557–78, and Wright 1972, pp. 145, 444. Knaus felt that Heinrich, Engelbert's nephew, who spent time in Spain, probably also owned the Harley manuscript, because of notations written in a Spanish hand in some of the margins, e.g., on fols. 8 and 9.

2. Wright 1972, p. 444 (see also pp. 145, 153, 238, 358–59), places Mesmes' ownership after that of Fléchier. Mesmes' armorial binding is represented in fragments on one of the first flyleaves. However, since Fléchier's books were not sold until 1725–26, and a notation in the Harley binding dated one day after the sale seems to corroborate its identification with lot 67 there, Mesmes, who died in 1723, would likely have owned it before Fléchier or not at all. The date January 25, 1725–26 is inscribed in the manuscript and in the diary of Humfrey Wanley; see Wright/Wright 1966, II, p. 403.

3. Luria 1982, p. 14.

4. For a partial list, see Kuhn 1913–14, pp. 64–66. Philip the Bold had a tapestry of the *Roman de la Rose*; see Doutrepont 1909, p. 329, and Biryukova 1966, pp. 107–16.

5. Luria 1982, pp. 17–18.

6. Bourdillon 1906, p. 12; see also Luria 1982, p. 17.

7. Winkler 1925, pp. 179, 194, 207.

8. Oxford, Bodleian Library, Douce Mss. 219–220; Alexander 1970.

9. Fols. 47–68v; ibid., pls. 41–58.

10. Scott 1980, p. 196, dates the manuscript circa 1490 on the basis of costume.

11. This is another instance of gender change from text to illustration. Lorris' chaperone was an old woman. The bearded figure could instead represent Jealousy, although Lorris also described that emotion as feminine.

12. There has been much discussion of the meaning of such changes of gender in illustrations accompanying fifteenth-century versions of the *Roman*. See, for example, Tuve 1966, p. 322; Fleming 1969, pp. 29–30.

13. On the Master of the Prayer Books of c. 1500, see Winkler 1915, pp. 334–42, and 1925, p. 128.

14. On the illustration of the *Roman de la Rose*, see Kuhn 1913–14, pp. 1–66; for the most recent historiography, see Luria 1982, chap. 2. The Harley codex is treated only cursorily in Kuhn, Tuve 1966, Fleming 1969, and other studies dealing with *Roman de la Rose* illustrations.

15. Winkler 1915, pp. 337–40, figs. 48–56, discusses especially Vienna, Österreichische Nationalbibliothek, Cod. 1862, and Berlin, Kupferstichkabinett, Ms. 78 B 15. A prayer book with illuminations by the master is British Library, Egerton Ms. 1149; see Winkler 1925, p. 180.

16. Winkler 1925, p. 187. The calendar is illustrated in its entirety in Leidinger 1936. Leidinger disagrees with Winkler, who attributed the full-page miniatures in this manuscript to the Hortulus Master and, rightly, only the smaller scenes to the Master of the Prayer Books of c. 1500.

17. London (Royal Academy) 1953, no. 610; Hassall 1970, p. 33. Geirnaert in Bruges 1981, no. 192, doubted the present attribution. Winkler 1925, p. 187, however, had already remarked that these miniatures are very close to the Munich calendar.

18. Hassall 1970, pl. 159.

19. Royal Ms. 16 F II; Gagnebin 1976, no. 74; London (Royal Academy) 1953, nos. 611, 615; see also Loomis/Loomis 1938, p. 129, and Winkler 1925, p. 171. However, the attribution of a single miniature in Oxford, Bodleian Library, Douce Ms. 383, fol. 1 (Pächt/Alexander 1966–73, I, pl. 29, no. 362) does not seem convincing to this observer.

20. On Engelbert as a bibliophile, see Knaus 1960, and Schweinsfert 1975.

21. Geneva, Bibliothèque Publique et Universitaire, Ms. fr. 79; Gagnebin 1976, no. 74.

22. Cleveland Museum of Art, no. 63.256; de Winter 1981, pp. 420–21, figs. 29, 37–39, 139–141.

23. London (Royal Academy) 1953, no. 615.

24. Winkler 1925, p. 128.

25. Bruges 1981, pp. 176–80, n. 87.

7 Hours of Joanna of Castile

Use of Rome; Bruges or Ghent, 1496–1506. Additional Ms. 18852

MANUSCRIPT *Vellum, 422 leaves; 10.9 × 7.5 cm. 24 full calendar borders, 54 other large and small miniatures. Full coats of arms of Joanna and her husband, Philip the Handsome, in the right border of fol. 26, Joanna's repeated in the* bas-de-page *flanked by lions rampant and the mottoes, "Qui vouldra" and "je le veus." Script imitative of rounded Italian gothic.*

BINDING *Modern red velvet, with a clasp and corner pieces of chased silver gilt which may be seventeenth century.*

PROVENANCE *The Infanta Joanna of Castile; Philip A. Hanrott; Sir John Tobin, Liverpool; Rev. John Tobin, Liscard, Cheshire; British Museum purchase from the book dealer William Boone, 1852.*

THOUGH relatively small, even for a private devotional book, this manuscript is abundantly illuminated. In addition to the nearly eighty miniatures and historiated borders, every page has elements of painted decoration. Executed for a princess, Joanna of Castile, daughter of Queen Isabella of Castile and King Ferdinand of Aragon (Cat. 5), the British Library hours is a luxury manuscript. Yet, for all its copious and finely executed decoration, the Hours of Joanna of Castile constitutes one of the most ambitious examples of a manuscript conceived on the basis of designs gathered from diverse artists' workshops. The use of patterns was a time-honored medieval illuminator's practice that flourished into the sixteenth century due in no small part to the large demand for devotional books. Books of hours share so many subjects — the Life of the Virgin, the saints, frequently the Passion of Christ, and so on—that the circulation of patterns to facilitate their execution was widespread. Illuminators employed the compositions of older painters and illuminators (Pl. VI, Figs. 3d, 3e, 8a, 8b), and they repeated their own designs (Figs. 8e, 8f), or allowed them to be copied in their workshops (Figs. 4k, 4l). Most of the miniatures in the Hours of Joanna of Castile are closely derived—often simply copied—from patterns in earlier books of hours, including the Huth Hours (Cat. 4), the Hours of Mary of Burgundy and Maximilian in Berlin, and others. Furthermore, many of the borders, including an unusual type of architectural border (Fig. 7a), clearly also derive from illuminators' workshop patterns. Nevertheless, the illuminator, the Master of the David Scenes in the Grimani Breviary, has adapted some of his sources in novel ways, and the Hours of Joanna of Castile contains unique miniatures of considerable artistic interest (Figs. 7a, 7c). The result is a sumptuous book of hours with an original character, a product of

both the personal requirements of the patron and the resourcefulness of the illuminator.

Folio 26 of this small, deluxe book of hours contains the arms, mottoes, and initials of both the Infanta Joanna and her husband, Philip the Handsome (d. 1506), son of Emperor Maximilian I and Mary of Burgundy, whom she married in 1496. Joanna commissioned a number of Flemish tapestries and paintings while residing in Ghent,[1] and that this manuscript was intended for her is affirmed by the fact that her portrait appears twice: in one miniature she is accompanied by a guardian angel and John the Baptist (fol. 26) and in another, by John the Evangelist (fol. 288).

The Hours of Joanna of Castile is the most luxurious example of a particular group of manuscripts probably produced primarily at Bruges that share a number of distinctive decorative and codicological features. The most striking is an architectural border design representing a spacious interior with the miniature or text block set into the rear wall (Fig. 7a); so that the miniature takes on the appearance of an interior within the interior, or a view through a window.[2] Like the typical Flemish illusionistic borders of flowers and insects, the scale of the architectural border is distinct from the scale of the miniature; border and miniature seem to embody separate realities. On the other hand, the illuminator of the Hours of Joanna of Castile occasionally adapted the border for narrative purposes, as in this *Temptation of Adam and Eve* (Fig. 7a) where Adam and Eve are depicted fleeing the Garden of Eden through a doorway in the decorative border; they are escaping into another pictorial realm. The same two scenes from the Fall of Man and a nearly identical border appear in a miniature in the Brukenthal Museum, Sibiu (Romania), which appears to be later in date and by a different illuminator.[3]

Other manuscripts that feature this distinctive architectural interior border—only occasionally is exterior architecture depicted—include books of hours in the Beinecke Library, Yale University;[4] Bibliothèque Nationale, Paris;[5] Walters Art Gallery, Baltimore;[6] The Detroit Institute of Arts;[7] Österreichische Nationalbibliothek, Vienna;[8] Museo Correr, Venice;[9] the Biblioteca Apostolica Vaticana;[10] the Houghton Library, Harvard University;[11] and the Huntington Library, San Marino.[12] The group also includes two prayer books in the Bodleian Library, Oxford.[13] As is the case with the Hours of Joanna of Castile, the architectural borders of these manuscripts are derived from illuminators' patterns.[14] For example, the borders on fols. 45 and 241 in the Joanna hours also appear with only minor variations in the Beinecke hours (fols. 102 and 168, respectively) and in the Paris hours (fols. 48 and 113, respectively). It is difficult to determine which of the

Fig. 7a [LEFT]. Master of the David Scenes in the Grimani Breviary. *Temptation of Adam and Eve*; *Expulsion from Paradise*; *Speculum consciencie*, fols. 14v–15.

Fig. 7b [RIGHT]. Master of the David Scenes in the Grimani Breviary. *Temptation of Adam and Eve*; border with the *Expulsion from Paradise* and other scenes, Hours of Marie de' Medici. Oxford, Bodleian Library, Douce Ms. 112, fol. 36.

manuscripts is the earliest because none of the group except this Joanna hours is securely dated. However the Joanna hours cannot be the earliest in the sequence since it contains a miniature developed from a prototype that is copied in the Beinecke (Figs. 7d and 7f) and Detroit hours and the Bodleian prayer books. Therefore, the Master of the David Scenes in the Grimani Breviary, who was active only in the Joanna hours among the manuscripts in this group, was probably not the inventor of the patterns for the borders. A workshop from the circle of the Master of the Dresden Prayer Book probably invented the architectural borders, along with some of the miniatures.[15]

In addition to the architectural borders, the group of devotional books is interrelated in other ways. Except for the Joanna and Paris hours, the manuscripts all feature a rounded Italian gothic script; and the Joanna and Paris hours, which are the finest and most richly illuminated, have an elegant variation on this script with elongated descenders. All the manuscripts are relatively small, while several are tiny. The hours in Paris and Vienna measure 7.5 × 6.2 cm and 6.9 × 4.9 cm, respectively. Finally, many of the manuscripts have a number of miniatures in common. For example, the twenty-four calendar landscape borders in the Joanna, Paris, and Beinecke hours feature some scenes that are nearly identical, down to details of setting and figural motifs (Figs. 7e and 7f).[16] A program of twenty-four landscape borders in a calendar is unusual in late Flemish illumination.[17] A number of other compositions, including the *Temptation* (Fig. 7a), the *Betrayal of Christ* (fol. 50), *St. Luke* (Fig. 7c), and *St. Mark* (fol. 189),

are derived from common patterns in the Joanna hours, Beinecke hours (Fig. 7d), and both Bodleian prayer books. In some of these manuscripts the decoration seems to have been highly organized. Although, as noted, the use of patterns was extremely common in late Flemish illumination, evidence of such systematic use of groups of patterns is unusual. The illuminator of the Joanna hours may have had access to pattern books organized by entire pictorial cycles or decorative motifs such as the calendar (see also Cat. 10), a Passion cycle, the Evangelists, and architectural borders. Perhaps a workshop of book production, directed by a scribe or illuminator, assembled the artist's pattern books and distributed them to the several illuminators responsible for these various manuscripts. Except for the Joanna and Paris hours, the manuscripts in this group are routine illuminated devotional books, but all relied heavily on patterns to hasten their production and probably reduce costs.

The quality of the illumination in the Hours of Joanna of Castile, the only manuscript of royal patronage in this group, is significantly higher than in the others. Winkler thought the hours might be by Gerard Horenbout, but as indicated above it is more likely an early work by his follower, the Master of the David Scenes in the Grimani Breviary.[18] The figure types, landscape setting, and buxom serpent of the London *Temptation* recall closely the miniature and border of this subject in the Bodleian hours (Fig. 7b) illuminated by this master.[19] Even the vignettes with Adam and Eve expelled from the garden betray a similar quality of movement and gesture. As his name suggests, the Master of the David Scenes executed some Old Testa-

Fig. 7c [RIGHT]. Master of the David Scenes in the Grimani Breviary. *St. Luke in His Chamber*, fol. 184.

Fig. 7d [BOTTOM RIGHT]. Flemish Master. *St. Luke in His Chamber*, Book of Hours. New Haven, Yale University, Beinecke Rare Book and Manuscript Library, Ms. 287, fol. 40.

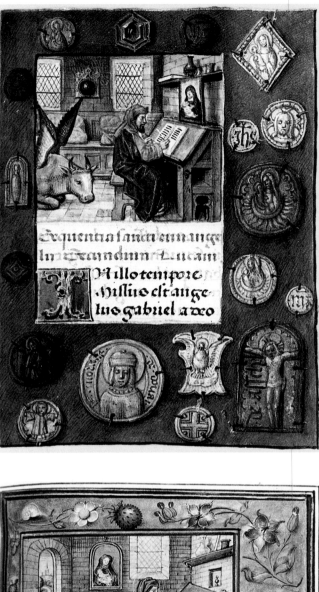

ment and other miniatures in the Grimani Breviary in the following decade.[20]

In addition to the large number of scenes in the Hours of Joanna of Castile that the Master of the David Scenes based directly on familiar patterns from miniatures in such deluxe manuscripts as the Hours of Mary of Burgundy and Maximilian and the Huth Hours (Cat. 4), the full-page *Madonna and Child* is copied from a panel painting from the circle of Rogier van der Weyden (Brussels, Musées Royaux des Beaux-Arts).[21] At the same time, the Master of the David Scenes in the Grimani Breviary has created in this manuscript several of the most striking and original miniatures in Flemish illumination, above all, the small *Speculum consciencie* ("Mirror of Conscience"; Fig. 7a). It shows a framed convex mirror containing a skull, with the words "SPECULUM CONSCIENCIE" inscribed in the frame. It is placed opposite the *Temptation* and at the beginning of a collection of texts that include the Ten Commandments, the Seven Deadly Sins, and the Articles of the Faith. Marrow has demonstrated the strong moralizing effect of the *Speculum consciencie* image, which traditionally is depicted within a larger, narrative scene.[22] Here the Master of the David Scenes has represented the mirror by itself, a chilling emblem of contemplation and a superb example of Flemish realism. The artist deftly defines the convexity of the mirror and its translucence. He inserted a convex mirror into another miniature, *St. Luke in His Chamber* (Fig. 7c), which shows this illuminator at the height of his powers in the handling of light, color, and spatial effects.[23]

The manuscripts identified here as related to the Hours of Joanna of Castile on the basis of codicological features were probably produced in Bruges. Several have original Bruges bindings, and many of their miniatures seem to derive from the Bruges illuminator, the Master of the Dresden Prayer Book.[24] On the other hand, the Master of the David Scenes may have been active in Ghent, where Joanna resided, so it is difficult to be certain which of the two cities was responsible for the production of her book of hours.

BIBLIOGRAPHY London (British Museum) 1868, p. 160; Millar 1928, p. 17, pl. XLVII; Durrieu 1927, p. 67, pl. LXXXVI; Winkler 1943, p. 59; Schwarz 1959, p. 94, fig. 10; Winkler 1964, p. 175; Köster 1965, pp. 468–69, 478, 483–84, 492, 494, 503, pl. 4; Turner 1967, no. 63; Pächt 1973, pp. 88, 90, n. 9, fig. 84a; Kren 1974, pp. 21–34, cat. 3; Cahn/Marrow 1977–78, pp. 261–62, under no. 78; Pächt 1981, p. 23, fig. 3; de Winter 1981, pp. 346–47, 394, figs. 5, 41; Marrow 1983, pp. 156–58, 161, fig. 2; Cambridge 1983, under no. 28.

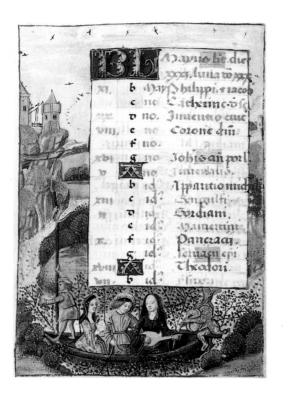

Fig. 7e [FAR LEFT]. Workshop of the Master of the David Scenes in the Grimani Breviary. *May*, fol. 5v.

Fig. 7f [LEFT]. Flemish Master. *May*, Book of Hours. New Haven, Yale University, Beinecke Rare Book and Manuscript Library, Ms. 287, fol. 5v.

NOTES

1. On the tapestries, see de Winter 1981, p. 346, and Hulst 1967, pp. 115–20. On an altarpiece commissioned by Philip and Joanna, now in the Groeningemuseum, see Bruges 1969, no. 59.

2. Kren 1974, pp. 8–30, cats. 1–10.

3. Known to me only in a single reproduction, the miniature probably belongs to a luxurious book of hours; see Ionescu 1964, p. 9, no. 3 (ill.) as "Simon Bening or Gerard Horenbout."

4. Ms. 287; Kren 1974, no. 4; and Cahn/Marrow 1977–78, under no. 78.

5. Ms. lat. 10555; Kren 1974, no. 7; Leroquais 1927, II, no. 175.

6. Mss. W. 427 and W. 428; Ricci 1935–40, I, p. 807, under Baltimore, Walters Art Gallery, nos. 315 and 316; Baltimore 1957, no. 180; Ithaca 1968, no. 108; Kren 1974, nos. 1, 2.

7. No. 63.146; see Warner 1920, I, no. 103; sale, Sotheby's, London, December 1, 1959, lot. 87, and Kren 1974, no. 10.

8. Cod. 2032; Unterkircher 1957–59, I, p. 59, and Vienna 1962, no. 61.

9. Ms. V, 4; Torresan 1974, pp. 80–81, figs. 11–12.

10. Ms. Vat. lat. 10293; Vatican City 1979, no. 63, pl. XI. I am grateful to James Marrow for calling this example to my attention.

11. Ms. Richardson 8; Cambridge 1983, no. 28. Roger Wieck kindly brought this manuscript to my notice.

12. HM.1174; to be published by Consuelo Dutschke in her forthcoming catalogue of medieval manuscripts in the Huntington Library.

13. Douce Mss. 8 and 12; Pächt/Alexander 1966–73, II, nos. 371, 372; Kren 1974, nos. 5, 6.

14. See the discussion under Cat. 3.

15. Kren 1974, pp. 57–58.

16. Casier/Bergmans 1914–22, II, pp. 86–88, pls. CLXII–CLXIII, compared the calendar miniatures in the Joanna hours to a manuscript then in the collection of Paul Durrieu.

17. Twelve full-border calendar landscapes by the workshop of the Master of the Dresden Prayer Book appear in the breviary owned by Queen Isabella of Castile (Cat. 5), Joanna's mother.

18. Winkler 1943; p. 59; Otto Pächt suggested to me the possible attribution to the Master of the David Scenes.

19. Pächt/Alexander 1966–73, II, no. 396, pl. XXXI.

20. Venice, Biblioteca Marciana, Ms. lat. XI 67 (7531), fols. 288v, 310v, 321v, 348v, 357v; Pächt/Alexander (1966–73, II, no. 397) also attribute to this illuminator Douce Ms. 256 in the Bodleian Library.

21. The Passion miniatures and two with Saints on fols. 81, 88, 93, 100, 107, 115, 121, 411v, and 413v are derived from the Huth Hours (fols. 20v, 22v, 23v, 25, 26v, 28, 29v, 135v, 139v, respectively). The Rogierian painting is illustrated in de Winter 1981, fig. 6.

22. Marrow 1983, p. 158.

23. Schwarz 1959, p. 94, fig. 10, discusses this miniature in the context of the convex mirror motif and St. Luke iconography in the fifteenth century.

24. Bruges bindings are found on Walters Ms. W. 428 and the Detroit hours; see Kren 1974, nos. 2, 10, and, on the sources for the miniatures, pp. 57–58.

8 Book of Hours

Use of Rome; Bruges or Ghent, circa 1500. Additional Ms. 35313

MANUSCRIPT *Vellum, ii + 237 + ii leaves; 23.7 × 15.2 cm. 75 miniatures plus a dozen historiated* bas-de-page *in the calendar. On fol.* 159, *with the* Mass of the Dead *miniature, an unidentified coat of arms.[1] Rounded gothic script.*

BINDING *Brown calf, gold-tooled, probably late eighteenth century.*

PROVENANCE *Baron Ferdinand de Rothschild, Ms. IV; his bequest to the British Museum,* 1898.

THE innovative two-page spreads in this book of hours illustrate how the Master of James IV of Scotland transformed the decorated text opening in a Flemish prayer book into a unified design that is nearly entirely illuminated (Pl. x). Miniatures in a Flemish prayer book were included customarily at the beginning of each collection of devotions, its subdivisions, or before individual prayers. Full-page miniatures on the left announce the devotional text commencing on the opposite page, as in the Hastings Hours (Pls. II, III). The illuminator thus faced the problem of unifying an asymmetrical two-page design. In the Hastings Hours, executed about two decades earlier, effective unification is achieved through the use of color and, occasionally, identical border styles on the facing leaves. A solution found in late-fifteenth-century Flemish illumination, which offers a more balanced two-page design, provides a smaller, complementary miniature on the text page, as in the Hours of Joanna of Castile (Fig. 7a).[2]

In the present book of hours, the Master of James IV of Scotland takes this latter solution one step further. He enlarges the right-hand miniature as fully as possible, without completely eliminating the text. However, he reduces it to two lines (Pl. x). As a result the two-page spread is almost entirely illuminated and the design of the opening is nearly symmetrical. In the Spinola Hours he advances this decorative concept to achieve a spectacular effect: he extends the pictorial space of the miniature into the border by representing the narrative scene in an architectural interior, with the border as its corresponding exterior (see Ill. 4, p. 9); in other miniatures, he continues the landscape of the miniature into the border.

The narrative potential for such designs is rich, as demonstrated by the Passion cycle that illustrates the Hours of the Cross in the British Library manuscript. The miniatures of the Passion begin with Christ's entry into Jerusalem and end with his Entombment.[3] The Hours of

the Cross were normally illustrated by a cycle of miniatures located at the eight canonical subdivisions. Under the more conservative system of decoration this generally resulted in narrative cycles composed of seven or eight miniatures. The system illustrated here, with two large miniatures at each opening, allows for twice that number, so that the Passion cycle (Pl. x, Fig. 8a) consists of fourteen miniatures. The nearly equal size of the two miniatures on each spread gives greater continuity to the narrative sequence. Following the tradition of elaborate Passion iconography during this period, the illuminator unfolded the emotionally charged narrative in ever more vivid detail.[4]

With a breadth of handling quite unlike the Master of Mary of Burgundy or any of his Flemish contemporaries, this illuminator seems to be striving for a monumental scale that belies the small dimensions and essentially intimate character of a devotional book. The painterly handling and graphic depiction of torture throughout the Passion cycle are typical of his early work. In the *Flagellation* and *Christ Crowned with Thorns* (Pl. x), tactile values are emphasized in a rich variety of textures—the figure of Christ in both, for example, is evenly covered with drops of blood—while the decorative borders, which imitate carved architectural relief panels with Gothic finials, crockets, and sculpture in niches, enhance the scale of the page.

The *Road to Calvary* miniature (Fig. 8a) is copied loosely from a miniature of several decades earlier in the Hours of Mary of Burgundy by an anonymous Flemish illuminator (Fig. 8b).[5] Here the fragile Christ looks downward. His suffering seems internalized. The Master of James IV of Scotland crops the miniature somewhat and, along with the prominence of the spearheads and the massing of the landscape, this cropping serves to press the figures forward, bringing the scene closer to the viewer. Close framing of a devotional subject reflects the popularity of the pictorial half-length in the late fifteenth century (see Ill. 5, p. 10), an attempt to heighten the supplicant's experience of the devotional subject. In the London miniatures, figures are more fully and broadly modeled, Christ himself looms larger, and he appears more vulnerable as he casts an exhausted glance at the soldier in front of him. Thus his suffering is expressed outwardly. In the later Spinola Hours (Fig. 8c) the Master of James IV of Scotland draws on some of the figures from the Vienna *Road to Calvary* (Fig. 8b) as well as on an engraving by Martin Schongauer.[6] In the process the master cropped the composition even more tightly, further raised Christ's head, and provided a more immediate statement of his suffering—Christ directly confronts the viewer. The Spinola *Road to Calvary* is one of the artist's most powerful illuminations.

Fig. 8a [ABOVE]. Master of James IV of Scotland. *Road to Calvary*, fol. 28v.

Fig. 8b [TOP RIGHT]. Flemish Master. *Road to Calvary*, Hours of Mary of Burgundy. Vienna, Österreichische Nationalbibliothek, Cod. 1857, fol. 94.

Fig. 8c [RIGHT]. Master of James IV of Scotland. *Road to Calvary with St. Veronica*, Spinola Hours. Malibu, Calif., The J. Paul Getty Museum, Ms. Ludwig IX 18, fols. 8v–9.

Pl. X [OPPOSITE]. Master of James IV of Scotland. *Flagellation of Christ* and *Christ Crowned with Thorns*, Book of Hours. Add. Ms. 35313, fols. 24v–25.

Fig. 8d [LEFT]. Master of the *Hortulus Animae*. *St. Mark*, fol. 16v.

Fig. 8e [BOTTOM LEFT]. Master of James IV of Scotland. *Visitation*, fol. 76v.

Fig. 8f [BELOW]. Master of James IV of Scotland. *Visitation*, Rothschild Prayer Book. Vienna, Österreichische Nationalbibliothek, Cod. ser. nov. 2844, fol. 99v.

The London book of hours deserves to be grouped with the Rothschild Prayer Book and Spinola Hours, the Master of James IV of Scotland's most important commissions after the Grimani Breviary.[7] They are not only his most luxurious and impressive productions, but the first three contain a significant number of similarities beyond the controlling participation of the master. They share a rounded gothic script, comparable acanthus initials, and a collaborating illuminator.[8] In all three manuscripts the Master of the *Hortulus animae* was largely responsible for long sequences of half-length miniatures of saints (Fig. 8d). In addition, the Rothschild Prayer Book exhibits the same style of architectural relief borders as the hours in London (Pl. x); and a number of miniatures are nearly identical in the two manuscripts, notably the *Annunciation*, the *Visitation* (Figs. 8e and 8f), the *Death of the Virgin*, and the *Coronation of the Virgin* (Fig. 8h).[9]

Both the Rothschild Prayer Book and the Spinola Hours are more accomplished productions than the hours in London, and it seems likely that the London hours dates significantly earlier.[10] The Rothschild Prayer Book and the Spinola Hours are plausibly dated to the second decade of the sixteenth century.[11] In both the pictorial treatment of the two-page spread and the Road to Calvary subject, the Spinola Hours represents a further stage in development over the London hours. In the Rothschild Prayer Book, a subtle development beyond the London hours toward a more convincing spatial recession is evident. For example, in the Rothschild *Visitation*, the small mound with the trees in the left foreground is made lower and flatter than in the London miniature of this subject (Figs. 8e and 8f). Moreover, the handling is more atmospheric, and the features of Elizabeth are less broadly drawn in the former than in the latter.

The Master of James IV of Scotland seems to have undergone a steady evolution toward tighter brushwork and more monumental space, which helps to locate the London work chronologically within his oeuvre. In his earliest dated manuscript, a breviary from Namur of 1488–89 (Fig. 8g), the very broad treatment reflects the youth of the master, and traces of this loose brushwork are still apparent in the hours in London.[12] However, the treatment of the *Coronation of the Virgin* in the latter (Fig. 8h) is more ambitious and grander in scale than his well-known treatment of the subject in the Breviary of Isabella of Castile, which is datable to about 1495 (Fig. 5d).[13] So a date of circa 1500 for the London manuscript, or at the latest within the first decade of the sixteenth century, seems plausible.[14]

Winkler attributed the half-length miniatures of the saints and some others in this manuscript to the aforementioned illuminator he named the Master of the *Hortulus animae*, after a sumptuous manuscript in Vienna.[15] He subsequently identified this artist with Simon Bening; he believed that the *St. Mark, St. Matthew,* and *St. Luke* miniatures, as well as a half-dozen other miniatures of saints, were by Bening. However, the identification of the anonymous master with the famous illuminator from

Fig. 8g [BELOW]. Master of James IV of Scotland. *Nativity*, Breviary from Namur. Berlin, Staatsbibliothek, Ms. theol. lat. 2°285, fol. 33.

Fig. 8h [BOTTOM]. Master of James IV of Scotland. *Coronation of the Virgin*, fol. 120.

Bruges is difficult to sustain.[16] Bening is a more gifted colorist and a superior draughtsman, and his characterizations are more deeply felt (see Cats. 9 and 10).

Like the Rothschild Prayer Book and the Spinola Hours, the hours in the British Library was an important commission probably carried out under the auspices of a noble patron. Unfortunately, none of these manuscripts provides firm indications regarding the identity of its patron. References to John the Baptist and John the Evangelist in the calendar, the litany, and the suffrages of the saints suggest that the hours in the British Library was commissioned by a patron or patroness with this Christian name. Several saints in the litany, including St. Ildefonso and St. Isidore of Seville, were particularly venerated in Spain, and this argues for a possible Spanish patron for the manuscript.[17] A plausible candidate would be Juan of Asturia (1478–1497) or, more likely, his sister Joanna of Castile (see Cat. 7). Winkler believed that the manuscript was probably executed in Bruges.[18] However, if the Master of James IV of Scotland should be identified with Gerard Horenbout (see Cat. 15), Ghent is a more likely place of origin.[19]

BIBLIOGRAPHY London (British Museum) 1901, pp. 253–54; Herbert 1911, pp. 320–21; Winkler 1913a, pp. 275–76; Winkler 1913b, p. 52; Winkler 1915, p. 284, n. 2, and fig. 5; Millar 1914–20, pp. 96–101, 103–04; Millar 1928, no. XXXVI; Winkler 1925, pp. 127, 178, 197; Durrieu 1927, pp. 42, 93, pl. XCVII; Hulin de Loo 1939a, pp. 16, 17, fig. 2; Winkler 1943, pp. 60, 61; Winkler 1962–63, p. 11; Winkler 1964, pp. 120, 149, fig. 93; Turner 1967, p. 50; Trenkler 1979, pp. 79–80; de Winter 1981, p. 417, fig. 127; Euw/Plotzek 1979–82, II, pp. 275, 279, 282–84.

NOTES

1. Argent, à chevron azure.

2. Another example appears in the Hours of Engelbert of Nassau illuminated by the Master of Mary of Burgundy, Oxford, Bodleian Library, Douce Mss. 219–220; see Alexander 1970, pls. 72–91. The name "Master of James IV of Scotland" derives from his miniature depicting the Scottish ruler in a book of hours in Vienna (Österreichische Nationalbibliothek, codex 1897, fol. 24v). See Winkler 1925, pl. 74.

3. Fols. 18v–31 inclusive.

4. On the development of Passion iconography in this period, see Marrow 1979. At the beginning of the fifteenth century the Limbourg brothers employed a symmetrical two-page design with facing miniatures in, for example, the Belles Heures of Jean, duc de Berry (New York, Cloisters). See Meiss/Beatson 1974, fols. 123v–124, 131v–132.

5. On this manuscript, see de Schryver 1969a; also Winkler 1915, p. 284, n. 2, pl. XIII and fig. 5. Pächt 1948, p. 26, attributed the miniature to the Master of Mary of Burgundy.

6. The Schongauer engraving is *Christ Bearing the Cross* (Lehrs 1908–34, no. 26). On pictorial sources for the Spinola miniature, see Euw/Plotzek 1979–82, II, pp. 281–82.

7. On the Rothschild Prayer Book, see Trenkler 1979; on the Spinola Hours, Euw/Plotzek 1979–82, II, no. IX 18, figs. 367–468.

8. The miniatures by this collaborating illuminator in the Rothschild Prayer Book include fols. 203v–238v (see Trenkler 1979); for those in the Spinola Hours, see Euw/Plotzek 1979–82, II, pp. 275–76 and figs. 444–449, 451, 459–464, 467–468.

9. In the Rothschild Prayer Book, fols. 84v, 99v, 130v, and 134v; see Trenkler 1979. In the London hours, fols. 56v, 76v, 119v, and 120. Both manuscripts also include a prayer to the Virgin with indulgences granted by Pope Sixtus IV (1471–84), a type of prayer found at the end of the fifteenth century and in the first quarter of the sixteenth. In the London hours this leaf with its one miniature (fol. 237) was inserted apparently not long after the completion of the manuscript.

10. Winkler 1943, p. 60, called the London hours "a typical, good workshop example by the artist," whom he identified as Gerard Horenbout. He originally attributed fols. 10v, 18v–34, 56v–126, 158v, and 159 without qualification to the Master of James IV of Scotland (1931b, p. 52, n. 4).

11. Trenkler 1979, p. 89, and Euw/Plotzek 1979–82, II, p. 256. However, de Winter 1981, p. 424, n. 20, dates both the Spinola Hours and the Rothschild Prayer Book considerably earlier, i.e., "c. 1500" and "c. 1505," respectively.

12. Berlin 1975, no. 158, color plate; Berlin 1980, no. 89, color plate 23.

13. See Cat. 5.

14. Winkler 1925, p. 178, suggested a dating of circa 1500.

15. Österreichische Nationalbibliothek, Codex 2706; ibid.

16. Winkler 1962–63, p. 11.

17. I am grateful to Derek Turner and Consuelo Dutschke for discussing liturgical aspects of this manuscript with me.

18. Winkler 1915, p. 284, n. 2.

19. Turner 1967, p. 50, and Winkler 1943, p. 60. Four miniatures from the Passion cycle in the British Library manuscript appear to be copied in a minor Flemish book of hours of the first quarter of the sixteenth century (London, Sir John Soane's Museum, Ms. 4); see Millar 1914–20, pp. 96–101, 103–04.

9 Genealogy of the Infante Dom Fernando of Portugal

Lisbon and Bruges, 1530–34. Additional Ms. 12531

MANUSCRIPT *Vellum, 13 detached leaves; 55.9 × 39.4 cm. On each leaf (except fol. 2) a large central miniature with genealogical trees and related historical scenes, or additional ancestors (fol. 10); on fol. 2 only an illuminated border with a genealogical tree; on fol. 1 the coat of arms of Infante Dom Fernando of Portugal and his motto, "Salus vite," on banderoles held by wild men.*

PROVENANCE *The Infante Dom Fernando of Portugal (1507–1534); 11 leaves (fols. 1–11) acquired by Newton Scott (or Smith?) in 1842 in Lisbon and subsequently sold to the British Museum; 2 leaves (fols. 5* and 9*) acquired by the British Museum from the collection of Baron Hortega, Madrid, in 1868.*[1]

THE artistic importance of the unfinished Genealogy of the Portuguese Infante Dom Fernando, brother of King John III (1521–27), rests mainly on the five magnificent leaves by Simon Bening, the finest Bruges illuminator of the sixteenth century (Pls. XI, XII, Figs. 9b–9e). Like most Flemish illuminators of the late fifteenth and early sixteenth centuries, Bening was a specialist in the execution of small devotional books, but the dimensions of the present leaves are much greater than a page from a typical book of hours, and they comprise the only illuminated genealogy in Flemish art. Not only are these the largest leaves Bening illuminated, but they are probably also the largest in Flemish illumination. The genealogy demonstrates his ability to work in dimensions greater even than some panel paintings, though he rarely, if ever, painted on panel. A keen observer of human nature, he provides the genealogy with lively characterizations, luscious coloring, and vivid textures typical of his finest devotional miniatures. The intriguing story of its genesis deserves to be recounted in detail.

The Genealogy of Dom Fernando contains a total of thirteen leaves, seven of the remainder illuminated by Antonio de Hollanda, an artist active in Lisbon, who designed all thirteen. They comprise one of the most richly documented of all manuscript commissions. Damião de Góis (1501–1573), a Portuguese humanist, historian, and diplomat who lived in Antwerp, records in his chronicle of King Manuel I the circumstances behind the creation of the genealogy. He tells that while he was in Flanders in the service of King John III, Dom Fernando, the king's brother

> ordered me to find whatever chronicles I could, either manuscript or printed, in whatever language, so I ordered them all. And to compose a Chronicle of the Kings of *Hispanha* since the time of Noah and thereafter, I paid a great deal to learned men: salaries, pensions, and other favors. I ordered a drawing of the

tree and trunk of this line since the time of Noah to King Manuel I, his father. [Dom Fernando ordered it illuminated] for him by the principal master in this art in all of Europe, by name of Simon of Bruges in Flanders. For this tree and other things I spent a great deal of money.[2]

Góis' Simon of Bruges is certainly Simon Bening, an identification supported not merely by the wide evidence of Bening's own fame, as recorded by Vasari and Guicciardini,[3] but also by the style of some of the illuminations. In fols. 2, 4, 5, 5*, and 10 (Pls. XI, XII, Figs. 9b–9e), the modeling of the figures agrees well with the Dixmuiden *Crucifixion*, the illuminator's only known signed miniature, which unfortunately was destroyed in World War I.[4]

Several other documents illuminate the circumstances of the commission. Another contemporaneous source, the Portuguese artist Francisco de Hollanda's notation in his copy of Vasari, confirms that his father, Antonio de Hollanda, designed the genealogy. Hollanda executed the drawings that Dom Fernando sent to Bening one at a time.[5] Góis wrote to Dom Fernando on August 15, 1530, describing the progress on the illumination and telling him that Bening was disappointed because only a single drawing had arrived.[6] Bening had hoped to receive two, three, or even four, and he had even finished all his other commissions so that he could concentrate on this project, which he expected would take two years.[7] In 1539, five years after the death of Dom Fernando, Antonio still had not been paid for his work on the genealogy and the project was never completed. In the end, Bening illuminated only the aforementioned five leaves (Pls. XI, XII, Figs. 9b–9e), and Hollanda attempted to complete the remainder himself. In addition to the seven he illuminated (Fig. 9a), he drew another that was never completed (Fig. 9f).

Figanière, Ströhl, and Aguiar have transcribed the inscriptions on the leaves, identified the subjects, and analyzed their historical anomalies.[8] The opening plate represents the *Prologue* with the arms and device of Dom Fernando (Fig. 9a). The genealogy begins on the following leaf (fol. 2) and represents the Old Testament ancestors of the family: the descendants of Magog, grandson of Noah (Fig. 9b). It then moves ahead several millenniums to Favila, Duke of Cantabria (d. 700), and his descendants, described as the "Trunk of the Kings of León and Castile" (fol. 3). This is followed by three leaves depicting the lineage of the Kings of Aragon, commencing with Iñigo Arista (late eighth–early ninth century), founder of the house of Navarre (fol. 4; Fig. 9c), and continuing on fol. 5 with the lines of his son and successor, García Iñiguez (ninth century), and of Sancho Ramirez (fol. 5*; Fig. 9d), King of Aragon (1063–94) and Navarre (1076–94).

Fig. 9a. Antonio de Hollanda. *Prologue*, with arms of the Infante Dom Fernando of Portugal, fol. 1, detached leaf.

Despite the confusing labels of fols. 7 and 8 as the "First Table" and fols. 9 and 9* as the "Fourth," there is continuity of lineage, with no apparent gaps in these four leaves.

The last two tables represent the complex array of descendants of John of Gaunt, Duke of Lancaster and Aquitaine (d. 1399; Fig. 9e), whose progeny included fifteenth-century kings and queens of the houses of Lancaster, Burgundy, Hapsburg (Pl. xii), Portugal (Fig. 9f), and Castile.[9]

Despite their common subjects, there is no basis, either visual or historical, for suggesting that these last two leaves belonged to a two-page opening. Both have right-hand borders, indicating their placement on the right side of different, but probably consecutive, spreads; the corresponding left leaves, if executed, have been lost. These missing leaves would likely have depicted the ancestors of Manuel I of Portugal (1469–1521), as well as John of Gaunt's Castilian descendants through Isabella of Castile and her daughter Maria, wife of Manuel I and mother of the Infante Dom Fernando.

The ruling house of Portugal begins with Henry of Burgundy, first Count of Portugal (d. 1112). Henry is depicted at the head of a tree (fol. 6), which includes St. Stephen, King of Hungary (1001–38), and St. Stephen's relations. The first king of Portugal, Afonso I (1128–85), is represented as the trunk of the next tree (fol. 7), followed by later Portuguese kings (fol. 8).

Fols. 7 and 8 were undoubtedly conceived as a pair of facing leaves. Placed together, with fol. 7 on the left, the title for these tables reads "First Table: The Kings" on fol. 7, and "of Portugal" on fol. 8. The designs of the pages, and to some extent the trees themselves, are symmetrical, showing King Afonso II (1211–23) in the upper right quadrant of fol. 7, facing his wife, Queen Urraca, in the upper left corner of fol. 8. Folios 9 and 9* were likewise intended as facing leaves, with the title, "Fourth Table" (fol. 9) "of the Kings of Portugal" (fol. 9*). The immediate ancestors of King Afonso IV (1325–27) appear in fol. 9, while those of his wife, Beatriz, are depicted in fol. 9*.

Fig. 9b. Simon Bening. *Genealogical Tree of Magog*, fol. 2, detached leaf.

Pl. xi [OPPOSITE]. Actual size detail of Fig. 9b.

BÉLIER

OVCAR

OVELED

DAMA

OVEVO

Fig. 9c. Simon Bening. *Genealogical Tree of the Kings of Aragon*, fol. 4, detached leaf.

Fig. 9d. Simon Bening. *Genealogical Tree of the Kings of Aragon*, fol. 5*, detached leaf.

Fig. 9e. Simon Bening. *Genealogical Tree of John, Duke of Lancaster*, fol. 10, detached leaf.

Pl. XII [OPPOSITE]. Actual size detail of Fig. 9e.

In addition to these last, probably unrealized branches, several visual and genealogical lacunae among earlier folios strongly suggest that the genealogy was intended to be considerably more extensive than the existing thirteen leaves. Over thirty leaves may have been planned. As many as twenty-five may actually have been completed if, as Kaemmerer suggests, they were executed in chronological order.[10] However, the documents do not reveal anything about the organization of the project. According to Ströhl, there are genealogical errors within the existing folios,[11] but despite such ambiguities and gaps, Aguiar argues persuasively that the genealogy, hitherto considered that of the royal house of Portugal, is rather a genealogy of Dom Fernando himself.[12]

The allocation of leaves illuminated by Antonio de Hollanda and by Simon Bening appears to be as follows. The leaves executed by Hollanda are fols. 1, 3, 6, 7, 8, 9, and 9*; by Bening, fols. 2, 4, 5, 5*, and 10.[13] The borders in each leaf seem to have been illuminated by the artist who executed its miniature. Weale has observed that most of the border designs are superior to the design of the main miniatures and that they may therefore be by Bening. He points out that on both fols. 10 (Fig. 9e) and 11 a full or partial border has been left blank by Hollanda.[14] This may be true in some cases, for example fol. 3; but such scenes as the landscape in fol. 8 have none of the quality of Bening's landscapes and, in general, the types of subjects represented in the borders rarely occur in Bening's oeuvre.[15]

The designs and illuminations for the genealogy are Hollanda's most famous work (Fig. 9f). Relatively little of his art has been studied, but his career is well documented.[16] Probably born about 1480, possibly in Holland, he was named by King Manuel I to the post of heraldic officer ("passavant") in 1518, a post he continued to occupy into the reign of King John III.[17] He illuminated texts for various members of the Portuguese royal family, and in 1534 he visited Toledo to paint the portraits of Emperor Charles V and his wife, Isabella of Portugal.[18] Hollanda illuminated breviaries, psalters, altar books and choir books, chronicles, and probably other genealogies. He was alive in 1553, when his son Francisco wrote about him to Michelangelo,[19] but he probably died a few years later.[20]

Hollanda's contribution can best be assessed by examining his unilluminated and very beautiful drawing (Fig. 9f). Probably inspired by the technique of German draftsmen, especially Albrecht Dürer, Hollanda modeled his figures in fine, closely placed parallel hatchings and crosshatchings. The hatchings are short, and their arrangement gives the materials a velvety quality.

The primary prototype of a genealogical tree for Hollanda was Burgkmair's woodcut series, The Genealogy of the Emperor Maximilian I (1509–12).[21] Indeed, the poses of a number of the figures in Dom Fernando's genealogy exhibit similarities to Burgkmair's woodcuts. It is possible that Antonio de Hollanda knew the Burgkmair series, since knowledgeable agents such as Damião de Góis were busily assembling research materials and shipping them to Lisbon. Maximilian is even represented at the upper right of fol. 10 (Fig. 9e). However, Burgkmair's woodcuts depict only rows of single figures unrelated by arboreal motifs.

The compositional type of the Hollanda design recalls Tree of Jesse imagery, of which a number of prominent Netherlandish prototypes are known. In the Tree of Jesse by Geertgen tot Sint Jans (Amsterdam, Rijksmuseum), there is a similar interest in richly brocaded and courtly dress.[22] However, unlike this painting, Hollanda's designs have a plain background rather than a naturalistic setting, and the supporting trunks and branches function largely as connecting segments with no clear identity as a single tree on the page.

Hollanda seems to have followed the artistic mainstream in Lisbon, which had absorbed recent developments in other European art. Some of the designs—the Prologue, for example (Fig. 9a)—are clearly related to a Portuguese tradition of illumination. The tripartite division of the main miniature with the coat of arms in the central compartment recalls the program of a frontispiece designed by Alvaro Pires in 1527.[23] The compartmentalization of the borders in the Prologue is also anticipated in Pires' design. The bas-de-page with Nereids and Tritons represents an adaptation of Italian Renaissance motifs that was evident in Portuguese illumination some years earlier, as in the bas-de-page of another frontispiece, in the Leitura nova of 1516, one of the great monuments of Portuguese illumination.[24] The quality of Hollanda's painting, however, lacks the refinement of his drawing. His illumination appears competent but flat and dull in comparison to Bening's work, and the characters lack expression.

The leaves by Simon Bening tell quite a different story. He has taken the Portuguese artist's refined drawings and breathed life into them. In the border with the Genealogical Tree of Magog (Fig. 9b, Pl. XI), Bening animates the pattern of movement by the shadows cast against the recessed violet ground, and he also enlivens Hollanda's characterizations. Bening's figures more often interact with each other and their surroundings. A range of lively personalities is apparent in the Genealogical Tree of John, Duke of Lancaster (Fig. 9e, Pl. XII), one of the illuminator's most unusual and beautiful miniatures. These paintings have extraordinary presence.

Bening also gives his illuminations a sculptural quality and places them in a deeper, more tangible space. The colors, blues and reds in particular, are richer and the texture of a leaf, a brocade, velvet, or armor are differentiated in an even light. He had beautiful drawings to work with here, but his skill as an illuminator surpasses the draftsman's achievement. In his calendar miniatures (Cat. 10) he created monumental works in tiny format. Here he demonstrates his ability to illuminate in the dimensions of panel paintings, and in my view these leaves compare favorably with the work of the best painters of his day, including Bernaert van Orley and Joos van Cleve. Bening's five illuminated leaves in the Genealogy of the Infante Dom Fernando of Portugal rank among his finest work.

Fig. 9f. Antonio de Hollanda. *Genealogical Tree of the Kings of England and Castile*, fol. 11, detached leaf.

BIBLIOGRAPHY Góis 1619, pt. II, chap. xix, p. 65; London (British Museum) 1850, pp. 59–60; Figanière 1853, pp. 268–76; Weale 1872–73, p. 118; Kaemmerer/Ströhl 1903; Weale 1903, pp. 321–24; Haupt in Thieme/Becker 1907–50, I, p. 596; Durrieu 1910, pp. 166–67; Destrée 1923, pp. 23–28; Winkler 1925, pp. 139–40, 176, pls. 80, 81; Durrieu 1927, pp. 43, 90, pl. XCI; dos Santos 1930, pp. 23, 25–26, 30, 32; Wescher 1946, p. 209; dos Santos 1950; London (Royal Academy) 1953, no. 626; Aguiar 1959, pp. 119–20, 127, 129, 142, 144; Aguiar 1962; Smith 1968, p. 200; Baumgarten 1972; Baumgarten 1975; Biermann 1975, pp. 40, 42, 269–70; Segurado 1975, p. 157; Kupfer-Tarasulo 1979a, pp. 274–75, n. 5, 298, n. 73.

NOTES

1. Figanière (1853, p. 270) says that Newton Smith bought the leaves at an auction in Lisbon in 1842. He paid 40 pounds sterling and subsequently sold them to the British Museum for 600 guineas. However, other sources identify the purchaser as Newton Scott; see Aguiar 1962, pp. 48, 50, 52. Aguiar (1962, chap. 1, and p. 205) contends, however, that the leaves were stolen from the Royal Library in Madrid.

2. Góis 1619, p. 65. I am indebted to Barbara Anderson who has kindly translated the Portuguese sources cited in this entry.

3. Vasari 1927, VI, p. 254, and Guicciardini 1581, p. 143.

4. Winkler 1925, p. 169; Durrieu 1927, pl. 88.

5. Dos Santos 1950.

6. Destrée 1923, pp. 24–25, 89; see also dos Santos 1930, pp. 26–27, where a portion of the letter is quoted.

7. Destrée 1923, pp. 24–25.

8. Figanière 1853, pp. 271–76; Kaemmerer/Ströhl 1903, I, pp. 5–9; Aguiar 1962, chap. 4.

9. Kaemmerer/Ströhl 1903, I, p. 9.

10. Because at least some parts of the genealogy were evidently designed visually and historically in terms of two-page spreads, several existing folios (including 1 through 6, and 10) appear to be lacking their facing leaves. However, Aguiar does not believe that each illuminated leaf had a facing illuminated leaf (1962, pp. 102–03). Absent are the lines of three Portuguese rulers, from Pedro I (1357–67) through Fernando (1367–83) and John I (1384–1433), as Kaemmerer/Ströhl (1903, I, p. 8) and Aguiar

(loc. cit.) have pointed out. Each of these would likely have required at least one spread, thus adding another six leaves or more. Aguiar doubts that other leaves were executed since both artists were so rushed by Góis, they would not have had time (ibid., p. 178).

11. Ströhl has noted, for example, that on fol. 4 King Sancho I has been mistakenly labeled Sancho Abarqua (Kaemmerer/Ströhl 1903, I, p. 6), and that Philippa and Henry, depicted as the off-spring of John of Gaunt's second marriage, to Constance of Castile (Figs. 9e and 9f), were actually his children by Blanche of Bourbon (ibid., p. 9). Aguiar's exhaustive historical study includes detailed discussions of these and other anomalies in the genealogy (1962, pp. 69–84 and 159–90).

12. Aguiar 1962, pp. 78–79.

13. Winkler 1925, p. 176.

14. Weale 1903, p. 322. Aguiar, on the other hand, believes that Antonio executed almost all the borders except those of fols. 2, 3, and 10 (1962, p. 151).

15. Smith 1968, p. 200, points out that they are typical of early-sixteenth-century Portuguese illumination.

16. On the basis of the genealogy, dos Santos makes a number of attributions of illuminations in Portuguese collections (1923, pp. 23, 25, 30, 32, pls. XXVIIIb, XXXVII, XLVI). He also attributed to Antonio the *Genealogy of the Count of Feira* (whereabouts unknown). See also Segurado 1970, pp. 504–05.

17. Haupt in Thieme/Becker 1907–50, I, pp. 595–96, and Segurado 1970, pp. 12, 142, 175–77, 228, 454, 460, 503–05, 512.

18. Segurado 1970, pp. 504–05.

19. Ibid., pp. 142, 505f.

20. Ibid., p. 54.

21. Hollstein 1949–, V, nos. 324–415.

22. The Amsterdam painting has also been attributed to Jan Mostaert. For a good reproduction, see Snyder 1971, p. 444, fig. 1.

23. Lisbon, Arquivo Nacional, L° 11; dos Santos 1930, p. 30, pl. XLIV.

24. Lisbon, Arquivo Nacional, L° 3; ibid., p. 30, pl. XL.

10 Calendar Miniatures

Bruges, circa 1540. Additional Ms. 18855, fols. 108–109

MANUSCRIPT *Vellum, 2 detached leaves illuminated on both sides; 15.2 × 10.2 cm. 4 full-page miniatures, no borders. Formerly inserted in Add. Ms. 18855, a book of hours of the Bourdichon school.*

PROVENANCE *Sir John Tobin, Liverpool; Rev. John Tobin, Liscard, Cheshire; British Museum purchase from the book dealer William Boone, 1852.*

THE four full-page miniatures on these two leaves, among the most beautiful of Simon Bening's mature landscapes, have never been fully published. They have long been considered to be part of a dismembered set that includes two similar leaves in the Victoria and Albert Museum. These additional two also contain four landscape miniatures illustrating occupations of the different months of the year, the traditional subject matter of medieval and Renaissance illuminated calendars.[1] Sidney Cockerell attributed all four leaves to Simon Bening, and this view has been widely accepted.[2] Bening painted a number of the finest calendar cycles made during the first half of the sixteenth century, and the four leaves seem to belong at the end of a chronological sequence that includes calendar miniatures in the Da Costa Hours, the so-called "Golf Book," the Hennessy Hours, and a complete calendar cycle of detached leaves in Munich.[3]

Fig. 10a [LEFT]. Simon Bening. *March*, fol. 108, detached leaf.

Fig. 10b [RIGHT]. Simon Bening. *April*. London, Victoria and Albert Museum, Salting Ms. 2538, detached leaf.

Fig. 10c [LEFT]. Simon Bening. *May*. London, Victoria and Albert Museum, Salting Ms. 2538v, detached leaf.

Fig. 10d [RIGHT]. Simon Bening. *July*, fol. 109v, detached leaf.

By analogy with other Flemish calendars, the eight illustrations may be identified probably as representations of the occupations for *March* (Fig. 10a) and *December* (Pl. XIII); *June* (Fig. 10h) and *July* (Fig. 10d); *April* (Fig. 10b) and *May* (Fig. 10c); *August* or *September* (Fig. 10e) and *September* or *October* (Fig. 10f).[4] The iconography of Bening's calendar scenes reflects not only subjects common in other Flemish calendars of the fifteenth century, such as the lovers making music on a canal in *May* or the peasants lunching in the fields in Fig. 10e, but also the fresh impetus given to such cycles by the Très Riches Heures of Jean, duc de Berry, which was conceived and mostly executed by the Limbourg brothers at the beginning of the fifteenth century.[5] In the Grimani Breviary of circa 1515 (Fig. 10g), for example, the Master of James IV of Scotland provided a lively and influential reinterpretation of the famous French calendar illuminations.[6] The scene of hounds devouring a wild boar in the British Library leaf (Pl. XIII) derives ultimately from the December calendar scene in the Très Riches Heures, but the spearing equestrian figure in the background was first introduced in the Grimani Breviary free copy of the Très Riches Heures miniature.[7]

The four London leaves differ in two respects from other Flemish calendar cycles of the period. They have no texts, and they have miniatures on both their rectos and versos—unlike conventional Flemish calendar pages, such as those in the Da Costa or Hennessy hours, in which a calendar text of feasts appears on the recto of a leaf while a full-page miniature for the following month appears on the verso. Each two-page spread of the calendar section was thus devoted to a single month. Therefore, the leaf in the British Library with miniatures which appear to represent *March* on the recto and *December* on the verso could not —since the months are not consecutive—have been intended for a conventional book of hours. These anomalies suggest that the leaves were either intended as an independent collection of calendar miniatures, executed solely to delight (perhaps as specimens for the inspection of potential customers); or, what seems equally likely, as examples that may have been supplied by the illuminator as

Fig. 10e [LEFT]. Simon Bening. *August* or *September*. London, Victoria and Albert Museum, Salting Ms. 2600, detached leaf.

Fig. 10f [RIGHT]. Simon Bening. *September* or *October*. London, Victoria and Albert Museum, Salting Ms. 2600v, detached leaf.

patterns for his workshop.[8] Thus far, however, no other miniatures or calendar cycles based upon these eight miniatures have been identified.

The five calendar sets by Bening under consideration illustrate a dramatic evolution in the artist's treatment of landscape, in which he develops more variegated terrain, more clearly articulated spatial recession, and deeper, more atmospheric vistas. Moreover, the figures play an increasingly minor role. The four British Library and Victoria and Albert leaves seem to represent the culmination of this development. The miniatures of *June* (Fig. 10h) and *July* (Fig. 10d) have grand, hazy vistas viewed from a hilltop or a slope. Bening's treatment of June in the Da Costa Hours (Fig. 10i), which contains his earliest fully realized calendar cycle executed as many as thirty years earlier, demonstrates how he has opened up the space. In the London scene, the vantage point is much higher, the far distance shows a valley, and the winding river draws the viewer to the distant horizon. Here, especially in the river motif, the artist's debt to the visionary landscapes of the Antwerp painter

Joachim Patinir and his followers is apparent. Patinir's *Temptation of St. Anthony,* with figures by Quentin Massys, exemplifies the kind of landscape Bening emulated.[9] But Bening's landscape appears to be developed beyond Patinir's conception. The distant horizon is bathed in a soft haze, and the row of trees leads the viewer down the slope in a nearly regular rhythm. This device is echoed in the famous row of trees used by Pieter Bruegel in the *Return of the Hunters* (Fig. 10j), painted in 1565, only four years after Bening's death.[10]

Destrée placed the four London leaves in the second half of the illuminator's career and associated them with the Munich cycle, which is nearly as advanced in its treatment of landscape.[11] Gaspar agreed, dating both sets of leaves close to 1530.[12] On the basis of the costumes and the mature treatment of the landscape, however, the miniatures in London may date considerably later, perhaps as late as the 1540s (compare Figs. 10b and 10k).[13] Relatively little else is known of Bening's activity after the Genealogy of the Infante Dom Fernando of Portugal (Cat. 9), begun

Pl. xiii. Simon Bening. *December*. Add. Ms. 18855, fol. 108v, detached leaf.

Fig. 10g. Master of James IV of Scotland. *December*, Grimani
Breviary. Venice, Biblioteca Marciana, Ms. lat. XI 67 (7531),
fol. 12v.

Fig. 10h [LEFT]. Simon Bening. *June*, fol. 109, detached leaf.

Fig. 10i [ABOVE]. Simon Bening. *June*, Da Costa Hours. New York, The Pierpont Morgan Library, M.399, fol. 7v.

Fig. 10j. Pieter Bruegel. *Return of the Hunters*, oil on panel. Vienna, Kunsthistorisches Museum.

Fig. 10k. Simon Bening. *June*. Munich, Bayerische Staatsbibliothek, Clm. 23638, fol. 7v, detached leaf.

the Grimani Breviary (fol. 10v; Salmi 1974, pl. 19) and in the "Flora" Hours (fol. 12). Fol. 108 of the British Library miniatures, for *March* and *December*, merits discussion because the two leaves do not represent consecutive months. A scene with woodcutters and a gardener doffing his cap to ladies (Fig. 10a) appears as the *March* miniature in Bening's Golf Book (fol. 20v; London [British Museum] 1911, pl. XXII), while a boar hunt appears as the *December* miniature in the Très Riches Heures (fol. 12v; Longnon/Cazelles 1969, pl. 13), the Grimani Breviary (fol. 12v), and the Hennessy Hours (Destrée 1923, pl. XXIII). (However, in the British Library leaf [Pl. XIII], the figure holding the dog's ears is eliminated.) Warner 1910, III, p. 16, suggested that the scene represents February, but this seems unlikely, since no precedent for the same subject as February has been identified. London (British Museum) 1868, p. 161, identifies the subject as April, but again without a clear basis.

5. Fols. 1–12v; Longnon/Cazelles 1969, pls. 1–13.

6. For the Master of James IV, see Cats. 8 and 15.

7. Fol. 12v; Longnon/Cazelles 1969, pl. 13; Salmi 1974, pl. 23.

8. Janet Backhouse suggested to me the possibility that the leaves may be display specimens.

9. Koch 1968, no. 17, fig. 44.

10. On the significance of Bening's calendar landscape for Pieter Bruegel the Elder, see also Tolnay 1934, p. 125. Winkler 1962–63, p. 13, has discussed the importance for Bruegel of some of the landscapes and iconographical features of the Golf Book. See also Gibson 1977, pp. 146–48, figs. 103, 104; Hindman 1981, pp. 455–58.

11. Destrée 1923, pp. 38, 40.

12. Gaspar 1943, p. 15.

13. Winkler 1962–63, p. 13, places them "in his later years."

14. Bening was paid in 1537 for illuminations in a manuscript for the Order of the Golden Fleece; see Onghena 1968, pp. 187–215, and Marrow 1984, n. 64, for further references.

Damião de Góis reported toward the end of his life that in 1544 he sent to Queen Catherine of Portugal, wife of King John III, a book of hours illuminated by "Symon de Bruges." Dos Santos 1930, pp. 26–27, pl. XXXIII, has identified this manuscript with a book of hours illuminated by Bening in the Museu Nacional de Arte Antiga in Lisbon. It is known to me only in poor reproductions.

There is also a *Self-Portrait* from Bening's later period, dated 1558 (London, Victoria and Albert Museum, no. P. 159–1910), and a replica in New York, The Metropolitan Museum of Art; see Murdoch/Murrell/Noon/Strong 1981, pl. 1c. There is a prayer book dated 1545 in a Belgian private collection that I have not seen (Christie's, London, March 10, 1976, lot 203; Marrow 1984).

in 1530.[14] The London leaves are a testament to his poetic vision of landscape, an attitude sustained throughout a long and distinguished career.

BIBLIOGRAPHY London (British Museum) 1868, p. 161; London (Burlington) 1908, under no. 231; Warner 1910, III, p. 16, pl. L; Herbert 1911, p. 323; Delisle 1913, p. 26; London (Victoria and Albert Museum) 1923, pp. 30–31; Destrée 1923, pp. 40–41; Winkler 1925, pp. 140, 177; Gaspar 1932, p. 56; Gaspar 1943, pp. 5, 15; Winkler 1962–63, p. 13; Biermann 1975, p. 42.

NOTES

1. The leaves in the Victoria and Albert Museum were acquired from George Salting and belonged previously to Mr. Locker-Lampson; see London (Victoria and Albert Museum) 1923, pp. 30–31.

2. London (Burlington) 1908, under no. 231; see also Warner 1910, III, p. 16; Destrée 1923, pp. 40–41; Winkler 1925, pp. 140, 177; and, most recently, Biermann 1975, p. 42.

3. On the Da Costa Hours (New York, The Pierpont Morgan Library, M. 399), see Quaritch 1905, and Winkler 1962–63, p. 13, figs. 7, 8; on the Golf Book (London, British Library, Add. Ms. 24098), see London (British Museum) 1911; on the Hennessy Hours (Brussels, Bibliothèque Royale, Ms. II 158), see Destrée 1923; on the Munich leaves (Bayerische Staatsbibliothek, C.m. 23638), see Leidinger 1913.

4. In Flemish calendar illuminations a given occupation was not always strictly associated with a specific month. Sometimes it illustrated different months in different calendars. For example, the scene of sowers and plowers (Fig. 10f) represents September in the Hennessy Hours (fol. 9v; Destrée 1923, pl. XVIII) and in the Da Costa Hours (fol. 10v), but it represents October in

ITALIAN

MANUSCRIPT

ILLUMINATION

1460–1560

THE best-known works of Italian Renaissance art are monumental in scale, for example, Mantegna's *Triumphs of Caesar* (Ill. 8), Michelangelo's *David*, and Leonardo's *Last Supper*. By contrast, manuscript illumination occupies little more than a footnote in most general histories of the Italian Renaissance. As monumentality is more than a matter of size, just as it is but one aspect of Renaissance style, why this comparative neglect? It cannot be denied that large-scale painting offered more scope for the emphasis of the plastic and spatial values which so preoccupied artists during this period. The miniaturist was constantly brought face to face with the two-dimensionality of the lines of text which he illustrated, but this very problem could provide a special spur to the imagination. We shall see that the manuscript page offered only slightly less opportunity for the display of artistic illusionism than the church wall or the altarpiece panel.

By their very nature small and private objects, seldom displayed to the public eye, illuminated manuscripts were less suitable for the communication of artistic ideas than large paintings and statues or mass-produced prints. During the Renaissance, as in earlier times, manuscripts nevertheless continued to serve as a medium for the interchange of motifs and compositions. Miniatures were more prone to be influenced by works on a larger scale than vice versa, but Renaissance illumination was not an especially derivative art form. Mantegna's San Zeno Altarpiece reflects Donatello's earlier altar for the Santo in Padua, and even Michelangelo's Vatican *Pietà* has an ultimately German iconographic source.[1] Originality, in any case a relative term, is more a question of temperament than of opportunity; and the extent to which illuminators could appropriate motifs from frescoes and panel paintings was limited by the small scale and special requirements of their medium. However, in Italy it was not uncommon for artists to work in a variety of mediums, including illumination and engraving as well as fresco and panel painting. The commonly held view that late manuscript illumination was a decrepit art form doomed by the new technology of printed illustration is a fallacy derived from hindsight and the misapplication of evolutionary theories to the history of art.

In view of the vast quantity and frequently exquisite quality of Renaissance illuminations, it is remarkable that they have received so little attention in recent years. The study of Quattrocento drawings, in particular, could benefit from the parallel examination of miniatures.[2] Manuscript illuminations also reveal a much wider iconographic range than any other artistic medium of the fifteenth century. Whereas the large majority of monumental Renaissance secular decorative cycles has disappeared, numerous series of secular illuminations survive. One can form a better idea of the splendor of the Sforza and Este courts or of the remarkable Italianate milieu of Buda under Matthias Corvinus from the illuminated manuscripts which these princes commissioned than from the scanty remains of their palace decorations. However, the greatest interest of Renaissance miniatures lies in their unique association with the written word. They represent the visual arts in their most intimate contact with the classical and humanistic texts upon which the foundation of the Renaissance depended.

The revival of interest in the forms and content of classical antiquity puts Italian art of the Quattrocento in a different category from that of the rest of Western Europe. Since the Italian Renaissance was originally a literary movement, its consequences were speedily apparent in manuscripts. The clear and easily readable form of the Western alphabet, which is the lineal ancestor of that in common use today, originated in Florence at the beginning of the fifteenth century. Although Poggio Bracciolini and the other early exponents of this script stressed its classical

Ill. 8. Andrea Mantegna. *The Vase Bearer*, from the *Triumphs of Caesar*, tempera on canvas. Hampton Court. Reproduced by gracious permission of Her Majesty the Queen.

Donatello and the painter Mantegna, it has been pointed out that they were already common accessories in Italian manuscripts of the second half of the fourteenth century.[4] The early medieval origins of *bianchi girari* and the Trecento antecedents of putti indicate the continuity of medieval ideas in the Renaissance and remind us that the early humanists lacked the strict archaeological method which is often taken for granted today. One may cite instances of comparable antiquarianism from both Italy and the North. During the early Quattrocento in Florence, the twelfth-century Baptistery was sometimes mistaken for an ancient Roman building; and in the Netherlands, the painter Jan van Eyck juxtaposed the archaic forms of Romanesque architecture with those of contemporary Northern Gothic to evoke the contrast between the Old and New Testaments.[5] Viewed literally, many elements of the early-fifteenth-century Florentine revival seem incongruous. However, the enthusiasm of the earlier humanists for the classical past initiated an increasingly rigorous program of antiquarian research, among both writers and artists.

Although artists as diverse as the French architect Villard de Honnecourt and the Italian sculptor Nicola Pisano had copied antique sculpture since the thirteenth century and earlier, little systematic attempt was made to record and imitate classical remains before the fifteenth century.[6] The way was led by the traveler and scholar Cyriacus of Ancona. In Italy and the Levant he studied Greek and Roman monuments, such as the grave altar now at Port Sunlight (Ill. 10) which he saw in the treasury of the church of Santa Maria Maggiore at Rome in either 1424 or 1432–33.[7] His enthusiasm for recording ancient sculptures rapidly fired the imagination of other North Italian humanists and artists, of whom the most famous were the Veronese scholar Felice Feliciano and the Paduan painter Andrea Mantegna. It is recorded that in 1464 Mantegna accompanied Feliciano and other antiquaries on a visit to Lake Garda, where they copied classical inscriptions.[8] The painter's passionate interest in antiquity had been established much earlier, as is evident from the numerous motifs derived from Roman art in his early frescoes at the church of the Eremitani in Padua.

Mantegna may have worked as an illuminator himself, although it is unlikely that the decorations in the manuscript of the *Life and Passion of St. Maurice* at Paris, which have sometimes been attributed to him, are actually by his hand.[9] His influence on North Italian miniaturists and painters of the second half of the fifteenth century was clearly greater than that of any of his contemporaries, but there is the danger of overestimating his role in the development of what one might term "archaeological antiquarianism." The older Venetian artist Jacopo Bellini, whose daughter Mantegna married in 1453 or 1454, was

antecedents and dubbed it littera antiqua, their actual sources were manuscripts of the eleventh and twelfth centuries, which derived from ninth-century Carolingian models. Together with the new script came a form of decoration known as "white vine," from the Italian *bianchi girari*.

An early example of a manuscript with such decoration is the copy of Plautus' *Comedies* at the British Library (Ill. 9), completed by Sozomeno of Pistoia on August 1, 1415. The schematic white interlaced scroll set against a brightly colored background is derived from the decorated initials of eleventh- and twelfth-century manuscripts.[3] It rapidly achieved widespread acceptance and remained popular for many years, developing into increasingly complex forms, such as appear in the British Library Petrarch of circa 1463–83 (Cat. 11). The playful nude figures of putti are a recurrent motif in Italian Renaissance illuminated manuscripts, appearing, for example, in the volume of St. Augustine's commentary on the Psalms decorated by Cristofano Mayorana (Cat. 12) and the books illustrated by Giovan Pietro Birago (Cats. 14, 15). Although these little figures are ultimately of classical origin and were popularized during the Quattrocento by the sculptor

deeply interested in classical remains, as his London and Paris sketchbooks indicate.[10] It has been pointed out that the similarities between the two versions of the *Agony in the Garden* (London, National Gallery) by Mantegna and his brother-in-law Giovanni Bellini, may well reflect a common knowledge of a composition by Jacopo rather than the influence of one of the younger painters upon the other.[11] Similarly, while the Mantuan miniaturist Pietro Guindaleri was subjected to the full force of Mantegna's powerful style at the court of the Gonzaga, some of his illuminations suggest direct points of contact with Jacopo Bellini (see Cat. 11).

The manuscripts written and possibly decorated by Bartolommeo Sanvito, such as the British Library Eusebius (Cat. 13), present an analogous problem. The scribe and scholar Sanvito was himself a Paduan, a fellow citizen of Mantegna, but he was only twenty-five when the painter moved to Mantua. Faceted epigraphic capitals, similar to those which appear in Mantegna's paintings, are a standard feature of Sanvito's manuscripts. Felice Feliciano, a great scholar but an indifferent scribe, wrote the earliest-known treatise on the design of such letters, and it has been suggested that Mantegna reinterpreted his Veronese friend's ideas in a beautifully decorated manuscript of Strabo's *Geography*.[12] Were this the case, Mantegna would appear as the designer of the epigraphic capital, as used by Sanvito and others. However, it seems more likely that the capitals which appear in Mantegna's documented paintings and Sanvito's known manuscripts reflect not the dependence of the scribe upon the painter but their mutual knowledge of the North Italian circle of Feliciano.

North Italian antiquarianism was rapidly influential in many different regions of Italy. Sanvito himself worked principally at Rome. The Neapolitan miniaturist Cristofano Mayorana specialized in decorative frontispieces, of which the one in the British Library St. Augustine (Pl. XIV) is a typical and exquisite example; here the text appears to be a placard resting against an architectural backdrop inhabited by putti. The derivation of this compositional idea, probably via a North Italian source, from classical sculptures such as the Port Sunlight grave altar is readily apparent. Giovan Pietro Birago's text pages (Pl. XV, Figs. 15c, 15f), in which the "placards" of script are more immediately illusionistic and the framing pilasters of disparate objects piled one on top of the other are distinctly reminiscent of antique carvings, have a similar provenance.

The decorated pages of Mayorana and Birago remind us of the common problem of fifteenth-century illuminators, both Northern and Italian. In Mayorana's folios, the lines of text were transformed into a placard leaning against an architectural structure. In Birago's, the text appears to be written on a piece of paper loosely affixed between pilasters—the latter at once architectural, sculptural, and purely decorative. Inexorably increasing artistic naturalism presented the danger of driving a destructive wedge between the representational requirements of the artist and the inevitable two-dimensionality of the page of text. It has been pointed out elsewhere that the use of illusionistic "text placards" by Jean Fouquet was more a development of the practice of earlier Northern miniaturists such as the Bedford Master than a response to Italian painting and sculpture of the Quattrocento.[13] In this context, it is significant that Matteo da Milano utilized decorative borders composed of illusionistic flowers and insects on a gold ground, a system derived from Netherlandish models (Fig. 16c), as well as the North Italian type of border, consisting of carefully delineated classicizing motifs, ultimately based upon antique carvings. Both types of border function in an analogous way, providing an intermediate zone, partly decorative and partly illusionistic, between the real world beyond the book and the text or the pictorial space of the miniatures. The ingenious responses of North Italian miniaturists to the fundamental irreconcilability of the outer world of visual experience and the textual or pictorial plane are comparable to those formulated in a monumental context by Mantegna in the Camera degli Sposi.

Florentine manuscripts of the later fifteenth century were, if anything, even more lavishly decorated than those produced in Northern Italy. Attavante degli Attavanti, the most celebrated Florentine miniaturist of his day, was the head of a large workshop which produced deluxe volumes for clients from many parts of Italy and beyond. Although Attavante has sometimes been criticized for the very rich-

Ill. 10. Roman, second century A.D. Grave altar, marble. Port Sunlight, Great Britain, Lady Lever Art Gallery.

ness of his taste, a manuscript such as the Philostratus at Budapest, which he executed in 1488–90 for Matthias Corvinus, King of Hungary, reveals that he too was intrigued by the problems of reconciling text and decoration.[14] The endpaper and title page of this volume are completely covered with decoration, so that the underlying vellum is almost entirely concealed; even the text is written in gold on a colored ground. Although executed many years later, Attavante's double folio 3v–4 in the British Library copy of Collenuccio's *Apologues* (Pl. XXII) is an essentially similar conception. It has been pointed out that Attavante's florid style suggests points of contact with the painter Ghirlandaio and with Verrocchio, who was both painter and sculptor.[15] Indeed, his contemporaries, the Florentine miniaturists Gherardo and Monte di Giovanni, also worked as panel painters and mosaicists, assisting Ghirlandaio and Botticelli in the latter capacity in 1491.[16] However, it is unrealistic to propose a general order of priority in the flow of ideas between Florentine painters, sculptors, and illuminators at the end of the Quattrocento, since specialists in a wide variety of mediums often worked side by side, especially in the larger ateliers, such as that of Verrocchio.

At the turn of the sixteenth century, the ornate style of the generation of Ghirlandaio and Attavante was rapidly overtaken by the new monumentality and compositional clarity of Leonardo, Raphael, and Michelangelo. During the High Renaissance and the Mannerist epoch that succeeded it, the significance of Italian manuscript illuminators became increasingly peripheral. It must be admitted that the illuminations of the Croatian-born Giulio Clovio (1498–1578), such as appear in the De Rothesay Hours at the British Library (Ill. 11), are not readily accessible to twentieth-century taste. In 1911 the British scholar J. A. Herbert wrote, "Giulio Clovio is a typical master of the decadence [of manuscript illumination]; fond of weak suave forms, cheap sentiment and soft broken colours."[17] However, in 1568 Giorgio Vasari had observed, "For many centuries, and perhaps for yet other centuries, there has been no more excellent illuminator or painter of small things than Giulio Clovio, who has far surpassed all others in this exercise."[18] This dramatic contrast of opinion is indicative of the respective authors' attitudes toward the style known as Mannerism (from the Italian *maniera*).[19] But the comments of both Herbert and Vasari are in the nature of art criticism, rather than art history. For our present purpose, it seems more profitable to investigate the position of illuminated manuscripts during the first half of the sixteenth century in relation to monumental paintings, printed illustrations, and the printed book.

Book illustration, whether hand painted or printed, served as an adjunct to text, just as monumental painting,

whether altarpiece or fresco, belonged to a given room or building. Manuscript illuminators of the late fifteenth and early sixteenth centuries either painted their miniatures as though they occupied a world separate from the adjacent text or, more daringly, combined the two, so that the reality of the text simultaneously amplified and denied that of the illustrations. Giovan Pietro Birago, for example, employed both solutions, as a comparison of the full-page miniatures of the Sforza Hours (Pls. XVI, XVII) with the decorated frontispiece of the British Library *Sforziada* (Pl. XV) readily indicates. However, the source of Giulio Clovio's decorated pages, with an intermediate zone of seemingly sculptural motifs around a central cartouche containing the main scene, is to be found in ceiling frescoes, such as those by Michelangelo in the Sistine Chapel. This shift of emphasis may reflect the intentional caprice of an artist schooled in the style of Giulio Romano, rather than a lack of inventiveness, but it positively denied the actual function of manuscript illumination—as a component of a book.[20]

Even the best late-fifteenth-century Italian woodcut book illustrations, such as appear in Francesco Colonna's *Hypnerotomachia Poliphili* (Ill. 12), printed by the great

Ill. 11. Giulio Clovio. *King David*, De Rothesay Hours. London, British Library, Add. Ms. 20927, fol. 91v.

Aldus Manutius at Venice in 1499, could hardly compare with the better sort of contemporary manuscript illuminations in expressive range, narrative clarity, or subtlety of execution. The major breakthrough in the quality of printed illustration was made not in Italy, but in Germany during the opening decades of the sixteenth century. At Nuremberg, Albrecht Dürer was one of the first artists to approach woodcut and engraving as art forms in their own right, rather than as substitutes for painting or illumination. Through a combination of the efforts of Dürer and his contemporaries, the distinguished patronage of figures such as Emperor Maximilian I, and the increasing demand for beautifully illustrated books of moderate cost, the standard of woodcut and engraving was permanently raised. The increased regard in which graphic illustration was held during the early sixteenth century is apparent in the terms with which the great Dutch humanist Erasmus favorably compared the genius of Dürer with that of the semi-mythical antique painter Apelles: Dürer had achieved with black lines what Apelles had needed the assistance of colors to do.[21] The new Northern school of printmaking was rapidly influential upon Italian engravers and illuminators, as may be illustrated by the presence of a landscape background ultimately derived from Dürer in the *Annunciation* miniature in the Ghislieri Hours (Fig. 16c). In the mid-sixteenth century, the inability of manuscript illumination to endure as an innovatory medium is apparent in the British Library miniatures of the *Triumphs of Charles V* (Cat. 18), which are copies of, rather than models for, prints.

That the invention of printing rendered the scribal profession redundant is a dangerous half-truth. Printers could certainly provide a larger and cheaper edition of a given text more speedily than the best-organized scriptorium. While this ruined the living of the humble copyists who

were to be found in the university cities of Europe supplying students with the standard texts that they required, other classes of scribes were comparatively unaffected by the new technology. Until the invention of the typewriter, clerks and most educated people prized the ability to write clearly and elegantly. In this context, it is significant that Bartolommeo Sanvito, the scribe of the British Library Eusebius (Cat. 13), was himself a scholar and that Pierantonio Sallando, who wrote the text of the Ghislieri Hours (Cat. 16), was a teacher of writing. Moreover, certain sorts of texts, such as personalized books of hours with special prayers, were less amenable to the large editions that printing entailed. Nevertheless, the spread of typography naturally popularized a limited range of scripts, the consequence of which is apparent in the growing uniformity of handwriting in the work of early-sixteenth-century Italian scribes.[22] It is ironic and not a little poignant to observe that *La Operina,* the treatise by Ludovico degli Arrighi on the formation of chancery script, was issued in 1522 as a printed book illustrated with woodblocks cut by the famous chiaroscuro printmaker Ugo da Carpi.[23]

Social and economic factors exercised a formative influence on the remarkable century of Italian manuscript illumination which followed the invention of printing. Although some of the manuscripts considered here, such as the Sforza Hours, belong to a category of religious books common throughout Europe, most are closely associated with humanist and princely libraries. While they were not identical, the composition of humanist libraries determined that of noble ones, since rulers such as Ludovico Gonzaga of Mantua and Federigo da Montefeltro of Urbino (Ill. 13) were themselves educated by humanists and came to share their cultural values. Even though the great prototypes of the aristocratic library, those of the kings of France and the Visconti dukes of Milan, were founded before the end of the fourteenth century, the great age of such institutions came later, during the Quattrocento. The inventory of new acquisitions compiled in the Sforza ducal library for the decade 1459–69 lists 123 new titles, the majority of which were classical texts or recent works by humanist authors.[24] After the Aragonese capture of Naples in 1442, an impressive library was assembled by Alfonso V and his son Ferrante, of which the four-volume St. Augustine written by Rodolfo Brancalupo (Cat. 12) formed a part. Similar libraries were established in Mantua, Ferrara, and Urbino during the second half of the Quattrocento. The Medici of Florence, princes in all but name, were also enthusiastic bibliophiles. Under Sixtus IV the Vatican library was reorganized, with a new building and a permanent librarian. Matthias Corvinus, King of Hungary, emulating his Italian contemporaries, founded the first major humanist-inspired library in Northern Europe. By

Ill. 13. Joos van Ghent. *Federigo da Montefeltro and His Son, Guidobaldo, Attending a Lecture*, oil on panel. Hampton Court. Reproduced by gracious permission of Her Majesty the Queen.

the turn of the sixteenth century, the Corvinian collection had grown into one of the largest libraries in the Western world, only to be dispersed and largely destroyed after the Turkish invasion a few decades later.[25]

One cannot doubt the scholarly enthusiasm of a prince such as Federigo da Montefeltro, of whom the Florentine bookseller and scribe Vespasiano da Bisticci wrote: "He spared neither cost nor labour, and when he knew of a fine book, whether in Italy or not, he would send for it. It is now fourteen or more years since he began the library, and he always employed, in Urbino, in Florence and in other places, thirty or forty scribes in his service. . . . In this library all the books are superlatively good, and written with the pen, and had there been one printed volume it would have been ashamed in such company."[26] One might tactlessly object that had the Duke of Urbino been prepared to tolerate printed books, he would have been able to assemble a far larger library with the thirty thousand ducats that Vespasiano claimed he disbursed on this grand project. To do so, however, would betray a misunderstanding of the aristocratic patrons who commissioned most of the richly illuminated manuscripts in this exhibition. Erudition, like piety and military ability, was a widely recognized and applauded virtue in a Renaissance prince, but it was not enough for his books to be numerous and well chosen, any more than it was sufficient for his chapel to be merely in a good state of repair or his armor to be no more than serviceable. As all three reflected his status, it was necessary that they be richly decorated and of the highest quality. The younger sons of aristocrats, such as Cardinal Francesco Gonzaga (see Cat. 11), and patricians such as Bernardo Bembo and the Ghislieri (see Cats. 13, 16) recognized similar values, although their means were more limited. The cheapness and wide availability of printed books rendered them positively unsuitable for the purpose of such display, unless they were printed on vellum, decorated by hand, and finely bound, as was the British Library *Sforziada* (Cat. 14).[27] Illuminated manu-

scripts, no less than monumental statues and fresco cycles, panel paintings, and noble buildings, were a vital medium through which the Italian Renaissance elite displayed its erudition, good taste, wealth, and power.

NOTES

1. For the association of Mantegna's altarpiece with that of Donatello, see Janson 1957, II, pp. 180–81. For the iconographical derivation of Michelangelo's *Pietà*, perhaps via Italian or French intermediaries, from German sculptures of the fourteenth century, see Weinberger 1967, I, pp. 68–69.

2. The distinction between manuscript illuminations and drawings is not always entirely clear, especially in the case of drawings by artists who worked both as painters and illuminators. See, for example, the drawing *A Pope with a Hawk on His Fist, Riding away from a Woman*, attributed to a member of Fra Angelico's school, which derives iconographically from Joachim of Fiore's *Prophecies of the Popes* and may itself have been a model for a miniature in a copy of the *Prophecies* at the British Library (Harley Ms. 1340), attributed to the circle of Benozzo Gozzoli; see Popham/Pouncey 1950, pp. 2–3.

3. See Alexander/de la Mare 1969, pp. xxxiii–xxxiv.

4. Ibid., pp. xxxiv–xxxv.

5. For the mistaken dating of the Florence Baptistery during the Quattrocento, see Heydenreich/Lotz 1974, p. 34. For the architectural symbolism of Jan van Eyck and other early-fifteenth-century Netherlandish painters, see Panofsky 1953, I, pp. 131ff.

6. Drawings after antique sculpture by Villard de Honnecourt appear on fols. 11v and 22 of his sketchbook (Paris, Bibliothèque Nationale, Ms. fr. 19093); see Hahnloser 1972, pp. 59–60, 130–32. The derivation of Nicola Pisano's Pisa Baptistery statue of *Fortitude* and the relief of the *Annunciation* and *Nativity* from antique sarcophagus sculpture is well known; see White 1966, p. 43.

7. Lady Lever Art Gallery, Port Sunlight, Great Britain; see Waywell 1982.

8. Meiss 1957, pp. 55–56.

9. Paris, Bibliothèque de l'Arsenal, Ms. 940. For the attribution of the decorations in this book to Mantegna, see Meiss 1957, pp. 17–29.

10. British Museum, Department of Prints and Drawings and Musée du Louvre, Cabinet des Dessins; see, above all, Goloubew 1908–12.

11. Davies 1961, p. 336.

12. Albi, Bibliothèque Rochegude, Ms. 4; see Meiss 1957, pp. 52–63.

13. Evans 1981.

14. Budapest, National Széchényi Library, Clmae 417; see Berkovits 1964, pp. 55–58.

15. Marle 1923–38, XIII, pp. 467–70.

16. Ibid., pp. 470–78.

17. Herbert 1911, p. 304.

18. For Vasari's account in translation, see Vasari 1927, IV, pp. 244–49.

19. By far the best concise analysis of the Mannerist style is Shearman 1967.

20. A similar sense of caprice, in a monumental context, is apparent in Giulio Romano's frescoes in the Sala dei Giganti in the Palazzo del Te at Mantua, which give the illusionistic impression that the room is collapsing. Giulio Clovio's friendship with Giulio Romano is mentioned by Vasari 1927, IV, p. 244.

21. For Erasmus' comparison of Dürer with Apelles, see Nuremberg 1971, p. 41.

22. Alexander/de la Mare 1969, p. xxii.

23. For Arrighi's treatise, with further bibliography, see Baltimore 1965, pp. 79–80.

24. For the Sforza library inventory of 1459 and the inventory of new acquisitions of 1469, see Pellegrin 1955, pp. 290–352.

25. For an account of the Corvinian library, see Berkovits 1964, pp. 9–104.

26. For Vespasiano's account in translation, see Vespasiano 1926, pp. 99–100, 102–05.

27. That vellum was used primarily for reasons of display is apparent from the fact that it is a less suitable ground for printing than paper, being more malleable and lacking absorbency.

11 Petrarch, *Canzoniere* and *Trionfi*

Mantua, 1463–83. Harley Ms. 3567

MANUSCRIPT *Vellum, 190 leaves; 26.2 × 17.5 cm. 6 decorated pages with full-page decorative borders surrounding large miniatures and capitals; numerous decorated initials. Partly erased arms of Cardinal Francesco Gonzaga on fol. 9. Antiqua script.*

BINDING *Brown calf, gold fillets, early eighteenth century.*

PROVENANCE *Cardinal Francesco Gonzaga, c. 1463–83; Bartolommeo Sanvito; Guidotti family, Modena, sixteenth century;*[1] *Nathaniel Noel, bookseller, London, January 1724; Robert Harley, 1st Earl of Oxford; Edward, 2nd Earl of Oxford (d. 1741); sold by Lady Oxford to the British Museum on its foundation in 1753.*

FRANCESCO Petrarch's series of Italian poems, the *Canzoniere*, and his long allegorical poem, the *Trionfi*, are two of the poet's most famous works and enjoyed widespread popularity during the Quattrocento.[2] Francesco Gonzaga is known to have owned a second, and possibly a third, copy of the *Canzoniere*.[3]

The Harley manuscript at the British Library is signed on fol. 189 by the scribe Matteo Contugi of Volterra, who worked at Mantua for the Gonzaga from circa 1463 until 1486.[4] In 1463–68 Contugi wrote a manuscript of Pliny's *Naturalis historia* for the Gonzaga, which is probably identical with the volume now at Turin.[5] The miniatures in this manuscript, which are stylistically comparable to those in the British Library Petrarch, have been attributed to Pietro Guindaleri of Cremona, who was in the service of the Gonzaga from 1464 until his death in 1506.[6] Guindaleri was also probably responsible for the miniatures in a sumptuous copy of Boccaccio's *Il Filocolo* at Oxford, written for Marquis Ludovico Gonzaga, the father of Francesco.[7]

At Mantua, Guindaleri was a contemporary of the Paduan artist Andrea Mantegna, who worked for the Gonzaga from 1460 until his death, which also occurred in 1506.[8] Mantegna's influence on the Cremonese miniaturist is most apparent in the antiquarian details of the Turin Pliny, which was executed between 1489 and 1506.[9] The

Fig. 11a [TOP RIGHT]. Pietro Guindaleri. *Triumph of Cupid*, fol. 149.

Fig. 11b [RIGHT]. Pietro Guindaleri. *Horsemen in a Piazza* (detail), in Boccaccio, IL FILOCOLO. Oxford, Bodleian Library, Ms. Canonici Italiani 85, fol. 114v.

Fig. 11c [ABOVE]. Jacopo Bellini. *Flagellation of Christ*, Bellini Sketchbook, fol. 8. Paris, Musée du Louvre, Cabinet des Dessins.

Fig. 11d [RIGHT]. Pietro Guindaleri. *Triumph of Time*, fol. 184.

British Library and Oxford manuscripts reveal an earlier stage of the artist's stylistic development, before he had fallen more deeply under Mantegna's spell. The foreshortened horses, for example, which appear in the *Triumph of Cupid* in the British Library Petrarch (Fig. 11a) and *Horsemen in a Piazza* in the Oxford Boccaccio (Fig. 11b), are of a type that derives ultimately from Pisanello.[10] It has already been pointed out that some of the miniatures in the latter volume seem to imply a knowledge of the Ferrarese frescoes in the Palazzo Schifanoia.[11] The archway in the British Library *Triumph of Cupid* is reminiscent of that in a drawing of the *Flagellation of Christ* by the Venetian painter Jacopo Bellini (Fig. 11c).[12] In the *Triumph of Time* minia-

ture (Fig. 11d), the rendering of the front edge of the row of tiles, which emphasizes the termination of pictorial space, also appears to have been borrowed from the drawings of Jacopo.[13] That Guindaleri was familiar with the work of the Venetian artist, who was the father of Gentile and Giovanni Bellini and the father-in-law of Mantegna, is confirmed by fol. 22 of the Turin Pliny (Fig. 11e). In this page, the archway with a keystone carved in the form of a cupid is a device which also appears in Jacopo's drawings of the *Flagellation of Christ* and *Christ before Pilate*.[14]

As a court miniaturist at Mantua, Guindaleri could hardly avoid the influence of Mantegna. However, it does him an injustice merely to categorize his style as "Mantegnesque."

Fig. 11e. Pietro Guindaleri. Text page decoration, in Pliny, NATURALIS HISTORIA. Turin, Biblioteca Nazionale, Cod. I–I, 22–23, fol. 22.

NOTES

1. Mann 1975, p. 298.

2. Together with Dante and Boccaccio, Francesco Petrarch (1304–1374) was one of the three most significant Italian authors of the fourteenth century. His *Canzoniere* is a collection of 366 Italian poems which he composed over a period of many years; his *Trionfi* was probably begun during the 1350s.

3. Rome, Vatican Library, Ms. Vat. urb. 681, and London, Victoria and Albert Museum, L 101–1947; see London (Victoria and Albert Museum) 1981, pp. 114–15.

4. See ibid., p. 114, and Mantua 1966, pp. 28, 57–58, 80–81.

5. See Mantua 1966, pp. 28, 57–58, 80–81, and Mariani Canova 1969, p. 147.

6. Mantua 1966, pp. 28, 56–57, 80–81, and Pächt/Alexander 1966–73, II, p. 40.

7. Oxford, Bodleian Library, Ms. Canonici Italiani 85; Mantua 1966, pp. 56–57, and Pächt/Alexander 1966–73, II, p. 40.

8. For a summary of Mantegna's activity at the court of the Gonzaga, see London (Victoria and Albert Museum) 1981, pp. 15–25, 51–54, 118–24, 142–45, 164–65, 171–72.

9. Mantua 1966, pp. 56, 80–81.

10. Compare, for example, Pisanello's drawing *Two Horses, One Viewed from the Front and the Other from the Back*, Paris, Musée du Louvre, Cabinet des Dessins, no. 2468; see Fossi Todorow 1966, pp. 72–73 and pl. XLIII.

11. Pächt/Alexander 1966–73, II, p. 40.

12. Fol. 8 of the Paris sketchbook of Jacopo Bellini (Louvre, Cabinet des Dessins); see Goloubew 1908–12, II, pl. III.

13. See, for example, Jacopo's drawings of the *Presentation in the Temple* and the *Presentation of the Head of Hannibal to Prusias* on fols. 28 and 41 of his Paris sketchbook; ibid., II, pls. XXVII and XL.

14. Fols. 8 and 35 of the Paris sketchbook, ibid., II, pls. III and XXXIV.

15. Wardrop 1963, pp. 32, 51.

His chosen medium precluded the use of sweeping spatial illusionism, such as the great Paduan employed in his monumental fresco cycle in the Camera degli Sposi at the Gonzaga castle in Mantua. Not only the specific motifs mentioned above, but also Guindaleri's general preference for small figures juxtaposed against monumental architectural settings indicate that his style was directly associated with that of Jacopo Bellini, who was also influential on Mantegna. In this respect, he may be regarded as Mantegna's contemporary as much as his follower.

Since the white-vine leaf and latticework borders in the British Library Petrarch are quite unlike those in the Oxford Boccaccio, it would appear that either of these, or possibly both, were executed by illuminators who specialized in such work rather than by Guindaleri himself. At a later date, the completed Petrarch came into the hands of Bartolommeo Sanvito, the scribe of the British Library Eusebius (Cat. 13), who added the rubrics and commentaries.[15]

BIBLIOGRAPHY Wardrop 1963, pp. 32, 51; Mantua 1966, pp. 28, 57, 60; Pächt/Alexander 1966–73, II, p. 40; Wright 1972, p. 167; Mann 1975, pp. 296–98; London (Victoria and Albert Museum) 1981, pp. 114–15.

12 St. Augustine, *Explanatio psalmorum*

Naples, 1480. Additional Ms. 14781

MANUSCRIPT *Vellum, 287 leaves; 41 × 28 cm. 1 decorated title page, 1 decorated frontispiece, numerous decorated capitals and borders. The royal arms of Aragon at the sides of the text on fol. 1v (Fig. 12a) and at the foot of fol. 2 (Pl. XIV). Antiqua script.*

BINDING *Brown russia, gold-tooled border, late eighteenth century.*

PROVENANCE *Ferrante I, King of Naples (1480–94); by 1764 in library of the college of the Society of Jesus at Paris; seized by the French government upon the dissolution of the Jesuits in France; Baron Gerard Meerman (d. 1771); (?) Count Jean Meerman (d. 1815); the London booksellers Payne & Foss; from whom purchased (as part of a lot comprising Add. Mss. 14759–14841) by the British Museum, November 16, 1843.*

S T. AUGUSTINE'S commentary on the Psalms, written between 391 and 420, is a fundamental work of biblical exegesis, read and copied throughout the Middle Ages and long after. This manuscript is part three, covering Psalms 72 to 112, of the four-part copy in the British Library.[1] The book is one of a considerable number added to the Neapolitan royal library during the reign of Ferrante I.[2] That it was written by the Neapolitan scribe Rodolfo Brancalupo is evident from the inscription "RODULPHUS BRANCALUPUS EXCRIPSI," which appears, together with the date 1480, on the last folio of the final volume.[3] In 1481 Brancalupo also signed a copy of St. Augustine's *Homiliae*, commissioned by Ferrante I, and now in Valencia.[4] The British Library *Explanatio psalmorum* is almost certainly identical with the copy of this work for which a certain "Randolfo, chancery scribe to the king," received cloth to the value of forty-six ducats, four tari, and nine grani on February 13, 1481.[5] It is notoriously difficult to calculate relative prices during the fifteenth century, but some idea of the value of this sum may be apparent from the fact that, during approximately the same period, one could purchase a horse for around twelve ducats, twenty tari; a house in the San Luca quarter of Messina for some thirty-six ducats, fifteen tari; and a major altarpiece by Antonello da Messina, arguably the most prestigious painter in Southern Italy, for about sixty-six ducats.[6] The Neapolitan archives also relate that on October 13, 1480, a certain "*Christofano*

. . . *miniator*" received part payment of cloth to the value of thirteen ducats, four tari, and two grani, out of a total owed of twenty-seven ducats, four tari, for the task of decorating a copy of St. Augustine's *Explanatio psalmorum*, evidently identical with the four-volume manuscript in the British Library.[7]

For this payment, the miniaturist Cristofano presumably undertook to execute not only the decorated title page and frontispiece in the third part of *Explanatio psalmorum* (Fig. 12a, Pl. XIV) and the small *King David* miniature on the opening folio of the first part of the book, but also the capitals and borders of white vine in all four volumes (Fig. 12b). The latter are very numerous: there are no less than seventy-two in the third part of the manuscript and a similar number in the other three volumes.

Mayorana, documented in the employ of Ferrante I from 1480 until 1492, was clearly the illuminator of the British

Fig. 12a. Cristofano Mayorana. Decorated title page, fol. 1v.

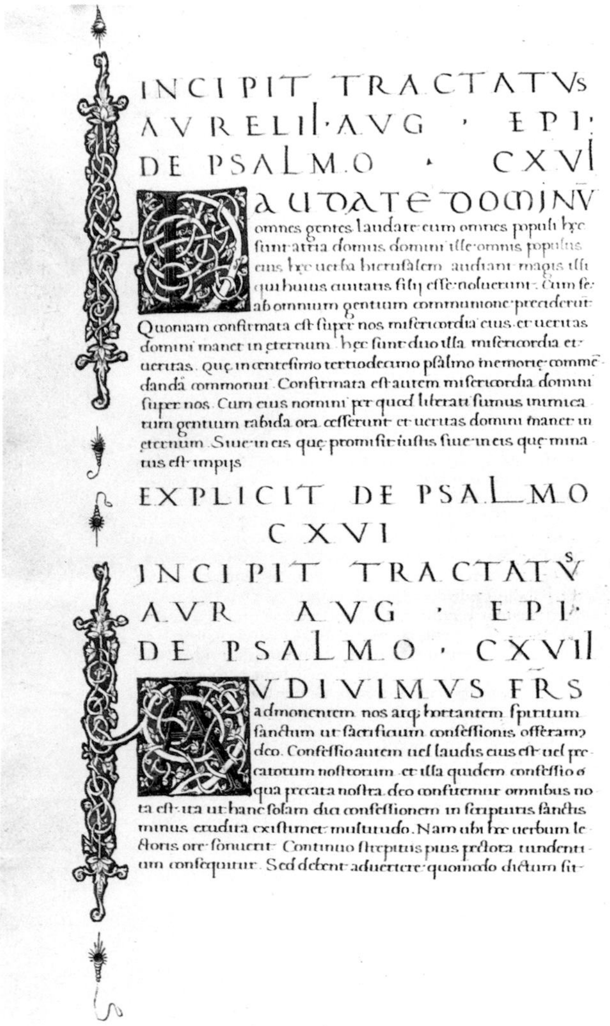

paintings of the fifteenth century, its original prototype seems to have been Altichiero's fresco *Petrarch in His Study* in the Sala Virorum Illustrium at Padua, the composition of which already reappears in an Italian illuminated manuscript of circa 1400 in Darmstadt.[12] Other frontispieces attributed to Mayorana, such as that in a copy of Tacitus' *Opera* in Vienna, incorporate a different image of the scholar, depicted at half-length, facing outward with his book, within a sort of window embrasure.[13] Paintings by Andrea Mantegna, perhaps his early *St. Mark* in Frankfurt, are the probable source of the latter compositional type.[14]

Pl. XIV [OPPOSITE]. Cristofano Mayorana. *St. Augustine in His Study*; decorated border. Add. Ms. 14781, fol. 2.

Fig. 12c [BELOW]. Cristofano Mayorana. *Pliny in His Study*; decorated border, in Pliny, EPISTOLAE. Turin, Biblioteca Nazionale, Ms. D II 24, fol. 1.

Library *Explanatio psalmorum*.[8] He worked on a considerable number of books for the king, his friends and associates, including Alfonso, Duke of Calabria, and Matthias Corvinus, King of Hungary.[9] The starting point for an analysis of Mayorana's style is the frontispiece of a copy of Aesop's *Vita et fabulae*, currently in Valencia and described in a Neapolitan archival reference of February 16, 1481, as the work of "*Christofaro Mayorana*."[10] Like the decorated title page and frontispiece of *Explanatio psalmorum*, this consists of a text placard set against a pseudo-architectural construction of classicizing form. Such decorated pages were something of a specialty with Mayorana, and they appear in many of his manuscripts, a representative example being that in a volume of Pliny's *Epistolae*, now in Turin (Fig. 12c).[11]

These frontispieces consist of a minor and a major element: the miniature of the scholar in his study and the classicizing architectural surround. Both motifs are ultimately of Paduan origin, although their pedigrees are quite different. While the image of the scholar at work is common in both Italian and Northern manuscripts and panel

AVDITE AV DITE DILEC TISSIMA, VISERa

Corporis christi quorum spes domin
deus uester est et non respicitis in ua
nitates et insanias mendaces. Et qui
ad huc respicitis uidete ne respici
atis. Psalmus inscriptionem habet
idest titulum. DEFECERVNT HY
MNI DAVID FILII IESSE PSAL
MVS IPSI ASAPH. Tot habemus psalmos in quorum titulis e
scriptum est nomen Dauid nusquam additum est filii Iesse nisi in hoc
solo. Quod credendum est non frustra factum neque inaniter. Ubique
enim nobis innuit deus et ad intellectum uocat pium studium caritatis. Quid est Defecerunt hymni dauid filii iesse hymni laudes
sunt dei cum cantico. hymni cantus cantici sunt continentes Laude
dei. Si sit laus et non sit dei non est hymnus. Si sit laus et dei laus et
non cantatur non est hymnus. Oportet ergo ut sit hymnus habeat
haec tria. et Laudem et dei et canticum. Quid ergo est Defecerunt
hymni dauid Defecerunt Laudes que cantantur in deum Molesta
rem. & quasi luctuosam uidetur nuntiare. qui enim cantat Laudem
non solum laudat sed etiam hilariter laudat. Qui cantat laudem
non solum cantat sed etiam amat eum quem cantat in laude con
fitentis est predicatio. In cantico amantis affectio. Defecerunt ergo
hymni dauid ait. Et addidit filii iesse. Erat enim dauid rex ifra
el filius iesse tempore quodam ueteris testamenti. quo tempore no
uum testamentum occultum ibi erat tanquam fructus in radice. Si ergo
enim queris fructum in radice non inuenis. Nec tamen inuenis in
ramis fructum nisi qui de radice processit. Illo ergo tempore popu
lo primo ueniente ex semine habrae carnaliter. Nam et populus secu
dus pertinens ad nouum testamentum ad semen habrae pertinet sed
iam spiritaliter. Illi ergo populo primo adhuc carnali ubi pauci pro
phete intelligerent. et quid desideraretur a deo et quando haberet
publice predicari prenuntiauerunt futura haec tempora et aduen
tum domini nostri iesu christi. Et quemadmodum christus ipse
secundum carnem nasciturus in radice erat occultus in semine pa
triarcharum. et quodam tempore reuelandus tanquam fructu apparete

Mayorana's illusionistic frontispieces, with the text placard resting against an antique monument—reminiscent, for example, of the grave altar at Port Sunlight (see Ill. 10, p. 91), derive from earlier Veneto-Paduan illuminations, such as that on fol. 1 of a copy of Pliny's *Naturalis historia*, printed at Venice in 1469.[15] Analogous "architectural" text pages also appear in manuscripts attributed to Pietro Guindaleri (Fig. 11e) and Bartolommeo Sanvito (Fig. 13f). It is noteworthy that, while Mayorana made extensive use of this Paduan classicizing motif, he sometimes could not refrain from combining it with old-fashioned decorative foliage patterns, as in the frontispiece here (Pl. XIV) or fol. II of a breviary, formerly in the possession of W. H. Robinson Ltd.[16]

Mayorana was not a particularly original miniaturist, but his high standards and professionalism are not in doubt. Presumably trained in Padua, he was one of the first artists to introduce the North Italian antiquarian style of illumination to Naples, which had previously been dominated by a mixture of influences from Spain and Northern Europe.[17]

BIBLIOGRAPHY Marinis 1947–52, I, pp. 150–56, 210, 213–14, II, pp. 5, 21, 268–73; Salmi 1957, pp. 64–70; Alexander/de la Mare 1969, pp. 84–85; Csapodi/Csapodi-Gárdonyi 1969, pp. 65, 228–29; Marinis 1969, I, pp. 25, 72, 86.

NOTES

1. Add. Mss. 14779–14782.

2. The task of building up the Neapolitan collection was initiated by Ferrante's father, Alfonso, who captured Naples from his French rival René of Anjou in 1442. For the composition of the Aragonese library see, above all, Marinis 1947–52 and 1969.

3. Add. Ms. 14782, fol. 282.

4. Valencia, Biblioteca Universitaria, Ms. 730; see Marinis 1947–52, II, p. 21.

5. Ibid., pp. 21, 272: "*Misser Francesco Copula donate a Randolfo Ccanceller scriptor del Senior Rey in panno o altre robbe de la corte la valuta de ducati quaranta sey, tari quactro et grana nove . . . per lo scrivere ha facto de vinti quaterni de forma reale de uno libro intitulato Augustino super salterium. . . .*"

6. The calculations are based upon the rate of six ducats to the Sicilian money of account known as the oncia or onza; see Ryder 1976, p. 5, n. 14. For the prices of a horse at two onze, twenty tari, the house which Antonello da Messina purchased from Naldo Lancza in 1464 for six onze, fifteen tari, and Antonello's *Annunciation* (1474, now in Syracuse) at eleven onze, see Messina 1981, pp. 25, 232, 235.

7. Marinis 1947–52, II, pp. 21, 268: "*Messer Francesco Coppola donau a Christofano de Maiorana miniator per lo miniar de Augustino super salmis pro rata de vint e sent ducats, quatre terins la valor de treze ducats, quatre terins, deu grans en drap ho altres robes de la cort. . . .*"

8. For Mayorana, see ibid., I, pp. 150–56.

9. For the copy of Martial's *Epigrammata* decorated by Mayorana for Alfonso and formerly in the collection of Major J. R. Abbey (J.A. 3183), see Alexander/de la Mare 1969, pp. 84–85. For the copy of Arrianus, *De expeditione Alexandri Magni*, decorated by Mayorana for Matthias Corvinus, now in the Vatican Library (Cod. Vat. lat. 5268), see Csapodi/Csapodi-Gárdonyi 1969, pp. 65, 228–29.

10. Valencia, Biblioteca Universitaria, Ms. 758; Marinis 1947–52, II, pp. 5, 273: "*Pro Christofaro Mayorana . . . per lo principio ha facto con spiritello, animalii et altri lavuri antichi et in la lictera grande sta uno homo antiche che czappa uno jardino et altre lictere maiuscole tucto de oro azuro, laccha et altre colury. In uno libro de metate de foglie bolunniese nominato Ysopo del Senyor Rey. . . .*"

11. Fol. 1; ibid., I, pp. 154, 213–14.

12. Darmstadt, Hessische Landes- und Hochschulbibliothek, Hs. 101, fol. 1v. For Altichiero's fresco and the manuscript illumination copy, see Cologne 1978, III, pp. 192–93.

13. Vienna, Österreichische Nationalbibliothek, Cod. 49, fol. 1; see Marinis 1947–52, II, pp. 154–55.

14. This signed work at the Städelsches Kunstinstitut, Frankfurt, is usually dated to the beginning of Mantegna's career; see Bellonci/Garavaglia 1967, pp. 87–88.

15. Ravenna, Biblioteca Classense, N.C. 670, fol. 1; see Salmi 1957, p. 64.

16. Marinis 1947–52, I, p. 210. Fol. 3 of the copy of Arrianus (see n. 9 above) is similarly decorated with an architectural motif within a margin of acanthus.

17. For an account of the artistic situation in Naples during the second half of the fifteenth century, see Bologna 1977.

13 Eusebius, *Chronica*

Padua or Rome, circa 1480–90. Royal Ms. 14 C III

MANUSCRIPT *Vellum, 150 leaves; 33.2 × 23.2 cm. Decorated frontispiece, 1 miniature (fol. 119v), 2 large ink drawings (fols. 17, 138), various small ink drawings, numerous decorated capitals and flourishes. Arms of Bernardo Bembo on the bases of the columns in the frontispiece (Fig. 13b). Cursive script.*

BINDING *Brown leather; nineteenth-century British Museum binding.*

PROVENANCE *Bernardo Bembo (d. 1519); (?) Pietro Bembo (d. 1547); presented by George II to the British Museum, 1757.*

EUSEBIUS OF CAESAREA (act. c. 300–40) is best known for his *Ecclesiastical History*, a fundamental source for the history of the Early Christian Church. His earlier *Chronica* is an epitome of world history, consisting of chronological lists of important events arranged by country. Originally written in Greek, Eusebius' book was revised and translated into Latin by St. Jerome.

The British Library *Chronica* is one of a large number of manuscripts written by the Paduan scribe Bartolommeo Sanvito.[1] It is one of four known volumes which Sanvito wrote for Bernardo Bembo, father of Pietro the celebrated author and cardinal.[2] Bernardo Bembo, born in Padua, a city under Venetian control but with a lively cultural tradition of its own, was himself an accomplished scholar. He enjoyed a glittering political career as a leading Venetian senator, serving as govenor successively of Ravenna, Bergamo, and Verona.

Sanvito was evidently a close friend of Bernardo Bembo; Bembo described him as "the Reverend Dominus Bartolommeo Sanvito, my honored compatriot" and apparently named his bastard son Bartolommeo after the scribe.[3] Born in 1435, Sanvito was working as a notary at Padua in 1466, although by 1474 he was in Rome, where he was still active during the 1490s. In 1509 the aging Sanvito was a canon of the church of Monselice, near his native city of Padua. He was still alive in 1518.[4]

Although the original humanist script, the so-called "littera antiqua," retained its position as a book hand until the end of the Quattrocento and later, being used by Matteo

Contugi (Cat. 11) and, in a modified form, by Pierantonio Sallando (Cat. 16), professional humanists generally wrote their essays and letters in a less formal and speedier script, known as cursive.[5] Around the middle of the fifteenth century, there was a growing interest in Roman inscriptions, centered chiefly around the North Italian circle of Cyriacus of Ancona and Felice Feliciano (see p. 90). Cyriacus and Feliciano were also particularly fond of the use of tinted inks of various colors.[6] In the manuscripts written by Bartolommeo Sanvito, these three elements—cursive script, epigraphic capitals, and colored inks—were combined to constitute a professional book hand quite distinct from those of his predecessors.

It has been pointed out that there is little difference between Sanvito's cursive book hand, such as appears in the British Library *Chronica* (Fig. 13a), and the informal script

Fig. 13a. Bartolommeo Sanvito. *Nativity* and text, fol. 119v.

he employed, for example, in his additions to the copy of Petrarch's *Canzoniere* and *Trionfi* which had come into his possession (Cat. 11).[7] His interest in Roman inscriptions is apparent in his use of both faceted epigraphic capitals (Fig. 13b) and ink drawings of classicizing monuments as text cartouches (Figs. 13c, 13d). The latter are closely related to copies of actual antique inscriptions collected by humanists, such as those that appear in the volumes compiled by the Veronese Fra Giovanni Giocondo (1443–1515), apparently written by Sanvito himself.[8] A memorable feature of the British Library *Chronica* is Sanvito's use of a wide range of colored inks, including gold, red, green, violet, and light blue, as well as black. This well-judged polychromy combines with Sanvito's feathery cursive

hand and his delicate drawings of classicizing decorations to endow the *Chronica* with that peculiarly ethereal quality so characteristic of his best work.

The style of the frontispiece and the *Nativity* miniature (Figs. 13b, 13a) is similar to that which appears in a number of manuscripts written by Sanvito, including the *Works* of Vergil in the British Library (Fig. 13e).[9] It has recently been noted that the specific motif of a putto wearing a mask, such as appears at the foot of the *Chronica* frontispiece, may again be found in a copy of Suetonius' *Lives of the Caesars* in Paris, also written by Sanvito (Fig. 13f).[10] Comparable miniatures also appear in a number of manuscripts not thought to have been written by Sanvito, and an attempt has been made to distinguish the hands

Fig. 13b. Bartolommeo Sanvito. *St. Jerome*; text; decorated border, fol. 2.

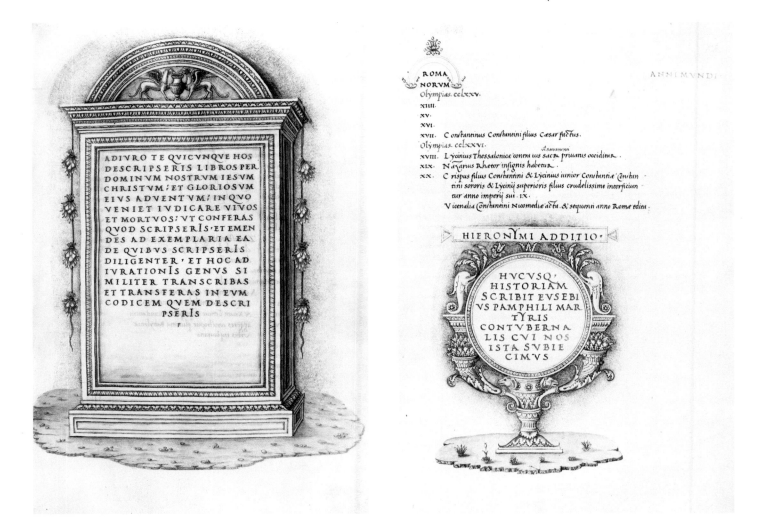

Fig. 13c [LEFT]. Bartolommeo Sanvito. Text and ink drawing of a classicizing monument, fol. 17.

Fig. 13d [RIGHT]. Bartolommeo Sanvito. Text and ink drawing of a classicizing ornament, fol. 138.

responsible for a group of manuscript illuminations in the Veneto-Paduan style associated with Mantegna and the Bellini family.[11] Much research on this problem remains to be done. The most immediate issue to be considered is the personal role of Sanvito in the illumination of this group of manuscripts. It has been suggested that the key figure in this complicated attributional problem may be the artist Lauro Padovano, who seems to have been known to Sanvito.[12] Lauro was evidently a miniaturist, but his only loosely documentable works are a series of panel paintings from the predella of the St. Vincent Ferrer Altarpiece, usually assumed to have been painted within the workshop of Giovanni Bellini.[13] The stylistic similarity between these panels and the manuscript illuminations associated with Sanvito is acceptable inasmuch as both belong to the circle of Mantegna and the Bellini, but it is not compelling.

Toward the end of his life, Sanvito presented two Epistolaries to the college at Monselice, with a Latin inscription stating that both were decorated and written by the scribe at his own expense.[14] This clearly implies that he was both scribe and illuminator. Even during the fifteenth century, when the production of illuminated manuscripts was generally dominated by scribes and illuminators who specialized in one or the other profession, a number of men both wrote and decorated manuscripts.[15] The stylistic difference between the miniatures in various books written by Sanvito may partly be explained by the arthritis that afflicted him in later years and apparently affected his handwriting.[16] Unless further information on the identity of the Veneto-Paduan miniaturist with whom Sanvito collaborated so successfully on a number of occasions is forthcoming, it seems justified to identify this artist with none other than the scribe himself. Viewed in this context, Bartolommeo Sanvito strikes a fascinating and uniquely apt comparison with his Paduan compatriot Mantegna, who was also an antiquary, artist, and gentleman.[17]

BIBLIOGRAPHY Wardrop 1963, pp. 24, 25, 29, 51; Robertson 1968, pp. 47–51; Alexander/de la Mare 1969, pp. 104–10; Alexander 1977, pp. 64–67; Alexander 1978, pp. 114–15.

Fig. 13e [FAR LEFT]. Bartolommeo Sanvito. *Aeneas and Dido*; text; decorated border, in Vergil, WORKS. London, British Library, Kings Ms. 24, fol. 59.

Fig. 13f [LEFT]. Bartolommeo Sanvito. Text and decorated frontispiece, in Suetonius, LIVES OF THE CAESARS. Paris, Bibliothèque Nationale, Ms. lat. 5814, fol. 1.

NOTES

1. Wardrop 1963, pp. 23–35, 50–53.

2. Ibid., p. 29. The *Chronica* was once incorrectly believed to have been commissioned by Pietro Bembo; see Warner/Gilson 1921, II, p. 133.

3. The inscription on fol. 43 of Bernardo Bembo's commonplace book (British Library, Add. Ms. 41068), cited by Wardrop 1963, pp. 29–30.

4. Ibid., pp. 25, 26, 27–30.

5. Ibid., pp. 7–12.

6. Ibid., pp. 15–18.

7. Ibid., pp. 33–34, for the similarity between Sanvito's book hand and his informal hand.

8. The attribution of Fra Giovanni Giocondo's volumes of inscriptions to Sanvito was made by Wardrop 1963, pp. 27–28.

9. See Warner/Gilson 1921, III, p. 9, and Alexander 1978, pp. 114–15. This manuscript has been dated to 1497–99. For a list of manuscripts with comparable illuminations, written by both Sanvito and other scribes, see Alexander/de la Mare 1969, pp. 108–09.

10. See Alexander 1977, pp. 64–67.

11. Alexander/de la Mare 1969, pp. 108–09, where it is proposed that these illuminations are the work of two Padua-trained art-

ists, called the "Master of the Vatican Homer" and the "Sanvito Illuminator," the latter possibly identical with Sanvito himself.

12. Alexander 1977, p. 64. Lauro Padovano is apparently mentioned in an entry for October 4, 1508, in the journal of Bartolommeo Sanvito, examined by S. de Kunert in 1907 but since untraceable; see Kunert 1907, pp. 70–73.

13. These predella panels, now in the Wittelsbach Collection, were attributed to Lauro Padovano by the early-sixteenth-century Venetian connoisseur known as the "Anonimo Morelliano." It has recently been suggested that the entire St. Vincent Ferrer Altarpiece should be attributed to Lauro Padovano, for whom see Robertson 1968, pp. 47–51.

14. "*Manu sua impensaque conscripta ornataque*"; see Alexander/de la Mare 1969, p. 107.

15. For example, the copyist and miniaturist Giovanni Martinengo of Padua, who complained in 1471 of the shortage of work, presumably a result of the introduction of printing, and threatened to move to Venice; see Wardrop 1963, p. 39.

16. Toward the end of his life, Sanvito complained in his journal of arthritis. For this and its apparent effect upon his writing, see ibid., pp. 24, 31, and Alexander/de la Mare 1969, p. 105.

17. Sanvito's comparatively elevated social standing is manifest in his friendship with Bernardo Bembo and is alluded to by the entries in his journal. Like Mantegna, he also seems to have been a collector; see Wardrop 1963, p. 27.

14 Giovanni Simonetta, *Sforziada*

Printed Milan, Antonio Zarotto, 1490. Presentation copy, for Ludovico Sforza, decorated Milan, circa 1490. Department of Printed Books

BOOK *Vellum, 202 leaves; 35 × 24 cm. Decorated frontispiece, numerous decorated capitals. In the frontispiece (Pl. XV), the arms of Ludovico Sforza; profile portraits of Ludovico and Francesco Sforza; Ludovico's symbol, the head of a Moor; and the Sforza motto "Merito et tempore" enclosing the Sforza symbol, the spazzola or "brush," in the left border. The device of a pair of towers with water flowing between them emblazoned on Ludovico's breastplate and on a shield between the tails of the pair of dragons in the right border.*

BINDING *Original; dark red velvet, the outer covers decorated with silver gilt bosses at the corners and, on each, a roundel of niello decorated with the device of two towers and a badly rubbed and indecipherable motto. 2 silver clasp plates on the covers, one decorated with a Moor's head, the other with the spazzola and the motto "Merito et tempore."*

PROVENANCE *Ludovico Sforza, c. 1490–99; possibly acquired by Louis XII of France; Charles de Rohan, Prince de Soubise (by 1788); Count MacCarthy-Reagh; George Hibbert (until c. 1829); Philip Augustus Hanrott (until 1833–34); Thomas Grenville; his bequest to the British Museum, 1846.*

THE *Sforziada* or, to give its full and proper title, *La Historia delle cose facte dallo invictissimo duca Francesco Sforza,* is a lengthy account of the life and exploits of Francesco Sforza (1401–1466), Duke of Milan from 1450 and founder of the Sforza dynasty. The *Sforziada* was written in Latin by Giovanni Simonetta (d. 1491), a member of a Calabrian family who had entered Francesco's service during his early days as a condottiere and subsequently followed him to Milan. This Italian translation by the Florentine humanist Cristoforo Landino (1424–1498) was dedicated to Francesco's son Ludovico in 1489 and printed by Antonio Zarotto (1450–1510) at Milan in 1490.[1] Although a printed book, this deluxe edition is on vellum rather than paper and, like a manuscript, is richly decorated by hand.

An illuminated manuscript of Landino's translation, with corrections in the hand of Simonetta, is preserved at Milan.[2] It bears Sforza arms and, according to tradition,

belonged to Galeazzo Maria Sforza, son of Francesco and brother of Ludovico. Galeazzo was fifth Duke of Milan from 1466 to 1476; the manuscript was inherited by his son, Giangaleazzo, who succeeded to the duchy on the death of his father.[3] Three deluxe copies of Zarotto's 1490 edition are known, each printed on vellum with frontispieces decorated in the same style: the present volume (Pl. XV), one at the Bibliothèque Nationale in Paris (Fig. 14c), and one at the National Library in Warsaw (Fig. 14b).[4] These frontispieces are by the same hand as the Milanese miniatures in the Sforza Hours (Cat. 15). That the miniaturist of this work was Giovan Pietro Birago is apparent from the signature "PSBR IO. BIRAGUS FE" (an abbreviated form of "*Presbiter Joannes Petrus Biragus fecit*") on the base on which the shield-bearing putti stand at the foot of the right border of the Warsaw copy.[5]

It is evident that the London *Sforziada* was the property of Ludovico Sforza, since it bears his portrait, arms, and a Moor's head, one of his favorite symbols.[6] The putti playing around his coat of arms have no more than a decorative significance and are clearly related to the figures in the engraving *Twelve Naked Children Playing* (Fig. 14a), also attributed to Birago, and to the numerous putti in the Sforza Hours.[7] The portraits of both Francesco Sforza and Ludovico have the appearance of reversed versions of their likenesses in a pair of medals by Cristoforo Caradosso Foppa, cast for Ludovico in 1488–94 to commemorate his acquisition of Genoa (Figs. 14d and 14e).[8] This event is also alluded to in the London *Sforziada* frontispiece. The two towers with water flowing between them, which appear on Ludovico's breastplate and a shield in the right border, as well as in the niello roundels on the cover, are an emblematic representation of the harbor mouth at Genoa reminiscent of the view of the city that appears on the verso of Ludovico's portrait medal (Fig. 14f).[9] The use of this device, which alludes to Ludovico as Duke of Genoa, rather than to his later title of Duke of Milan, and the

Fig. 14a. Giovan Pietro Birago. *Twelve Naked Children Playing,* engraving. Berlin, Staatliche Museen Preussischer Kulturbesitz, Kupferstichkabinett.

LIBRO PRIMO DELLA HISTORIA DELLE COSE FACTE DALLO
INVICTISSIMO DVCA FRANCESCO SFORZA SCRIPTA IN LA
TINO DA GIOVANNI SIMONETTA ET TRADOCTA IN LIN
GVA FIORENTINA DA CHRISTOPHORO LANDINO FIOREN
TINO.

FRAN·SFOR·VIC
DVX
MLI
IIII
PATER PATRIAE

NE TEMPI CHE LA REGINA GIOVANNA SE
conda figliuola di Carlo Re regnaua:perche era fuc
ceduta nel regno Neapolitano a Latiflao Re fuo fra
tello:elquale parti di uita fanza figliuoli.Alphonfo
Re daragona con grande armata mouendo di Cata
logna uenne in Sicilia : Ifola di fuo Imperio.La cui
uenuta excito gli huomini del Neapolitano regno a
uarii fauori:& a diuerfi configli:& non con piccoli
mouimenti di quel regno:Impero che Giouána Regina per molti & uarii
fuoi impudichi amori era caduta in fóma infamia.Et defperandofi che lei
femina poteffi adempiere lofficio del Re:& adminiftrare tanto regno:fece
a fe marito Iacopo di Nerbona Conte di Marcia:elquale per nobilita di fan
gue:& belleza di corpo:ne meno per uirtu era tra Principi di Francia excel
lente . Ma accorgendofi in breue che quello defideraua piu effere Re : che
marito:& quella non molto ftimaua:moffo da feminile leuita lo rifiuto:&
priuo dogni adminiftratice . Questo fu cagione chel fuo regno:elquale per
fua natura e prono alle diffenfioni & difcordie:arrogendouifi e nó honefti
coftumi della Regina : ritorno nelle antiche factioni & partialita:& comin
cio ogni giorno piu a fluctuare & uacillare.Erano alcuni a quali nó difpia
ceua la fignoria della dóna:perche benche il nome fuffi in lei:loro niente di
meno comádauono.Altri defiderauano:che Lodouico tertio Duca dangiox
figliuolo di Lodouico e'quale era nomato Re di Puglia:& di unolantenatai
della Reale ftirpe daragonia:fuffi adoptato dalla Regina.Coftui poco auáti
pe conforti di Martino tertio fómo Pontefice:& di Sforza Attendolo excel
lentiffimo Duca in militare difciplina : & padre di Francefco sforza de cui
egregii facti habbiamo a fcriuere era uenuto a liti di Campagna:Et cógiun
tofi Sforza:hauea moffo guerra alla Regina . Ma quegli che repugnauano
a Lodouicho:metteuano ogni induftria : che Alphonfo fuffi adoptato in fi
gliuolo della Reina:accio che in Napoli fuffi tal Re:che con le fue forze &
di mare & di terra poteffi refiftere alla poffa de Franciofi . Adunque in cofi
uehemète contentione de baroni:& piu huomini del regno:Alphonfo chia
mato dalla Reina in herede & compagno del regno:diuene nó folo illuftre:
ma anchora horribile : Et el nome Catelano elquale infino a quegli tempi
nó era molto noto & celebre fe non a popoli maritimi:ma inuifo & odiofo:
comincio a crefcere : & farfi chiaro . Ma & da Lodouico & da Sforza tanto
ogni giorno piu erono oppreffi:el Re & la Regina:che diffidádofi nelle pro
prie forze: conduxono Braccio Perugino : el quale era el fecondo Capitano
di militia in Italia in quegli tépi có molte honoreuoli códitioni:& maxime

Fig. 14b. Giovan Pietro Birago. Decorated border, frontispiece in Giovanni Simonetta, Sforziada, printed book. Warsaw, National Library.

Pl. xv. Giovan Pietro Birago. Decorated border, frontispiece in Giovanni Simonetta, Sforziada, Milan, 1490.

courtiers, made on behalf of Giangaleazzo's children, Francesco and Bona, the rightful heirs of the Milanese duchy.[15]

Although Ludovico is honored in the frontispieces of the London and Paris copies and roundly condemned in that of the Warsaw version, the three deluxe copies of the *Sforziada* have the appearance of being a single commission. Since Birago was in favor with both of the main Milanese political factions, working for Giangaleazzo's mother, Bona, on the Sforza Hours (Cat. 15) and supervising the decoration of Ludovico's Marriage Grant of 1494 (Fig. 14g), it is possible that the London and Paris copies of the *Sforziada* were executed for Ludovico and the Warsaw copy for an adherent of Giangaleazzo.[16] If this were the case, the iconography of the Warsaw frontispiece would suggest that it was commissioned with parody in mind. Another, more likely answer to this mystery may be that Giangaleazzo commissioned all three—the Paris copy for his own use, the London version for his uncle, and the Warsaw volume for one of his children, most probably Francesco—and that his death and Ludovico's usurpation of the dukedom occurred before the third of these was completed.[17] Under these circumstances, the remarkable change in the iconography of the Warsaw volume, presumably stipulated by Giangaleazzo's dispossessed widow, would cause little surprise.

As a decorative conception, the frontispiece of the London *Sforziada* is Birago's most impressive work. Meticulously executed, with the most exquisite attention to detail, it surpasses even the fine text pages in the Sforza Hours, where constant repetition led to a decline in the artist's inventiveness. The general impression of the *Sforziada* decoration is comparable with that of Ludovico's Marriage Grant (Fig. 14g), which is on a similarly large scale, but the execution of the latter is much cruder, indicating that members of Birago's atelier played a large part in its execution. Like the Sforza Hours, the frontispiece of the London *Sforziada* incorporates an abundance of images. Some, like the Milanese dragons on either side of the pedestal on which the putto bearing Ludovico's portrait stands, are of heraldic significance. Others, such as the pair of sphinxes at the foot of the right border, are entirely ornamental in purpose.[18] By shading the top edge of the main body of printed text, Birago transformed its appearance into that of a pasted-down piece of paper bending under the weight of the putto who seemingly lies upon it. He also painted the head of this figure so that it overlaps the bottom edge of the printed title above. In this way, the flat page of type is illusionistically transformed into a visually complex structure of a series of overlapping spatial planes. This perspectival capriciousness is in complete harmony with the witty and rich profusion of symbolic and ornamental images which constitutes the decoration of the frontispiece.

BIBLIOGRAPHY Warner 1894, pp. xxvii–xxxi; Schleinitz 1901, pp. 130–34; Warner 1903; Malaguzzi Valeri 1913–23, I, pp. 287, 379, III, pp. 155, 157; London (British Museum) 1930, pp. xxii, 708–24; Hind 1938–48, V, pp. 73–81; Pellegrin 1955, p. 365; Horodyski 1956, pp. 251–55; Milan 1958, pp. 141–45; Hill/Pollard 1967, p. 38; Munby 1972, p. 79.

NOTES

1. Pellegrin 1955, pp. 365, 369. Zarotto had already published Simonetta's book in the original Latin, likewise dedicated to Ludovico Sforza, in 1482; see London (British Museum) 1930, p. 718. Zarotto also published books illustrated with woodcuts; see Hind 1935, I, p. 195, II, p. 521.

2. Milan, Biblioteca Ambrosiana, Ms. A 271; Pellegrin 1955, p. 369.

3. The manuscript bears a seventeenth-century inscription to this effect; see ibid., p. 369.

4. Warner 1894, pp. xxvii–xxxi; Horodyski 1956. Another copy of this book, also printed on vellum but with the first page missing, is in the Vatican Library; see Warner 1903.

5. Horodyski 1956, p. 251.

6. On account of his swarthy complexion and dark hair, Ludovico was nicknamed "Il Moro" (The Moor).

7. Hind 1938–48, V, pp. 76, 79.

8. For the medals, see Hill/Pollard 1967, p. 38.

9. Warner 1894, pp. xxix–xxx, suggested that this device might be intended to represent the mythical Pillars of Hercules. For a view of Genoa, approximately contemporary to those on Ludovico's portrait medal and the frontispiece of the London *Sforziada,* see the woodcut on page LVIIv of Hartmann Schedel's *Weltchronik,* printed at Nuremburg in 1493, which also includes a pair of lofty towers guarding the harbor mouth.

10. Ludovico's Marriage Grant of lands to his wife (for which see n. 16 below) depicts his arms impaled with those of his wife.

11. Warner 1894, pp. xxx–xxxi, and Milan 1958, pp. 144–45.

12. Ludovico's symbol is literally "steering the ship of state."

13. Horodyski 1956, p. 255, points out that the book was subsequently in the possession of Bona, who presumably brought it to Poland on her marriage to Sigismund I in 1518.

14. Ibid.

15. For this interpretation of the iconography of the Warsaw frontispiece, together with an attempt to identify the courtiers, see ibid., pp. 253–54. Birago also depicted saints as putti in the Sforza Hours (Fig. 15c). For the miniature *Francesco Sforza and Famous Generals of Antiquity,* see Milan 1958, pp. 142–43.

16. For the Marriage Grant, see Warner 1894, pp. xxxii–xxxiii.

17. The *Sforziada* was a particularly suitable gift for Ludovico, Giangaleazzo, and Francesco, as the three of them constituted three generations of descendants of Duke Francesco I. That the manuscript of the *Sforziada* (see nn. 2, 3 above), upon which the printed edition of 1490 was presumably based, was in the possession of Giangaleazzo is consistent with his having been the patron of the three deluxe printed copies.

18. It has been pointed out that the base of the Cross of Matthias Corvinus, attributed to Cristoforo Caradosso Foppa and at Esztergom Cathedral, is closely analogous to the decorative sphinxes in the London *Sforziada* frontispiece; see Schloss Schallaburg 1982, p. 476.

15 Hours of Bona Sforza

Use of Rome; Milan, circa 1490 and Ghent, circa 1517–21.
Additional Ms. 34294

MANUSCRIPT *Vellum, 348 leaves; 13.1 × 9.3 cm. 64 full-page miniatures, 139 text pages with decorated borders and small miniatures, decorated initials. Various inscriptions of Bona's name and initials are included on several folios: "Diva Bona," "Bona Duc[issa]," "B.M." On fol. 93, the motto "Sola fata, dolum Deum sequor" combined with a phoenix. On fol. 61, a portrait of Margaret of Austria as St. Elizabeth in the miniature of the Visitation (Fig. 15g); on fol. 213, a medallion of Charles V in the decorated border. 1 detached miniature (Fig. 15i) acquired subsequently, Add. Ms. 45722. Rounded gothic script.*

BINDING *Dark red morocco binding, British Museum, c. 1900; the leaves have been separated and tipped into 4 volumes.*

PROVENANCE *Bona Sforza, c. 1490–1503; (?) Philibert of Savoy, c. 1503; his wife, Margaret of Austria, by 1517; (?) Emperor Charles V, c. 1521; by 1871 property of a Spanish noble; purchased in Spain by Sir J. C. Robinson, 1871; purchased by John Malcolm of Poltalloch, c. 1871; presented by him to the British Museum, 1893.*

THE lavish decorations of this book were undertaken in two separate campaigns: the first for Bona Sforza, widow of Galeazzo Sforza, Duke of Milan; and the second for her nephew's wife, Margaret of Austria, Regent of the Netherlands.[1] That Bona's miniaturist was Giovan Pietro Birago is apparent from numerous stylistic similarities between the Milanese illuminations in the Sforza Hours and the frontispieces to the printed copies of Giovanni Simonetta's *Sforziada* (Pl. XV). There can be little doubt that this book of hours is identical with an unfinished one ordered by Bona, mentioned in an undated letter by Birago.[2] Part of this book had already been completed and delivered to its patron when a substantial portion of the rest was stolen from Birago by a certain Fra Gian Jacopo. The motive for this crime is readily apparent from the artist's valuation of the stolen part at the enormous sum of over five hundred ducats, which may be compared with Leonardo da Vinci's own valuation of his London *Virgin of the Rocks* at one hundred ducats.[3] The stolen fragment of the Sforza Hours was subsequently acquired by Juan Maria Sforzino, a bastard half-brother of Bona's deceased husband and a future archbishop of Genoa.[4] Although Fra Gian Jacopo was imprisoned and Birago sought compensation, the missing folios were evidently not returned. To this day, only one of them has been identified, a full-page miniature of the *Adoration of the Magi* (Fig. 15i), which entered the British Library in 1941.[5] After the loss of so large a portion of her uncompleted manuscript, Bona seems to have abandoned the project. When the dowager duchess left Milan for her native Savoy

Fig. 15a [RIGHT]. Giovan Pietro Birago. *Martyrdom of St. Peter Martyr*, fol. 205v.

Fig. 15b [FAR RIGHT]. Giovan Pietro Birago. *Martyrdom of St. Catherine*, fol. 208v.

Fig. 15c. Giovan Pietro Birago. Decorated border with *St. Barnabas as an Infant*, fol. 14v.

of Milan, it embodies the Roman rite, rather than the local and time-honored Ambrosian liturgy.[9] However, the decorated border on fol. 14v (Fig. 15c) includes a *cartellino* describing St. Barnabas as the first to celebrate Mass in Milan, together with an illustration of the saint as a naked child with a chalice. These pointed references to the religious traditions of the city in which the book was commissioned were probably added on the initiative of Birago, who was himself a priest.[10]

As works of art, the decorated text pages of the Sforza Hours are of comparable importance to the full-page miniatures. All may be attributed to Birago and his workshop, with the exceptions of fol. 113 (which appears to be the work of a Ferrarese-trained artist of the late fifteenth century), fol. 48 (Fig. 15d), and the bottom part of fol. 213, which were added later by Horenbout. The format of these pages is generally standardized, with two decorative pilasters of classicizing form at either side and space for additional text or miniatures at top and bottom. These pilasters are of similar appearance to those on the *Sforziada* frontispieces, although their considerably smaller size dic-

in 1495, after the death of her son and the usurpation of the dukedom by Ludovico Sforza, she appears to have taken with her the unfinished book of hours. After her death at Fossano in 1503 it was probably inherited by her host and nephew, Philibert, Duke of Savoy. He died the following year, and in 1506 his widow, Margaret of Austria, moved to the Netherlands, presumably carrying the manuscript in her baggage. In 1517 Margaret commissioned the scribe Etienne de Lale to write the missing text pages and to put the manuscript in order; in 1519–21 she entrusted her court miniaturist Gerard Horenbout with the sixteen additional miniatures and two "vignettes" (presumably text page decorations).[6] As one of these is a portrait of Margaret's nephew, Emperor Charles V, added to one of the Milanese text pages (fol. 213), it is possible that the manuscript was completed as a gift for him.[7]

The liturgical divisions of the Sforza Hours constitute an ordinary book of hours, except for the absence of a calendar and the addition of an extra prayer at the end, which was probably inserted circa 1600.[8] Like the equally famous Visconti Hours, begun a century earlier for the first Duke

Fig. 15d. Gerard Horenbout. Decorated border, fol. 48.

Fig. 15e. Giovan Pietro Birago. Decorated border, engraving. London, British Museum, Department of Prints and Drawings.

text as though it were inscribed upon a tabernacle (Fig. 15f).

The framing of the decorated text pages of the Sforza Hours abounds with figures and animals. Some of these have a religious subject matter iconographically appropriate to the part of the text they surround. Those in the section devoted to the Hours of the Holy Cross (fols. 13–27v) include angels with symbols of Christ's Passion, emblematic scenes from the Passion itself, and saints in the unlikely guise of putti. The Hours of the Holy Spirit (fols. 28–40) have numerous representations of the third member of the Trinity in the familiar form of a dove, while the short Prayers to Our Lord on the Passion (fols. 167v–169v) include seven small scenes from the Passion. In the Office of the Dead (fols. 258–342v) the pictures of putti and snake-infested skulls are obvious symbols of mortality. A number of bust portraits appear in the borders of the Hours of the Virgin (fols. 41–136), some of which are copies of classical gems, others probably actual likenesses of Bona's family.[12] The richness of late medieval lore on the symbolic connotations of animals was such that it is not always easy to discern whether the numerous creatures in the borders of the Sforza Hours were intended as decorative extras, moral or religious exempla, or emblems of Bona and the Milanese ducal house. Many of the putti, mermaids, stags, hunting birds and dogs, cheetahs, and

tated that they be somewhat less ornate. Such pilasters appear to have been a specialty of Birago, who also executed a series of engravings of similar ornamental panels (Fig. 15e).[11] Within these framing elements, the main text is usually shaded at its upper and left edges to give the illusionistic impression that it is written upon a separate piece of paper stuck down on the page. This trompe-l'oeil effect is closely analogous to that of the text in the frontispiece of the British Library *Sforziada* (Pl. xv). On fols. 51, 53, 73, 90, and 95v, Birago combined text and decoration in a different but equally illusionistic way, rendering the

Fig. 15f. Giovan Pietro Birago. Decorated border, fol. 53.

apes probably fall into the first category. The Visconti serpents on many folios are specifically heraldic in intent. The peacock, such as also appears in a detached capital with a portrait of Galeazzo Sforza in the Wallace Collection, may be a symbol of Bona.[13] Rabbits and ermines are common symbols of purity, but they are so numerous, in both full-page miniatures and decorative borders of the Sforza Hours, that it seems probable that these animals were particularly popular emblems at the Sforza court. In this context, it is significant that a hutch of rabbits appears at the foot of fol. 124v of the Visconti Hours and that the Milanese sitter in Leonardo da Vinci's *Portrait of a Lady* in Cracow is prominently holding an ermine.[14]

It is unclear how many full-page miniatures were executed or intended to be executed by Birago for the Sforza Hours. His high estimate of the value of the stolen part of the manuscript indicates that it was lavishly illustrated, although the greater part of this cost probably covered decorated text pages, rather than full-page miniatures. Like the intact Prayers to Our Lord on the Passion, most of the sections of the book would originally have comprised a single large miniature, followed by text pages, many of which would have had decorated borders.[15] The Gospels extracts (fols. 1–12) and the Penitential Psalms (fols. 212v–235v) required four and seven full-page miniatures respectively, due to the number of their subdivisions.[16] As the most important part of the book, the Hours of the Virgin had an extensive Marian cycle of large miniatures, all of which were stolen and subsequently had to be replaced by Horenbout. The Passion cycle of full-page miniatures in the Passion according to St. Luke (fols. 136v–166v) may also be incomplete. Birago's finest remaining cycle of decoration is his series of twenty-five full-page miniatures in the Suffrages of the Saints (fols. 186–212; Pls. XVI, XVII, Figs. 15a, 15b), which appears to be almost intact. The *St. Andrew* (Pl. XVIII), however, is by Horenbout or a member of his workshop.

Each of Birago's full-page miniatures is bordered only with a simple, molded gold frame, much like that of a panel painting (Pls. XVI, XVII). The relevant opening words of text appear on a *cartellino,* which usually stands free within the pictorial space of the miniature or sometimes rests upon the molding, like an attached label.[17] The miniatures reveal a fairly consistent range of motifs, landscape details, and figure types. Birago's predilection for landscapes composed of rocky heaps of striated boulders interspersed with formalized trees and distant buildings is apparent both in the miniatures from the Sforza Hours and in his engravings.[18] Like the classicizing details of architecture and armor in his work, his landscape configurations derive ultimately from Mantegna, whose style had been introduced to Lombardy by Vincenzo Foppa as early as 1456. The extreme foreshortening of the dead soldier at the right of Birago's *St. Catherine* (Fig. 15b) is similarly Mantegnesque.[19] Birago's depiction of hair as a mass of wiry curls, as appears in his *St. Michael* (Pl. XVI), implies a knowledge of the work of Leonardo da Vinci, who had arrived at Milan circa 1482. To judge from the grotesque facial types that appear in such miniatures as *Christ before*

Annas on fol. 149v of the Sforza Hours, he may also have known some of Leonardo's famous caricatures.[20] Probably the most distinctive element in his own repertory of figures is a particular sort of chubby putto, such as appears in the *St. Augustine* miniature (Pl. XVII). This legendary child compared the saint's endeavors to explain the mysteries of the Trinity with attempting to empty the sea into a little hole.[21]

Arguably, Birago's most remarkable achievement was his use of color. A limited but distinguished color range, composed primarily of deep blues and greens and dark reds, unites both the borders and full-page miniatures of the Sforza Hours into a coherent whole. In the *St. Michael* (Pl. XVI), these prominent colors are also taken up in the stones scattered on the ground before the archangel. Birago used gold sparingly, as in the *St. Michael* and the *St. Augustine,* to suggest illumination, rather than as a merely decorative device. Color could also serve a narrative purpose. The gradual change of the sky from blue to green in the background of the *St. Michael* denotes both the effects of aerial perspective and the descent of the fallen angels, since the blue reappears in the costume of the archangel and the green in the skin of the devil. In the *St. Peter Martyr* miniature (Fig. 15a), the dramatic contrast between the agitated drapery of the friars and the tranquil colors of the landscape serves as a metaphor for the saint's innocence and the assassin's violence. That Birago could abandon his accustomed range of colors when required is apparent from his *St. Catherine* (Fig. 15b), where the warm reddish tones of the foreground figures suggest the fury of the storm that blasts the saint's executioners.

The sixteen miniatures and two "vignettes" added to the Sforza Hours in 1519 and 1520 are superb examples of Flemish illumination produced in the period when Flemish painting was strongly influenced by the art of the Italian Renaissance.[22] They are the only surviving documented miniatures by Gerard Horenbout, an artist from Ghent who enjoyed acclaim and the favor of important patrons.[23] Yet the illuminations appear to be stylistically unique; no others in the Italianate mode can be attributed to Horenbout through comparison with the Sforza miniatures alone.[24] On the basis of extensive circumstantial evidence, Hulin de Loo and Winkler identified Horenbout with the Master of James IV of Scotland, a major artistic figure but one whose illuminations exhibit a much broader manner.[25] If Hulin de Loo and Winkler are correct, the unique character of the supplemental Sforza miniatures may be explained by Horenbout's attempt to accommodate his work to both the style and format of Birago's miniatures.[26]

The influence of Birago on the sixteen miniatures by Horenbout is apparent in several ways. Birago's decorative borders (Fig. 15c) provided the model for one of the Flemish borders (Fig. 15d), where Horenbout softens the forms, especially contours, and the design loses some of the vitality of the Italian model. The bright reds, blues, and greens in Horenbout's *Martyrdom of St. Andrew* (Pl. XVIII) recall the dominant coloring of Birago's miniatures, such as *St. Augustine by the Seashore* (Pl. XVII), but again, in the

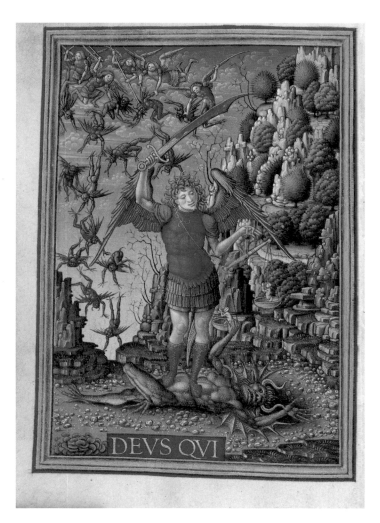

Pl. XVI [TOP LEFT]. Giovan Pietro Birago. *St. Michael*, Hours of Bona Sforza. Add. Ms. 34294, fol. 186v.

Pl. XVII [ABOVE]. Giovan Pietro Birago. *St. Augustine by the Seashore*, Hours of Bona Sforza. Add. Ms. 34294, fol. 199v.

Pl. XVIII [LEFT]. Gerard Horenbout or Workshop. *Martyrdom of St. Andrew*, Hours of Bona Sforza. Add. Ms. 34294, fol. 189v.

Flemish miniatures, the modeling is softer. An occasional detail in Horenbout's miniatures, such as the flowing locks of the angels in the *Madonna and Child Enthroned* (fol. 177v) or the full white beard and high forehead of David in the scene of *King David in Prayer* (fol. 212v) find correspondences in Birago's figure types. And the colored pebbles scattered in the foreground of Horenbout's *Visitation* (Fig. 15g) resemble those in Birago's *St. Michael* (Pl. XVI). Horenbout's miniatures also follow the decorative format of the ones they replace. They have similar gold borders, and they include text placards along the lower border. Horenbout seems to have been concerned primarily with adapting the miniatures to the existing format of the book's decorations.

The most striking Italianate features, especially in the architecture, do not derive strictly from the Birago miniatures. In this domain, Flemish painters influenced by Italian Renaissance art, such as the young Joos van Cleve in Antwerp, exerted a formative influence on the Sforza miniatures. The *Adoration* miniature (Fig. 15h) calls to mind the treatment of this subject by Joos and his shop probably just prior to the execution of the miniature itself.[27] The facial type of the kneeling king and the exotic costumes and architecture show familiarity with Joos' art, and in other miniatures the puffy cheeks of the angels betray his influence. It is known that Horenbout made at least one visit to nearby Antwerp in 1521.[28] The exotic Renaissance architectural motifs in the *St. Mark* and *King David in Prayer* (fols. 10v, 212v) reflect a fashion current in Flem-

ish painting from the time of Gossaert and apparent in the paintings of Joos and other Flemish mannerists.[29] A comparison of Horenbout's *Adoration* with Birago's (Fig. 15i) illustrates how thoroughly Flemish in character the Horenbout miniature remains.

Gerard Horenbout came from a family of Ghent artists, and he entered the guild there in 1487.[30] In addition to being an illuminator, he was a painter and is also known to have executed some designs for tapestries and stained glass. In 1515, Margaret of Austria, Regent of the Netherlands, who was residing at Malines, appointed him court painter. Over the next seven years he carried out a number of documented commissions for her. According to Carel van Mander, Horenbout was also in the service of Henry VIII of England.[31] He probably moved to England with his family in the mid-1520s; he died about 1540, most likely in England. Lucas and Suzanne Horenbout, his son and daughter, enjoyed considerable success as painters of portrait miniatures there, and Lucas was also a court painter to the English king.[32]

Traces of the style of the Master of James IV of Scotland are apparent in the Sforza miniatures, but the changes in this work are radical. If, for example, one compares the *Coronation of the Virgin* (Fig. 15k) in the Sforza Hours with two earlier representations of this subject by the Master of James IV of Scotland in the present exhibition (Figs. 5d, 8h), both the congruencies and disparities are apparent. The composition of the Sforza miniature is nearly a composite of the other two; the figures of Christ and God the Father resemble the version in the Breviary of Isabella of Castile (Fig. 5d), and the poses of the Virgin and the angels resemble more closely the version in another book of hours (Fig. 8h). The brushwork, especially in the handling of the hair, is looser in the earlier versions, and the male facial types have a superficial resemblance. However, what is unlike the miniatures by the Master of James IV of Scotland is the type of the Virgin. Her straggly hair and aquiline features are completely eliminated in the Sforza Virgin, and the drapery is drawn more crisply and finely. In these miniatures the angular contours and lumpy drapery folds of the Master of James IV of Scotland are barely detectable. Similar discrepancies are readily apparent by a comparison of the *Nativity* miniature (Fig. 15l) with earlier versions of this subject attributed to the Master of James IV of Scotland.[33] The quality of drawing in the Sforza miniatures, especially in the Life of the Virgin cycle, is superior to the illuminations of the Master of James IV of Scotland.

Winkler compared the Flemish miniatures in the Hours of Bona Sforza with the work of the Bruges illuminator Simon Bening (Cats. 9, 10). Despite the difference in figure types, the *Adoration* in the Sforza Hours shares the contained movement, delicate facial features, smooth textures, tight brushwork, and local color of Bening's *Adoration* (Fig. 15j) in the Prayer Book of Albrecht of Brandenburg, executed a few years later, about 1525–30.[34]

Fig. 15g. Gerard Horenbout. *Visitation*, fol. 61.

Fig. 15h [TOP LEFT]. Gerard Horenbout. *Adoration of the Magi,* fol. 97.

Fig. 15i [LEFT]. Giovan Pietro Birago. *Adoration of the Magi.* London, British Library, Add. Ms. 45722, detached leaf.

Fig. 15j [ABOVE]. Simon Bening. *Adoration of the Magi,* Prayer Book of Cardinal Albrecht of Brandenburg. Malibu, Calif., The J. Paul Getty Museum, Ms. Ludwig IX 19, fol. 36v.

the identification, three objections deserve to be aired. First, the quality of drawing in the Sforza miniatures is better than that usually found in the work of the Master of James IV of Scotland. Horenbout was a good draftsman, the anonymous illuminator less so. Second, and more important, it seems surprising that the illuminator of the calendar in the Grimani Breviary (Ill. 3, p. 8; Fig. 10g), of the Spinola Hours (Ill. 4, p. 9; Fig. 8c), and of the hours in the British Library (Pl. x, Figs. 8a, 8e, 8h) left little trace of his well-established and successful manner in the Sforza work. The dissimilarity in facial types, for example, is remarkable.

Third, there may be an even closer stylistic antecedent for Horenbout: a tiny panel in Prague, an *Ecce Homo* (Fig. 15m), which has sometimes been attributed to Juan de Flandes.[35] Although, as Lieftinck has shown, the painting derives from a miniature by the Master of Mary of Burgundy in the Hours of Engelbert of Nassau, the panel reveals a distinctive artistic personality, especially in the facial types, the attention to the painting of hands and gestures, architectural detail, and even the character of the animals.[36] The facial types of Christ and Pilate in the panel correspond closely with the types of Christ and God the Father

Similarities in scale and detail underscore this relationship. Although the Sforza miniatures were not illuminated by Simon Bening, they resemble Bening's style more closely than that of the Master of James IV of Scotland.

To accommodate the style of his miniatures to Birago's in the Sforza Hours, the Master of James IV of Scotland would have had to transform his style—to adopt not only the format and some motifs, and the odd facial type, but even aspects of coloring (albeit inconsistently) in the sixteen miniatures, the full border, and partial border. He did not choose to imitate Birago's style faithfully. Instead he seems to have adopted the Italianate characteristics of Flemish painting, a partial solution undoubtedly more suited to his own technique than to an Italian manner then thirty years old. Moreover, the localized color areas, the relatively more continuous, smooth contours, and refined facial types that recall Bening are further accommodations ultimately closer in spirit to the Italian tradition than to his own painterly style.

If the identification of Horenbout with the Master of James IV of Scotland is correct, the artist went to extraordinary lengths and explored several artistic avenues in order to devise a style complementary to Birago's miniatures. Although other circumstantial evidence supports

Fig. 15l. Gerard Horenbout. *Nativity,* fol. 82v.

Fig. 15m. (?) Gerard Horenbout. *Ecce Homo,*
oil on panel. Prague, Národnyí Galerie.

homogeneous, subtle differences in execution are apparent among them. In my view at least two closely related hands may be isolated. One is apparent in the scenes from the Life of the Virgin. A second hand, somewhat more Italianate in figure types, appears in the two miniatures with the Madonna and Child with angels in heaven (fols. 133v, 177v). The second hand may belong to one of Horenbout's gifted children. The careers of Suzanne and Lucas Horenbout deserve closer study, both in relationship to these miniatures and to their activity in England. This in turn may reveal further evidence to reconstruct their father's work.[37]

BIBLIOGRAPHY Warner 1894; Robinson 1895; Schleinitz 1901, pp. 135–41; Malaguzzi Valeri 1913–23, I, pp. 247, 260, 446, 481–82, III, pp. 157–75, 200; Warner/Gilson 1921, pp. 13–14, pls. XLII–XLIV; Ancona 1925, pp. 55–56; Winkler 1925, pp. 151, 177; Durrieu 1927, p. 95; Duverger 1930, pp. 87–90; *Mittelalterliche Miniaturen* 1931, no. 34 and frontispiece; Flower 1935–36; Hind 1938–48, V, pp. 73–81; Hulin de Loo 1939a, pp. 16–19; Winkler 1943, pp. 61–64; Pellegrin 1955, p. 364; Horodyski 1956; Salmi 1957, pp. 72–74; Milan 1958, pp. 141–45; London (British Museum) 1970, pp. 231–32; Euw/Plotzek 1979–82, II, p. 268.

NOTES

1. Warner 1894, pp. ii–viii, x, and Flower 1935–36.

2. Warner 1894, pp. viii–ix.

3. Warner 1894, p. ix, and Chambers 1970, pp. 206–08.

4. Warner 1894, p. ix.

5. British Library, Add. Ms. 45722; *Mittelalterliche Miniaturen* 1931, no. 34 and frontispiece, and London (British Museum) 1970, pp. 231–32.

6. Flower 1935–36, and Duverger 1930, p. 87. That the whole of the decorated text page (Fig. 15d) was executed by Horenbout rather than Birago, is evident from its style, which is unlike that of the Milanese text pages, although it is clearly based upon them, and from its range of coloring, which corresponds to that in the miniatures attributed to Horenbout.

7. Warner 1894, pp. x–xi. That most of this decorated text page was executed by Birago is obvious from its style and coloring. It is unclear whether the portrait of Charles V added by Horenbout was substituted for part of Birago's original design, or whether it merely fills a gap in an unfinished page.

8. Ibid., p. ii.

9. For the Use of the Visconti Hours, see Harthan 1977, p. 76.

10. In his letter of complaint about the theft, Birago signed himself *"Presbiter Johannes Petrus Biragus, Miniator."* See also Cat. 14 for a similar signature.

in the *Coronation of the Virgin* miniature (Fig. 15k). The crisply drawn whippet before the stairwell in the *Ecce Homo* reappears in the *Adoration of the Magi* miniature, and the facial types with strongly arched noses and full lips shown in profile in the *Ecce Homo* find correspondences in the crowd of the *St. Andrew* illumination (Pl. XVIII), where the physical type of the saint also recalls the Christ presented to the people. Even without any Italianate features, the panel, which may date as early as 1500, represents a plausible artistic antecedent to the Flemish miniatures in the Sforza Hours, and it may well be a relatively early work by Horenbout who, it will be recalled, is documented as both a painter and an illuminator. The panel is certainly not by the Master of James IV of Scotland.

The identification of Horenbout with the Master of James IV of Scotland is intriguing and possible, but not entirely persuasive. A more critical examination of the circumstantial evidence linking Horenbout's name with the anonymous master and a consideration of the artistic origins of the latter may shed further light on the problem.

Finally, it bears noting that Horenbout was not himself responsible for all the Flemish miniatures in the Sforza Hours. Although the style of the miniatures is fairly

11. There are twelve engravings in all; see Hind 1938–48, V, pp. 79–81, where they are attributed to the Master of the Sforza Hours, as Birago was known prior to 1956.

12. Fols. 45, 53, 55, 58, 74v, 77, 85v, 90v; see Warner 1894, pp. xxiii–xxv.

13. The Wallace Collection miniature was probably executed in 1477; see Alexander 1980, pp. 39–41.

14. Meiss/Kirsch 1972, fol. 124v and facing plate, and Pompilio/ Ottino della Chiesa 1967, pl. XXXVII and p. 101.

15. It is possible that Birago intended to decorate all the text pages. In the Hours of the Holy Cross and the Hours of the Holy Spirit they are completely decorated. The large miniature at the beginning of the former is a replacement by Horenbout, while the latter retains its original full-page miniature by Birago.

16. In the Gospels section, fols. 9–12 are Netherlandish replacements. The full-page miniature of *St. Mark* on fol. 10v is by Horenbout. It has been plausibly suggested that the other three full-page miniatures of the Evangelists (fols. 1, 4, 7) may be by an Italian artist other than Birago; see London (British Museum) 1970, p. 232. In the Penitential Psalms section, all the miniatures of *King David* are by Birago (Warner 1894, p. xii, disagrees), except for the opening miniature on fol. 212v, which is by Horenbout and is executed on the verso of one of the original Milanese text pages.

17. For an example of the latter arrangement, see fol. 170, the *Assumption of the Virgin*; Warner 1894, pl. vi.

18. See, for example, the *St. Michael* on fol. 186v, and his engraving of the *Lamentation*; Hind 1938–48, V, p. 77 and pl. 600.

19. For a generally comparable rock formation, classicizing armor, and foreshortened figure by Mantegna, see his *Agony in the Garden* at the National Gallery, London. Foppa was based at Pavia from circa 1456 to circa 1490, where he frequently worked for the Sforza.

20. Such patterns of hair were employed by both Leonardo and his followers in Milan. See, for example, Leonardo's London *Virgin of the Rocks* and its wing panels of musical angels by Ambrogio or Evangelista Preda. It has been pointed out that Birago's grotesque facial types reveal affinities with both the drawings of Leonardo and Northern art; see Warner 1894, pp. xiv–xv, xxv.

21. Ibid., pp. xvii–xviii.

22. A list of the sixteen Flemish miniatures is given by Warner 1894, pp. xi–xii. The two decorative borders are fols. 48, 213; see Duverger 1930, pp. 87–90, and Hulin de Loo 1939a, pp. 16–18.

23. Hulin de Loo 1939a, pp. 3–21 and Winkler 1943, pp. 55–64. See also Euw/Plotzek 1979–82, II, no. IX 18.

24. Prior to the discovery of the documents, Winkler 1925, p. 151 ascribed the manuscript tentatively to the Master of Emperor Charles V.

25. Hulin de Loo 1939a, pp. 16–20, and Winkler 1943. Horen-

bout has generally been identified as an illuminator of the Grimani Breviary (Venice, Biblioteca Marciana, Ms. lat. XI 67 [7531]) on the basis of Marcantonio Michiel's identification, made about 1520, of a "Girardo da Guant" as one of the three illuminators of the Grimani Breviary; see Frizzoni 1884, p. 201. The identification is supported in part by the fact that Horenbout's work in the calendar of the Grimani Breviary is copied from the Très Riches Heures, which was then in the possession of Margaret of Austria, whom he served as court painter at about the same time. However, Michiel also identified "Zuan Memelin" as one of the illuminators of the Grimani Breviary, but Memling was dead more than a decade before the decoration of the Breviary was undertaken. It seems possible, too, that the third artist mentioned by Michiel, "Lievene da Anversa," was Lieven van Latham, who also died before the manuscript was begun. Therefore, Horenbout's participation in the manuscript cannot be securely documented. Hulin de Loo 1939a analyzes the evidence for identifying the anonymous master with Horenbout.

26. Hulin de Loo 1939a, p. 18, and Winkler 1943, p. 55. See also Warner 1894, pp. xiv, xxxviii.

27. See the *Adoration* panel in Genoa, San Donato; Friedländer 1967–76, IXa, pl. 19, where it is dated circa 1518.

28. Goris/Marlier 1971, p. 94.

29. The *St. Mark* is illustrated in Durrieu 1927, pl. CI.

30. Hulin de Loo 1939a discusses the details of Horenbout's career recounted here.

31. Van Mander 1604, fol. 204v.

32. On Lucas Horenbout, see Murdoch/Murrell/Noon/Strong 1981, pp. 29–33. The dates of Suzanne Horenbout's birth and training have not been clearly established.

33. Compare, for example, this *Nativity* with the miniature of the subject in the British Library Hours, Add. Ms. 35313 (Cat. 8; Winkler 1964, fig. 93) and the Grimani Breviary (Hulin de Loo 1939a, p. 17, figs. 1, 2, 3).

34. Euw/Plotzek 1979–82, II, color pl., p. 289.

35. For the history of the attribution of this panel, which measures only 36.5 × 23 cm, see Bruges 1974, no. 5, illustrated p. 21.

36. Lieftinck 1969, I, p. 59, n. 14.

37. Warner 1894, pp. xli–xliii. Warner isolates four hands, the first of which includes apparently the two miniatures with the Virgin and Child and angels (fols. 133v, 177v); the second, the *Martyrdom of St. Andrew* (fol. 189v); the third, *Christ Nailed to the Cross* (fol. 12v), the *Entry into Jerusalem* (fol. 136v), and the *Raising of Lazarus* (fol. 257v); and the fourth, *King David in Prayer* (fol. 212v), the Life of the Virgin cycle (fols. 41, 61, 82v, 91, 97, 104v, 111, 124), and *St. Mark* (fol. 10v). However, Warner may be a bit severe in seeing so many hands at work. Certainly the *Martyrdom of St. Andrew* and *Christ Nailed to the Cross* are by the same hand, and they may well be by the same master as the *Adoration* miniature and others of the Life of the Virgin cycle.

16 Hours of Bonaparte Ghislieri

Use of Rome; Bologna, circa 1500. Yates Thompson Ms. 29.

MANUSCRIPT *Vellum, 136 leaves; 20.5 × 14.9 cm. 5 full-page miniatures, 15 portrait medallions, 15 historiated initials, numerous decorated borders, flourishes, and initials. Arms of the Ghislieri appear twice: at the foot of fol. 16, between the letters "BP GI," and on an archway in the background of the full-page miniature of the* Annunciation *on fol. 74v (Fig. 16c). At the bottom of fol. 7 a portrait of a middle-aged layman wearing a blue coat and red cap and holding a staff in his right hand (Fig. 16a). Fol. 132v (Pl. XXI) has been detached and is mounted separately. Rounded antiqua script.*

BINDING *Original binding of red leather tooled with small gold leaves and dots; the outer covers paneled with cut leather over green and blue silk and red and gold paper; in the center of each a (badly rubbed) miniature on vellum recessed within a silver ring. On the front cover, the Angel Gabriel; on the back, the Virgin. The inner covers of similarly tooled leather; in the center of each, an embossed leather medallion of Julius Caesar, inscribed "DIVI IVLII."*

PROVENANCE *Bonaparte Ghislieri, c. 1500–41; by the eighteenth century, Albani family, Urbino; James Dennistoun (purchase from Prince Filippo Albani, Rome), February 1838;[1] Bertram, 4th Earl of Ashburnham, 1847; Henry Yates Thompson (purchase from 5th Earl of Ashburnham), May 1897; bequeathed to the British Museum by Mrs. Henry Yates Thompson, 1941.*

THAT this book was commissioned by one of the Ghislieri, an ancient Bolognese patrician family, is evident from the coats of arms on fols. 16 and 74v (Fig. 16c).[2] Fol. 124v bears a collect for a pope, beginning "*Omn. semp. deus miserere famulo tuo pape nostro A.*" Evidently a reference to Pope Alexander VI, this limits the approximate dates for the writing of the book to the span of his pontificate, 1492–1503.[3] On the basis of the letters "BP GI" on either side of the coat of arms on fol. 16, the owner of the manuscript has been plausibly identified as Bonaparte Ghislieri.[4] Ghislieri was one of the many citizens banished from Bologna in 1506–07, after the capture of the city by Julius II, on suspicion of being partisans of the exiled Bentivoglio family who had previously ruled Bologna. After his return, Ghislieri held numerous civic offices, the most important being that of senator from 1523 until his death in 1541.[5] The portrait of the middle-aged man on fol. 7 (Fig. 16a), presumably a likeness of the person who commissioned the book, is usually thought to depict Bonaparte.[6] But it is doubtful that he would have looked so old circa 1500. Although Bonaparte's date of birth is unknown, his father Virgilio was himself relatively young at that date, since he remained active as an ambassador until he was murdered in 1523.[7] Possible solutions to this apparent anomaly are: that Virgilio commissioned the Ghislieri Hours, which was subsequently inherited by Bonaparte, who then added his initials to the family

Fig. 16a. Matteo da Milano. (?) *Portrait of Virgilio Ghislieri*; text page decoration (detail), fol. 7.

Fig. 16b. (?) Matteo da Milano. *St. Jerome in Penitence*; decorated border, fol. 127v.

to each word as a whole. This change of approach not only imparted greater legibility to their texts, but also greatly enhanced the sense of proportion and monumentality of their script. The apparent simplicity of Sallando's innovative style, which was of seminal importance for the development of sixteenth-century handwriting, is misleading. Rounded antiqua was an exacting script which required, as the Venetian writing master Giovan Antonio Tagliente pointed out, "profound understanding, both of proportion and art."[13]

The principal illuminator of the Ghislieri Hours was almost certainly Matteo da Milano, who is documented in 1502 as one of the three artists responsible for the sumptuous Breviary of Ercole I of Ferrara.[14] The hallmark of his style is the distinctive type of decorated border that appears, for example, around the full-page miniatures on fols. 74v, 104v, and 127v of the Ghislieri Hours (Fig. 16c, Pl. xx, Fig. 16b) and on various of its text pages. Based on Netherlandish decorated pages similar to those in the Hastings Hours (Cat. 3) and many other Flemish manuscripts, this border consists of a gold ground upon which are painted naturalistic flowers and insects. The illusionism of the border is belied by Matteo's inclusion of grotesque animals which, although also found in Northern illuminated books, were not employed by Netherlandish miniaturists in such a context. Matteo also painted more characteristically Milanese borders, such as the panels at either side of fol. 16 of the Ghislieri Hours. Composed of stylized leaves and tendrils and classical motifs such as cornucopias, vases, and cameos, these borders are reminiscent of the type habitually employed by Giovan Pietro Birago in the Sforza Hours (Figs. 15c, 15f) and in his frontispieces to copies of the *Sforziada* (Pl. xv, Figs. 14b, 14c). Although Matteo was presumably born and trained in Milan, his identified manuscripts suggest that his principal seat of activity lay in northeastern Italy. His role in the decoration of the Ghislieri Hours had probably come to an end by 1502 when he moved to Ferrara, where he worked on the Breviary of Ercole I and the missal of the duke's son, Cardinal Ippolito.[15] His latest manuscript, the Hours of Dionora of Urbino, also at the British Library (Fig. 16e), suggests that he reached Urbino between 1509 and 1520.[16]

The only full-page miniature in the Ghislieri Hours which may be firmly attributed to Matteo is that of the *Annunciation* (Fig. 16c).[17] In this illumination the facial types of the Virgin and the curiously wingless Gabriel are analogous to those in the numerous portrait medallions elsewhere in the manuscript, and the cameos that decorate the architecture may be compared with those in the decorated border on fol. 16. The Germanic half-timbered architecture visible beyond the archway is appropriated,

coat of arms; or that the father commissioned the book as a gift for his son.

The liturgical divisions of the Ghislieri Hours constitute a fairly standard book of hours of the Roman Use, although it lacks the customary section devoted to the Litany of the Saints. This may indicate that the book was never completed. Its elegant rounded antiqua script has been identified as that of the scribe Pierantonio Sallando.[8] Born at Reggio in Emilia, he settled at Bologna in 1489, where he worked as a scribe and as a teacher of writing at the university.[9] As a scribe, Sallando had several notable patrons, among them the connoisseur and bibliophile Duke Federigo da Montefeltro of Urbino; Nicolao Franco, bishop of Treviso from 1486 to 1499; Giovanni Bentivoglio, lord of Bologna until his deposition in 1507; and Mino Rossi who, like Virgilio and Bonaparte Ghislieri, was a member of the senate of the city.[10] Save for the Durazzo Hours in the Palazzo Bianco at Genoa, the Ghislieri Hours is probably Sallando's last manuscript, and it reveals him at the height of his powers.[11] Together with his younger colleague, Girolamo Pagliarolo, Sallando was a creator of the modified form of the littera antiqua script, known as the rounded antiqua.[12] Holding the pen at a different angle from that of earlier scribes, they took great pains to emphasize the autonomy of the individual letter, as opposed

with minor variations, from the background of the *Prodigal Son*, an Italian engraving which is itself a reversed variant of Dürer's famous print (Fig. 16d).[18]

Various artists have been proposed as the illuminators of the full-page miniatures on fols. 104v and 127v (Pl. xx, Fig. 16b), including Francesco Francia, Lorenzo Costa, and Amico Aspertini.[19] Unless further comparative material or documentary references come to light, it is unlikely that this attributional problem will be definitively solved, although it is evident that the Netherlandish-influenced borders of both folios were executed by Matteo da Milano. In view of the stylistic difference between the miniature of *St. Jerome* and that of *King David Playing the Harp*, it is improbable that both are by the same hand. The landscape in the former follows a more stylized convention than in the latter, and the handling of the faces of the two figures is quite

different. Moreover, the gradation of tones in the sky and distant landscape behind the figure of David is considerably more subtle than that in the background of the *St. Jerome*. To the present author, the *St. Jerome* seems acceptable as a work of Matteo da Milano, while the style of the *King David* appears to be sufficiently close to that of Amico Aspertini to permit an attribution to him.

Aspertini was active, principally at Bologna, from circa 1504 until his death in 1552.[20] Although he was probably also responsible for three miniatures detached from an antiphonal (Fig. 16f), his métier remained fresco and panel painting rather than manuscript illumination.[21] Like his closely analogous altarpiece of the *Adoration of the Shepherds* at Berlin (Fig. 16g), the miniature on fol. 15v of the Ghislieri Hours (Pl. xix) was executed shortly after his return from a visit to Rome, which took place about 1500–03.[22]

Fig. 16c [LEFT]. Matteo da Milano. *Annunciation;* decorated border, fol. 74v.

Fig. 16d [ABOVE]. Italian Master (after Albrecht Dürer). *The Prodigal Son,* engraving. Berlin, Staatliche Museen Preussischer Kulturbesitz, Kupferstichkabinett.

Pl. XIX. Amico Aspertini. *Adoration of the Shepherds*, Hours of Bonaparte Ghislieri.
Yates Thompson Ms. 29, fol. 15v.

Pl. xx. (?) Amico Aspertini. *King David Playing the Harp*; Matteo da Milano. Decorated border, Hours of Bonaparte Ghislieri. Yates Thompson Ms. 29, fol. 104v.

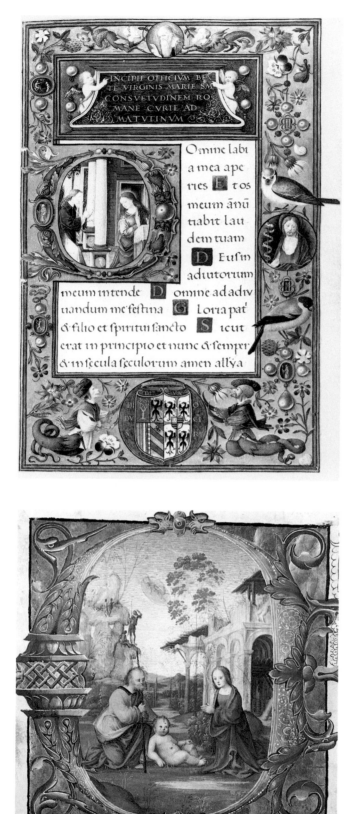

Fig. 16e [LEFT]. Matteo da Milano. Text page decoration, Hours of Dionora of Urbino. London, British Library, Yates Thompson Ms. 7, fol. 14.

Fig. 16g [BELOW]. Amico Aspertini. *Adoration of the Shepherds,* oil on panel. Berlin (DDR), Staatliche Museen, Gemäldegalerie.

Fig. 16f [ABOVE]. Amico Aspertini. Decorated initial with the *Nativity,* cutting from an Antiphonal. Liverpool, Liverpool City Libraries, O.R. 64–2.

Fig. 16h [RIGHT]. Pietro Perugino. *Martyrdom of St. Sebastian,* oil on panel. Perugia, Galleria Nazionale dell' Umbria.

Pl. XXI. Pietro Perugino. *Martyrdom of St. Sebastian*, Hours of Bonaparte Ghislieri.
Yates Thompson Ms. 29, fol. 132v, detached leaf.

Aspertini's passionate interest in Roman antiquities is strikingly apparent in the most remarkable feature of this illumination, its decorative border. By introducing trophies copied directly from antique reliefs and architectural motifs appropriated from recently discovered frescoes in the Golden House of Nero, he transformed the traditional type of decorated border.[23] In this respect, his style represents the turning point between the classicism of an earlier generation of antiquarians, who had never seen Roman paintings, and that of Raphael and his workshop, whose decorations, known as *grotteschi*, were based on newly uncovered ancient frescoes.

About 1490 a correspondent of the Duke of Milan aptly described Perugino, the illuminator of the *St. Sebastian* (Pl. XXI), as "an exceptional master, and particularly on walls. His things have an angelic air, and very sweet."[24] The latter characteristics of his style, which so endeared Perugino to nineteenth-century commentators, have provoked a vehement reaction against his work in the present century. In his own day, Pietro di Cristoforo di Vannucci, known as Perugino, was one of the most famous painters in Italy, with large workshop establishments in Florence and Perugia.[25] During his long career, which lasted from 1469 until his death in 1523, he was enormously prolific, although his later works often have a stereotyped quality. The *St. Sebastian* miniature from the Ghislieri Hours is his only identified manuscript illumination. Its crudely drawn border confirms the impression that he seldom worked as a miniaturist. Compositionally, the miniature is directly related to two later versions of the same subject by the artist: a fresco of 1505 in the church of San Sebastiano in Panicale (Perugia) and an altarpiece of 1518 from the church of San Francesco al Prato, in Perugia (Fig. 16h).[26] Like many painters of his day, Perugino evidently kept a considerable stock of figure drawings from which, over the years, favored types were repeatedly copied when required for a particular theme.

As all five of the full-page miniatures in the Ghislieri Hours are painted upon leaves with blank rectos tipped in between the text folios, it is possible that any or all of them are additions to the manuscript rather than an integral part of its original program of decoration. The positions of the *King David* and *St. Jerome* miniatures (Pl. XX, Fig. 16b) opposite, respectively, the opening pages of the Penitential Psalms and the Hours of the Cross, are liturgically appropriate, but there are inconsistencies in the disposition of the other large miniatures. The order of the *Adoration of the Shepherds* (Pl. XIX, before the opening of the Hours of the Virgin) and the *Annunciation* (Fig. 16c, before the section from Advent to Christmas of the Hours of the Virgin), could aptly be reversed. There is no obvious liturgical reason for the position of the *St. Sebastian* miniature directly before the Hours of the Holy Ghost, although it is possible that it was included for some personal devotional reason of the owner of the book.

There remains the problem of why at least two artists in addition to Matteo da Milano were employed on the Ghislieri Hours. The obvious hypotheses—that the book had to

be finished in a hurry for a special occasion, or that Matteo left for Ferrara before the manuscript was completed—share the same flaw. Neither Amico Aspertini nor Perugino was an obvious choice for such work, for the very good reason that neither seems to have been particularly well versed in the art of manuscript illumination. Their two miniatures, signed and with distinctive borders, one at the front of the book and the other at its back, stand out as a pair. But to what end? In this respect, a comparison with a contemporary large-scale decorative scheme may be revealing. About 1496 Isabella d'Este, the Duchess of Mantua, initiated a project of acquiring a small collection of panel paintings by celebrated artists with which to decorate her *studiolo*.[27] A decade later, after negotiations with various painters, including Leonardo da Vinci and Giovanni Bellini, the room was decorated with two pictures each by Mantegna and Costa and a single composition by Perugino. The patron of the Ghislieri Hours was of more limited means, but it is possible that he also had the instincts of a collector.

BIBLIOGRAPHY London (Palaeographical Society) 1884–94, II, pl. 38; Thompson 1907, pp. 145–52; Thompson 1907–18, VI, pp. 36–42, figs. 79–88; Ancona 1925, pp. 73, 88, figs. LXVIII, LXXXV; Wardrop 1946; Bober 1957, p. 36, fig. 135; Salmi 1957, pp. 57, 64, figs. 72, 80; Marinis 1960, pp. 57, 81, pls. CCC, CCCI; Turner 1965, pp. 23–25, figs. XLV–XLVI; Dacos 1969, p. 82; Alexander 1977, pp. 114–17; Tosetti Grandi a; Tosetti Grandi b.

NOTES

1. For Dennistoun's vivid and amusing account of his purchase of the Ghislieri Hours and the circumstances under which he was obliged to smuggle it out of Italy, see Thompson 1907–18, VI, pp. 39–41. According to Madden, who saw the Ghislieri Hours shortly before it was sold to the Earl of Ashburnham, the vellum roundels on the cover of the book were damaged by Dennistoun in a misguided attempt at conservation; see Frederic Madden, *Journal* (1847), Oxford, Bodleian Library, Ms. Eng. Hist. c 160, pp. 127–28.

2. Thompson 1907, p. 146. The coat of arms on fol. 16 shows signs of having been repainted: the bends originally ran from top right to bottom left. This should probably be seen merely as a mistake on the part of the miniaturist rather than as an indication that the book was originally commissioned by a different patron. Another example of a manuscript with a coat of arms reversed, presumably by mistake, occurs in British Library, Royal Ms. 8 G VII, fol. 2v, in which the lions in the English royal arms face the wrong way; London (British Library) 1977, p. 43.

3. Thompson 1907, p. 146.

4. Ibid. Dennistoun had previously believed, incorrectly, that the manuscript had been commissioned for the Florentine Giovanni Baroncelli; see Thompson 1907–18, VI, pp. 38–39.

5. For the biography of Bonaparte Ghislieri, see Dolci 1670, p. 363; Ghirardacci 1929–31; Tosetti Grandi a.

6. Thompson 1907, p. 148.

7. Dolfi 1670, p. 362.

8. Wardrop 1946, pp. 15–16, 28.

9. The University of Bologna had a long-standing reputation of excellence both in the practice and teaching of writing; ibid., pp. 9–11.

10. Ibid., pp. 11–15.

11. Ibid., pp. 15–16, 28.

12. Ibid., pp. 4–30.

13. "*Grande ingegno di misura et arte*"; Tagliente 1524, unpaginated. Tagliente was the first to classify this script as *littera antiqua tonda*; see Wardrop 1946, pp. 21–22.

14. The connection with Matteo da Milano was first pointed out by Turner 1965, p. 23. For the Breviary (Modena, Biblioteca Estense, Ms. V.G. II [Lat. 424]) see Fava/Salmi 1950–73, I, pp. 181–201; Ancona/Aeschlimann 1949, pp. 146–47.

15. For the Missal of Ippolito I (Innsbruck, Universitätsbibliothek, Cod. no. 43), see Hermann 1905, pp. 132–45.

16. London, British Library, Yates Thompson Ms. 7; James 1898, pp. 119–23, and Turner 1965, pp. 24–25.

17. That the *Annunciation* is by the same hand as the decorated borders has not, to my knowledge, been doubted since it was initially pointed out by Thompson 1907, pp. 148–49. The miniature had previously been attributed to Lorenzo di Credi by Dennistoun; see Thompson 1907–18, VI, pp. 37–38.

18. Dürer's engraving is usually dated to the later 1490s. For this anonymous copy, see Hind 1938–48, V, p. 302, no. 34. That the houses in the background of the *Annunciation* derive from this particular copy, rather than one of the many others, is indicated by Matteo's inclusion of the campanile, a motif peculiar to this variant of Dürer's composition.

19. Dennistoun attributed the *King David Playing the Harp* to Francia and the *St. Jerome* to a follower of Perugino; see Thompson 1907–18, VI, pp. 37–38. Thompson 1907, pp. 148–49, proposed Lorenzo Costa as the artist of the *King David* and attributed the *St. Jerome* to an unknown Bolognese painter. It has recently been suggested that the *King David* should be ascribed to Costa and the *St. Jerome* to an assistant of Costa; see Tosetti Grandi a. In the opinion of Dr. J. J. G. Alexander (letter to author), both of these miniatures may be attributed to Aspertini.

20. For Aspertini's life and career, see Longhi 1956, pp. 60–62, 146–52, 189–90; Bober 1957, pp. 3–4, 11–15.

21. All three detached miniatures, now framed together, are in the collection of the Liverpool City Libraries. They depict the *Assumption of the Virgin,* the *Nativity,* and the *Adoration of the Cross* within the initials A, G, and N, respectively. The miniatures were first attributed to Aspertini by Alexander in Manchester 1976, p. 37.

22. The *Adoration of the Shepherds* miniature is signed "AMICUS BONONIEMSIS." The Berlin *Adoration of the Shepherds* has been dated to the beginning of the artist's career, directly after his return from Rome; see Longhi 1956, p. 61.

23. For Aspertini's treatment of classical motifs, see Bober 1957, pp. 16–39.

24. For the opinion of the Duke of Milan's correspondent, see Baxandall 1972, p. 26. The *St. Sebastian* miniature is signed "PETRUS PRVSINVS PINXIT."

25. It has been suggested that Perugino visited Bologna about 1500–01, at which time he met Costa and presumably executed the *St. Sebastian* miniature in the Ghislieri Hours; see Tosetti Grandi b. For Perugino's career in general, see Canuti 1931.

26. Ibid., pp. 335, 339.

27. Chambers 1970, pp. 124–50, and London (Victoria and Albert Museum) 1981, pp. 164–66.

17 Pandolfo Collenuccio, *Apologues*; Lucian, *Dialogues*

Rome, circa 1509–17. Royal Ms. 12 C VIII

MANUSCRIPT *Vellum, 87 leaves; 20.7 × 13.5 cm. 1 decorated page with full-page borders and decorated capital; 5 pages with decorated borders and capitals, numerous colored plaques and flourishes. Fol. 4 decorated with several Tudor roses in the borders; in the border at the foot of the page, the royal arms of England supported by the Welsh dragon and the Beaufort greyhound, surrounded by a circular garter inscribed with the motto of the Order of the Garter,* Honny soit qui mal y pense, *surmounted by a crown and supported by angels. Chancery cursive script.*

BINDING *Original binding of red morocco tooled with gold, some tooled areas painted black.*

PROVENANCE *Henry VIII of England; thereafter in the English Royal Library; presented by George II to the British Museum, 1757.*

THE Greek author Lucian (c. A.D. 120–180) was a rhetorician and philosopher who wrote copiously in a variety of genres. This Latin translation of his dialogues, *De raptu Europae, Galene et Panope,* and *De Paridis iudicio,* is by Livius Guidoloctus of Urbino. Pandolfo Collenuccio of Pesaro (1444–1504) was, as well as a historian and poet, a jurist and diplomat, who served Giovanni Sforza of Pesaro and Ercole d'Este of Ferrara. His Latin *Apologues* in this manuscript, *Agenoria, Misopenes, Alithia,* and *Bombarda,* reveal Lucian's influence.

Collenuccio's *Apologues* (fols. 3v–71) and Lucian's *Dialogues* (fols. 71v–87v) are prefaced by a letter of dedication from Geoffrey Chamber to King Henry VIII (fols. 1v–3), in which the former alludes to his recent return to England and states that he had taken care that this presentation volume "should be written in the most elegant style of writing whereby the reading of the book should be rendered more enjoyable still" (Fig. 17a).[1] Chamber's claim was no idle boast, since he apparently entrusted this task to none other than Ludovico degli Arrighi (act. c. 1510–27), one of the most famous Italian scribes of the early sixteenth century.[2] Although born in Vicenza, Arrighi was employed at the Apostolic Chancery in Rome as a writer of briefs. Cursive script, related to that used by Bartolommeo Sanvito (Cat. 13), proved particularly suitable for these

Fig. 17a. Ludovico degli Arrighi. Text; Attavante degli Attavanti. Decorated capital, fols. 1v–2.

Fig. 17b [RIGHT]. Attavante degli Attavanti. *Visitation,* Hours of Laudomia de' Medici. London, British Library, Yates Thompson Ms. 30, fol. 20v.

Fig. 17c [BOTTOM RIGHT]. Circle of Attavante degli Attavanti. Decorated frontispiece, in the Statutes of the Hospital of Santa Maria Nuova, Florence. Oxford, Bodleian Library, Ms. 438, fol. 3.

papal letters, in which a speedy but easily legible hand was required.[3] The chancery scribes developed their own version of this hand, which came to be called *cancellaresca corsiva* (chancery cursive) or *lettera da brevi* (brief script). While Arrighi did not invent this script, he immortalized it in his book *La Operina,* published at Rome in 1522. One of the first and finest of all writing books, this treatise provided instruction on the formation of chancery cursive, illustrated with woodblocks cut by the celebrated printmaker Ugo da Carpi.[4] When Arrighi set up his own printing press at Rome in 1524, utilizing a typeface based on his own cursive script, he was, in a sense, taking the next logical step after the publication of *La Operina*. In our present context, it is noteworthy that in 1526 he published a printed edition of Collenuccio's *Apologues,* the same text that he had written for Geoffrey Chamber some years earlier.[5] As a scribe and printer, Arrighi is the major link in the chain that connects cursive script to the printed italic in use to this day.

The decorations on fol. 4 of the British Library copy of the *Apologues* and *Dialogues* (Pl. XXII) are characteristic of the style of the Florentine illuminator Attavante degli Attavanti. Henry VIII's presentation manuscript was not the only book on which Arrighi and Attavante collaborated, if we may judge from the stylistic similarity between the bust portrait of Collenuccio within the capital O on fol. 4 of the present work and the likeness of Aristotle within the capital C on the opening page of the second book of Aristotle's *Ethics*, in a volume at Amsterdam which Arrighi signed in 1517.[6]

Born in the Valdesa in 1452, Attavante was active during his youth in the workshop of Vespasiano da Bisticci, before setting up his own atelier in Florence.[7] He decorated numerous books, both for Italian patrons, including Laudomia de' Medici (Fig. 17b), and foreigners, such as Thomas James, archbishop of Dol in Brittany, and King Matthias Corvinus of Hungary.[8] The present manuscript was not the first product of Attavante's workshop to find its way to the Royal Library of the kings of England. A copy of the statutes of the Florentine hospital of Santa Maria Nuova, presented by Francesco Portinari to Henry VII, father of Henry VIII, includes a frontispiece that was evidently produced within Attavante's circle (Fig. 17c).[9] However, whereas the decoration of this page is marred by a certain crudity of execution, which indicates that it was executed by Attavante's students, the quality of the decorated page in the British Library manuscript is much higher and worthy of the master himself.

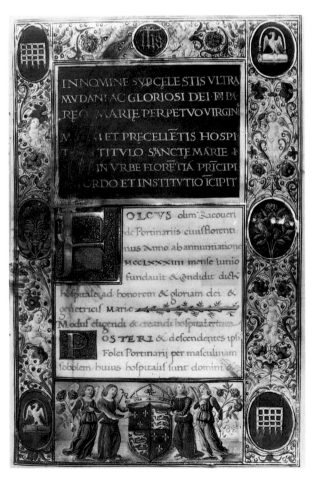

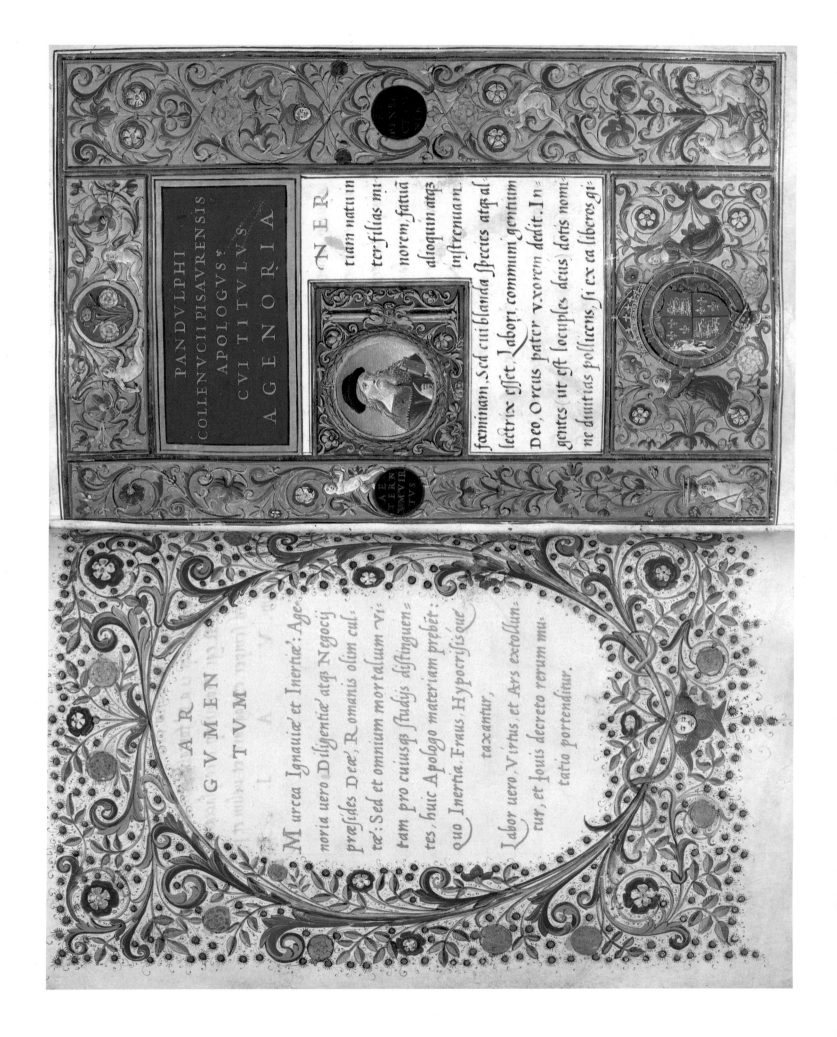

PANDVLPHI
COLLENVCII PISAVRENSIS
APOLOGVS
CVI TITVLVS
AGENORIA

NER
tiam natu in
ter filias mi-
norem, fatuā
alioquin atq3
instrenuam,
fœminam, sed cui blanda species atq3 al-
lectrix esset, labori, communi gentium
Deo, Orcus pater vxorem dedit. In=
gentes (ut est locuples deus) dotis nomi-
ne diuitias pollicens, si ex ea liberos gi=

ARGVMENTVM

M urcea Ignauiæ et Inertiæ: Age=
noria vero Diligentiæ atq3 Negocij
præsides Deæ, Romanis olim cul=
tæ: Sed et omnium mortalium vi=
tam pro cuiusq3 studijs distinguen=
tes, huic Apologo materiam prebēt:
quo Inertia, Fraus, Hypocrisísque
taxantur,
Labor vero, Virtus, et Ars extollun=
tur, et Iouis decreto rerum mu-
tatio portenditur.

Attavante's standing during his own day is attested by his many distinguished patrons. Vasari's opinion of his work—"no more perfect illuminations of that time can be seen, displaying such judgement and design, and, above all, the colours are laid on with incomparable delicacy"—is somewhat two-edged, since the Florentine biographer was under the misapprehension that Attavante was a contemporary of Fra Angelico (d. 1455), rather than of Leonardo da Vinci (b. 1452).[10] It must be admitted that much of Attavante's work has a distinctly stereotyped quality. For example, the pair of angels who appear holding the arms of England at the foot of fol. 4 in the British Library manuscript (Pl. XXII) are almost identical to those who hold a roundel picture of God the Father at the bottom of fol. 20v of the Hours of Laudomia de' Medici (Fig. 17b) and the pair supporting the arms of Pope Leo X at the top of fol. 1 of a volume of Cassiodorus' *Variae*, formerly in the library of Major J. R. Abbey.[11] Similarly, the bearded figure with his right index finger raised in a didactic gesture and a book in his left hand, who appears within the initial O on fol. 4 of the present work, has several close cousins in other manuscripts illuminated by Attavante. These include the figures of Aristotle in the Amsterdam *Ethics* and Cassiodorus on fol. 1 of the *Variae*, as well as the likeness of Appianus on fol. 7 of a volume at Florence, formerly in the collection of Pope Leo X.[12] These bearded and exotically garbed figures are of a type customarily reserved by Quattrocento artists for portraits of Old Testament prophets and figures from classical antiquity. While one would not quibble with Attavante's choice of such a standard type for the likenesses of Aristotle, Cassiodorus, and Appianus, it is questionable whether it was also appropriate for a portrait of Pandolfo Collenuccio, who died only in 1504.

BIBLIOGRAPHY Wardrop 1939; Ancona/Aeschlimann 1949, pp. 15–16; Fairbank/Wolpe 1960, pp. 83–84; Levi d'Ancona 1962, pp. 254–59; Wardrop 1963, pp. 45, 85–88; Baltimore 1965, pp. 79–80.

NOTES

1. See Fairbank/Wolpe 1960, pp. 83–84.

2. Arrighi is sometimes known as Arrighi Vicentino, from his birthplace, Vicenza. For the attribution of Royal Ms. 12 C VII to Arrighi, see ibid.

3. For a brief account of the development of chancery cursive script, see Wardrop 1963, pp. 36–49.

4. For *La Operina,* see Wardrop 1939, pp. 31–34, and Baltimore 1965, pp. 79–80.

5. Pointed out by Fairbank/Wolpe 1960, pp. 83–84. For Arrighi as a printer, see Wardrop 1963, pp. 34–39.

6. For the attribution to Arrighi of the text of Aristotle's *Ethics* (Amsterdam, Universiteits Bibliotheek, Ms. II A 19), see ibid., p. 45, pl. 48. The stylistic similarity between the miniature of Aristotle in this manuscript and that of Collenuccio in the British Library work was observed by Alexander/de la Mare 1969, p. 162.

7. It is usually thought that Attavante worked on the richly illuminated Bible of Federigo da Montefeltro (Vatican Library, Urb. lat. 1 and 2); see Ancona/Aeschlimann 1949, pp. 15–16, and Levi d'Ancona 1962, pp. 254–59, on this attribution, as well as for a general account of Attavante's career and patrons.

8. For the Hours of Laudomia de' Medici, see James 1902, pp. 294–98, and Turner 1965, p. 24.

9. Oxford, Bodleian Library, Ms. 488; for this manuscript, see Pächt/Alexander 1966–73, II, p. 32. There is a second copy of the Statutes of the Hospital of Santa Maria Nuova, also with Florentine decoration of the early sixteenth century, but of lower quality, similarly dedicated to Henry VII of England, in the British Library (Add. Ms. 40077).

10. See Vasari's life of Fra Angelico (Vasari 1927, I, pp. 343–45). Vasari opens his account with the line, "There lived at the same time as Fra Giovanni [Fra Angelico] a celebrated and famous illuminator named Attavante of Florence."

11. For the volume of Cassiodorus' *Variae* (formerly J.A. 2579), see Alexander/de la Mare 1969, pp. 161–63, pl. LXXVI.

12. For the volumes of Aristotle's *Ethics* and Cassiodorus' *Variae*, see nn. 6 and 11 above. For the manuscript of Appianus' *Romanorum liber Libycus, Syrius, Parthicus, Mithridaticus* (Florence, Biblioteca Medicea-Laurenziana, Plut. 68 Cod. 19), which was begun for Matthias Corvinus but, being unfinished on the Hungarian king's death, was eventually acquired by Pope Leo X, see Csapodi/Csapodi-Gárdonyi 1969, pp. 53, 122, pl. XVI.

Pl. XXII [OPPOSITE]. Attavante degli Attavanti. Decorated capital and borders; Ludovico degli Arrighi. Text, in Pandolfo Collenuccio, APOLOGUES; Lucian, DIALOGUES. Royal Ms. 12 C VIII, fols. 3v–4.

18 *Triumphs of Charles V*

Rome, circa 1550–75. Additional Ms. 33733

MANUSCRIPT *Vellum, 13 leaves; 20 × 29 cm. Leaves numbered 4 through 17. Fols. 1–3 comprise later notes and descriptions by Thomas Grenville; fol. 14, a drawing by Maerten van Heemskerck added to the volume in 1871, no longer bound in.*

BINDING *Violet velvet binding by Charles Lewis, c. 1816. Case of dark-blue morocco, velvet-lined, with an early-nineteenth-century magnifying glass recessed into it.*

PROVENANCE *(?) Philip II of Spain (d. 1598); (?) the royal library at the Escorial; Monsieur Trochon, rue Caumartin, Paris, who claimed to have purchased it from a French officer; sold, December 1815, to Samuel Woodburn; purchased before 1817 by Thomas Grenville (d. 1846); received by the British Museum as part of the Grenville Library, 1847; transferred to the Department of Manuscripts, 1890.*

To the connoisseurs of the late eighteenth and early nineteenth centuries, the work of Giorgio Giulio Clovio (1498–1578) represented the zenith of the illuminator's art.[1] The *Triumphs of Charles V*, which emerged from obscurity and was acquired for an English collection in 1815, the year of Waterloo, was hailed as a major example of the master's work and quickly became one of the most admired manuscripts in the British Isles. Its new binding was even supplied with a built-in magnifying glass for the benefit of those privileged to scrutinize it. Its proud owner, Thomas Grenville, statesman and book collector, enjoyed the envy of his fellow bibliophiles Francis Douce, William Young Ottley, and Richard Payne Knight.[2] Thomas Frognall Dibdin devoted six ecstatic pages to it in the *Bibliographical Decameron* of 1817.[3] When it eventually reached the British Museum in 1847 as part of Grenville's munificent bequest, it was the cause of much undignified skirmishing between Antonio Panizzi, Principal Keeper of Printed Books, and Sir Frederic Madden, Keeper of Manuscripts, each of whom considered that his own department had an unassailable right to the honor of housing it.[4]

Twentieth-century scholarship has viewed the *Triumphs* with more caution, and today the manuscript is regarded as the work of a pupil or follower of Clovio rather than as an achievement of the master himself. Clovio, who was Croatian by birth, worked in Italy for almost the whole of his life, and his style was heavily influenced by the Italian masters of the early sixteenth century. An early period in

Fig. 18a. Circle of Giulio Clovio. *Charles V Enthroned among His Enemies,* fol. 5.

Fig. 18b [LEFT]. Circle of Giulio Clovio. *Battle of Pavia*, fol. 6.

Fig. 18c [BOTTOM LEFT]. Circle of Giulio Clovio. *Submission of Egmont*, fol. 13.

Venice resulted in the patronage of several princes of the Church, including cardinals of the Grimani and Farnese families, and it was at the Palazzo Farnese in Rome that he spent virtually the entire second half of his long life. He owed a particular debt to Giulio Romano, the pupil of Raphael, and to the great Michelangelo, both of whom were active at the same time and within the same circles as Clovio himself. Vasari, writing of Clovio in his *Lives*, described him as the "little Michelangelo," and foretold for him the greatest fame enjoyed by any miniaturist who ever lived.[5] His illuminated pages are technically superb, and the detailed nature of their content is often awe-inspiring. They are, however, paintings in miniature rather than miniature paintings, even provided by their illuminator with appropriate heavy gilt frames. They require compari-

son with the monumental painting of the first half of the sixteenth century rather than with the book decoration of Clovio's predecessors.

The twelve miniatures that make up the *Triumphs of Charles V*[6] cannot very well have been painted before the end of 1556, the publication date of the engravings to which, as we shall see, they relate; and their outlines and colors are both much sharper and much clearer than those favored by Clovio at so advanced a stage of his career. The connoisseurs who admired them so much in the early nineteenth century should not, however, be judged too harshly for their insistence that the *Triumphs* were the work of Clovio, for they had little opportunity to see the master's work at first hand and no chance at all to own adequate reproductions of it.[7]

It was in 1554 that Emperor Charles V began to divest himself of the vast responsibilities he had accumulated as sole direct heir to the various sovereigns on both sides of his family. In that year he gave Naples and Milan to his son Philip and the next year made over to him the sovereignty of the Netherlands, which he had inherited as a child from his father, Philip the Handsome, the son of Duchess Mary of Burgundy. In 1556 Charles relinquished to Philip his Spanish kingdoms, which had descended to him through his mother, Joanna of Castile, from her parents Ferdinand V and Isabella, and in the same year he handed over to his brother Ferdinand the authority as emperor in Germany, which he had inherited from his paternal grandfather, Maximilian. In 1558 he formally abdicated as emperor. The *Triumphs* depicted in Thomas Grenville's manuscript represent some of the outstanding events of the Emperor's long reign and follow a series of commemorative engrav-

ings published in Antwerp in 1556 by Hieronymus Cock.[8] The drawings for this series were provided by Maerten van Heemskerck and they were engraved by Dirck Volkertsen Coornhert.[9] One of the original drawings, dated 1554, was purchased by the British Museum in 1853 and is now in the Department of Prints and Drawings (Fig. 18d). It may be compared here with the matching engraving in the series, photographed from the copy owned by Thomas Grenville and now in the British Library (Fig. 18e).

Tradition has it that Charles' son Philip II of Spain sent a set of the engravings to Clovio, requiring him to reproduce them in color on vellum, and that he also had them woven into a set of tapestries.[10] The full truth about the origin of the miniatures can probably never be known. The text that accompanies them (Fig. 18f) is identical with the sequence of Spanish verses found below the engravings in Cock's edition, and the omission of the companion verses

Fig. 18d [LEFT]. Maerten van Heemskerck. *Submission of the Duke of Saxony,* drawing, 1554. London, British Museum, Department of Prints and Drawings, no. 1853-8-11-50.

Fig. 18e [BOTTOM LEFT]. Dirck Coornheert (after Maerten van Heemskerck). *Submission of the Duke of Saxony,* engraving, 1556. London, British Library, Department of Printed Books, G. 2674*, pl. 10.

Pl. XXIII [OPPOSITE]. Circle of Giulio Clovio. *Battle of Mühlberg* 1547, in the *Triumphs of Emperor Charles V.* Add. Ms. 33733, fol. 15.

Fig. 18f. Circle of Giulio Clovio. Ornamented verse page accompanying the *Submission of the Duke of Saxony*, fol. 13v.

in both Latin and French does argue for a Spanish destination. That the miniatures derive from the engravings seems very likely, although there are some slight variations and the faces of the principal characters are often very different, those in the miniatures being more subtle and recognizably closer to other surviving portraits of their subjects. Stylistically, the miniatures are consistent with an origin in Italy soon after 1556. They do, however, have a certain Flemish flavor, due in part to the source from which they derive, and it is perfectly possible that they were made in the Netherlands by a Flemish artist trained in the Italian manner, or by an Italian artist working away from home. They could even have been made in Spain itself.

It is certainly not at all unlikely that the miniatures were once the property of Philip II. According to notes left by Grenville,[11] he acquired the volume from Woodburn,[12] who had bought it in December 1815 from a M. Trochon of the rue Caumartin in Paris. Trochon's source was said to be a French officer who "got them from the Escorial." Dibdin confused the issue when he suggested that the *Triumphs* must have been among the Escorial treasures seized from the abandoned baggage of Joseph Bonaparte at Vittoria,[13] an explanation which has since been discounted. The Escorial was in fact plundered by French troops under General La Houssaye in 1808, and the manuscript could well have been removed then. Many volumes were also lost when the library was temporarily housed in Madrid in 1809.[14] Grenville claims that the manuscript formerly had an Escorial ex libris on its first page. Such inscriptions do appear in other volumes taken from the Spanish royal library,[15] and the circumstantial evidence for an Escorial provenance for the *Triumphs* is at least equal to the objection that no trace of the book has been found in such earlier records of that enormous collection as are available.

The Grenville *Triumphs of Charles V* graphically demonstrates that even after a hundred years of printing there was still a demand for the illuminator's art at the top end of the book market. It also shows that the illuminator's art had reached a pinnacle of technical perfection and that, in spite of the superior prestige enjoyed by painters working on a far larger scale, miniatures could still be admired and commented upon as having an equal artistic status.

BIBLIOGRAPHY Dibdin 1817, pp. clxxxviii–cxciv; Stirling-Maxwell 1870, p. xxi; Bradley 1891, pp. 190–92, 217–30, 275–89; London (British Museum) 1894, p. 96; Herbert 1911, p. 305; Miller 1967, pp. 161, 174, 186; Munby 1972, pp. 25–26, 80; Miller 1973, pp. 165–66; Backhouse 1979, pl. 68.

NOTES

1. For reproductions of Clovio's work and a full bibliography, see Cionini-Visani/Gamulin 1980.

2. Noted by Grenville on fol. 2. These three men were among the greatest connoisseurs of the period. Francis Douce (1757–1834) was at one time Keeper of Manuscripts in the British Museum. His outstanding collection of illuminated books is now in the Bodleian Library at Oxford. William Young Ottley (1771–1836) amassed a vast collection of cuttings from Italian illuminated books. Richard Payne Knight (1750–1824), vice-president of the Society of Antiquaries, left his collection of coins and classical antiquities to the British Museum.

3. Dibdin 1817, pp. clxxxviii–cxciv.

4. The mutual antipathy between these two great men has become almost legendary, and the quarrel over the Grenville manu-

script was but one of multiple causes of friction. Panizzi (1797–1879), whose achievements included the building of the famous Reading Room of the British Museum, is at present the better known, because he has been the subject of a full-scale biography (Miller 1967). Madden (1801–1873), an outstanding scholar, has yet to be fully treated, partly because the materials for his life, including an immense series of diaries now in the Bodleian Library (Ms. Eng. Hist. c 160) are so very extensive. His intense hatred of Panizzi often flowed over into these diaries. At the end of 1847, the year of the Grenville bequest, he described him as "this scoundrel Italian, whose proper sphere is not to be at the head of the National library but to fill the odious post of a political spy; to lye, to cozen, to humbug, and to execute every other dirty and vile office, which no *gentleman* could be found to do!"

5. Vasari 1927, IV, pp. 244–49.

6. The events of Charles V's reign included in the series are: fol. 5, Charles V enthroned, surrounded by the contemporaries who feature in the *Triumphs*: Suleiman the Magnificent, Pope Clement VII, Francis I, the dukes of Cleves and Saxony, and the Landgrave of Hesse (Fig. 18a); fol. 6, the Battle of Pavia, 1525 (Fig. 18b); fol. 7, the death of the Duke of Bourbon at the capture of Rome, 1527; fol. 8, Clement VII imprisoned in the Castel Sant'Angelo treating for release, 1527; fol. 9, Suleiman and his army driven from the Siege of Vienna, 1529; fol. 10, the Spanish expedition to America, 1530; fol. 11, Charles V entering Tunis, 1535; fol. 12, the Duke of Cleves submitting to Charles V, 1543; fol. 13, Egmont submitting to Charles V, 1546 (Fig. 18c); fol. 15, the Duke of Saxony submitting to Charles V at the Battle of Mühlberg, 1547 (Pl. xxiii); fol. 16, the surrender of the German cities, 1547; fol. 17, the Landgrave of Hesse kneeling in submission before the emperor among clergy and courtiers, 1547.

7. One major Clovio manuscript was already in England at the relevant date, the Commentary of Cardinal Mario Grimani on St.

Paul's Epistle to the Romans, now Ms. 11 in the Library of Sir John Soane's Museum; see Millar 1914–20, pp. 36–48. When known to Grenville, it was owned by Henry Constantine Jennings (1731–1819). Adequate reproductions have, of course, been impossible until relatively recent times. The very comprehensive illustrations in Cionini-Visani/Gamulin 1980 provide the first overall view in color of Clovio's work.

8. Hieronymus Cock (c. 1510–1570) was a painter, engraver, publisher, and dealer in works of art. He traveled extensively in Italy and was influential in introducing the work of Italian artists, including Michelangelo, into Northern Europe. He was also a patron of Bruegel.

9. Heemskerck (1498–1574), who lived mainly in Haarlem, was much influenced by the work of Michelangelo. Coornhert (c. 1519–1590) made his living primarily as an engraver and calligrapher. His travels included visits to Spain and Portugal, and his circle comprised both Heemskerck and Bruegel.

10. This is recorded by Grenville in one of the notes on fol. 2 of the manuscript.

11. Ibid.

12. Samuel Woodburn was a well-known picture dealer operating in London during the first half of the nineteenth century.

13. Dibdin 1817, pp. cxciv–cxcv.

14. Edwards 1859, II, pp. 550–53.

15. One such in the British Library is Burney Ms. 19, a Greek Gospels, which is inscribed (fol. 3): "*San Lorenzo el R! del Escorial.*" The major loss of Greek manuscripts from the Escorial library is examined in Andrés 1968.

FRENCH

MANUSCRIPT

ILLUMINATION

1450–1530

THE miniature paintings concealed within the pages of a Renaissance illuminated book represent an art form which is essentially directed toward the individual. It is physically impossible for these paintings to be seen and admired by more than one or two people at once, nor can more than two facing pages be open to view at one time. From this it follows that the existence of a sufficient number of individual patrons, able and ready to pay for the making of illuminated books for their private enjoyment, was vital to the continued prosperity of the art, and that the books selected for the most ambitious schemes of decoration were bound to be those most attractive to such private individuals.

Both of these facts are reflected in the seven French manuscripts chosen for discussion in this catalogue. In three cases (Cats. 19, 22, 24) the identity of the original patron is known with certainty, and in a fourth (Cat. 21) with some probability. Furthermore, four of the manuscripts (Cats. 19, 21 23, 25) are books of hours and the other three works are in the French language, designed for private reading.

The book of hours has with justice been described as the biggest best seller of the Middle Ages and Renaissance.[1] It was the standard manual of private devotion throughout most of Europe from the mid-thirteenth century to the Reformation, and its varied contents, centering on the eight services of the Little Office of the Virgin Mary but usually including numerous other prayers and devotions, offered a wide scope to illuminators. The manuscript workshops of France were famous during the whole of the fifteenth century for the production of books of hours, destined not only for clients in France itself but often for export to customers in other countries. Many of the surviving books, which are now to be found in museums and libraries all over the world, are modest in content and design and were intended to satisfy demand at the lower end of the market. Some, however, are of the utmost magnificence, regarded as status symbols rather than practical prayer books for everyday use, and these are not infrequently lavishly supplied with the arms, badges, devices, and mottoes of their original owners. One of the most splendid of all is the Hours of Etienne Chevalier (Cat. 19), in which the owner's device appears on almost every surviving page.

Ill. 14. French Master. *Pentecost*, Book of Hours. London, British Library, Add. Ms. 25696, fol. 49.

The invention and introduction of printing had a radical effect upon the book of hours industry in France. The first known printed hours was issued in Paris in 1486 by Antoine Vérard, and during the 1490s both Paris and Lyons developed into major centers of production, providing for the different Uses of the various dioceses of France and also conducting an extensive export trade. It seems that many of the publishing houses, including that of Vérard, who was himself a calligrapher and illuminator, dealt in manuscripts as well as printed books, and certainly many of the printed hours were so designed that they could be illuminated by hand to satisfy the personal tastes of clients. Mass production thus quickly accounted for the lower end of a

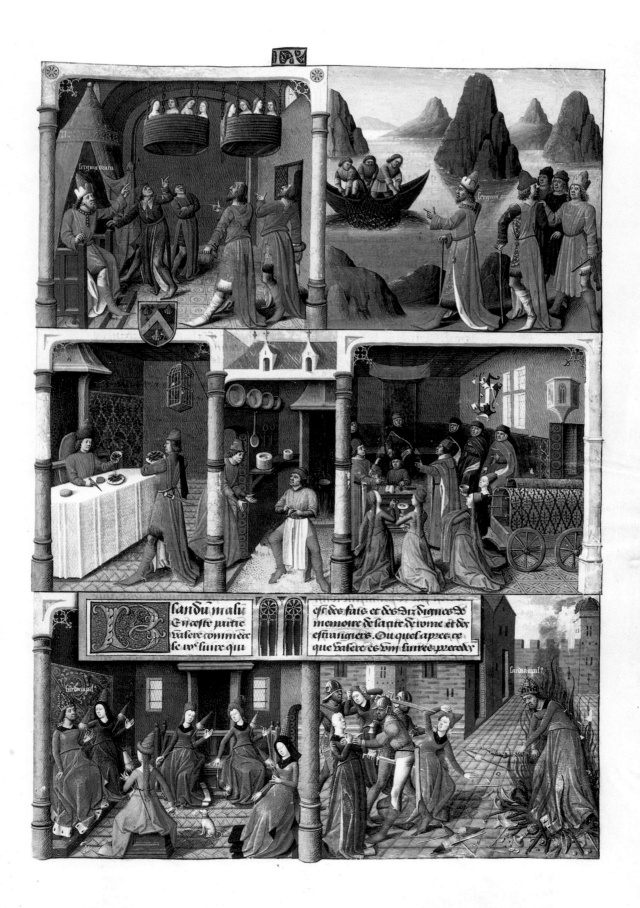

Ill. 15. French Master. Frontispiece to "Of Luxury," Book IX in Valerius Maximus,
FACTA ET DICTA MEMORABILIA. London, British Library, Harley Ms. 4375, fol. 179.

market formerly enjoyed exclusively by professional scribes and illuminators.

Manuscript books of hours continued to be made, however, and many anonymous but talented workshops flourished alongside the burgeoning printing industry. The seven manuscripts discussed in detail here present only a very limited picture of developments in France during our period, for they concentrate on the achievements of the artists of the Loire school and on work connected with the patronage of the French court. A single miniature from a fine book of hours in a style not shown elsewhere in this catalogue must stand here as representative of all the rest (Ill. 14). The British Library's collections of course include a large number of manuscripts representing other French work current at this time. Many of these are very little known, but an increasing interest is now being shown in the work of French Renaissance illuminators and year by year new publications are helping to provide a more comprehensive understanding of their achievements.[2]

French patronage in the late fifteenth and early sixteenth centuries was given a lead by royal example. Five kings, from Charles VII to Francis I, can each be associated with particular artists and their work. Successive queens, Charlotte of Savoy, Anne of Brittany, and Claude of France, together with Francis I's redoubtable mother, Louise of Savoy, are all well documented as patronesses of specific illuminators. Many other members of the royal family, followed by members of the court circle, were equally keen to own examples of fine workmanship. Patronage was not confined to the nobility. Etienne Chevalier, the owner of one of the greatest manuscripts of the fifteenth century (Cat. 19), is typical of a class of bourgeois patron emerging at this time. As an important official in the service of the king, he had a public position to maintain, and he was but one of several such officials to regard patronage of the arts as an important adjunct to his way of life.

Royal interest in the arts gave to several contemporary book painters, including Fouquet (Cat. 19), Bourdichon (Cat. 21), and Perréal (Cat. 22), official status as *peintres du roy,* and seems to have engendered at the court an atmosphere which also encouraged the more strictly amateur interest in patronage and, indeed, in the practice of the arts. Pierre Sala (Cat. 22) was one royal servant who himself wrote verse for the enjoyment of his friends and patrons and employed illuminators to make his presentation copies. The Lallemant family of Bourges, who lived on the fringe of courtly life, provides an example of similar interest at a local level of important bourgeoisie. The family house, the Hôtel Lallemant in Bourges, is a prime example of French Renaissance architecture, and various members of the family commissioned manuscripts, both books of hours and books for reading, over several decades.[3]

The books for reading covered in this catalogue are not at all typical of the taste of the period, because, owing to their immense size and weight, the real "coffee-table books" of the time cannot conveniently be transported or shown. The finest of these in the British Library is an enormous *Memorabilia* of Valerius Maximus (Ill. 15), made about 1475 for Louis XI's biographer, Philippe de Com-

mynes.[4] The two volumes of this work contain between them more than five hundred leaves of vellum, each measuring 47 × 34.3 cm. The two have in recent times been rebound as six for greater ease of handling, and each of the six is more than 5 cm thick. At much the same time, the same workshop could also produce a tiny book of hours (Egerton Ms. 2045) which measures only 8.9 × 6.4 cm. Both these manuscripts come from the studio of an illuminator known as Maître François, whose style provides some reminders of the work of book painters in the earlier part of the fifteenth century, and whose shop is now credited with the artist who painted miniatures into some of the books published by Antoine Vérard in the last years of the century, thus spanning the old and the new.

The artist whose workshop produced the Valerius Maximus is known to us under a Christian name gleaned from a documentary source which was recognized as relating to a specific manuscript.[5] A number of other painters of our period have been more specifically identified, and their careers can thus be traced through written records as well as through recognition of the manuscripts they made. Five of the seven manuscripts discussed here (Cats. 19, 20, 21, 22, 24) can be associated with named artists, and what is known of their lives and activities is outlined in the appropriate entries. Access to supplementary details concerning an illuminator through knowledge of his name of course has many advantages. It allows us to discover, through written records of other types of work in which he may have been engaged, additional information about the breadth of his practical experience, even though much of the work itself may now be lost. The French court painters mentioned above—Fouquet, Bourdichon, and Perréal—were all engaged from time to time in designing and carrying out the large-scale decorations required to support the pageantry of state entries and other court celebrations, some idea of which can be obtained from illuminated "souvenir programs" prepared at the time (Ill. 16). All three men also painted portraits, some of which survive, and other works on panel. We sometimes know also about activities not related to specific works. Documents have been found which tell us that Fouquet spent a period in central Italy, that Perréal's travels embraced both Northern Italy and England, and that Colombe was for a considerable time employed at the ducal court of Savoy, where he became familiar at first hand with the celebrated Très Riches Heures of the duc de Berry. One may assume from such records that the artists concerned would have enjoyed firsthand experience of works of art in the places to which their travels took them and that they also probably met their contemporaries who were employed there. Another of the named artists, Godefroy le Batave (Cat. 24), is known to have come to France from the Netherlands, and his style is certainly interconnected with that of the illuminators of the 1520s Hours Workshop (Cat. 25). It must not, of course, be forgotten that this traffic flowed both ways. Foreign artists visited and were employed in France, especially during the reign of Francis I, and the great Leonardo da Vinci himself died on French soil in 1519.

Ill. 16. French Master. Tableau presented outside the Palais Royal during the state entry of Mary Tudor into Paris in 1514 as Queen of Louis XII. In a contemporary manuscript probably made for presentation to Mary. London, British Library, Cotton Ms. Vespasian B II, fol. 15.

Scholars concentrating on an area and period such as this are often understandably tempted to rely too much on the evidence available through named artists and personalities and to neglect those who are anonymous. Those concerned with earlier centuries or with other parts of Europe are less affected, because to them names and records are a rarity rather than a commonplace. However, several outstanding French artists of this period have not been linked with any specific name and they are only now receiving adequate recognition, though the work which they produced stands equal to that of some of the best of their identified contemporaries. One such is the illuminator responsible for the miniatures of the Tilliot Hours (Cat. 23). Another is the artist known as the Master of Claude of France, because his output includes more than one book commissioned for the use of Francis I's queen. The British Library has examples of his work which include a very delicate little book of hours, which is as yet unpublished (Ills. 17, 18).

The adoption of outside ideas and influences did not necessarily result only from personal experience and travel. The increasing availability of the printed book, illustrations for which rapidly became more and more sophisticated, and the circulation of woodcuts and engravings from Italy and the Low Countries were also vastly influential.[6] It has already been mentioned that some printed books were hand-illuminated for customers of the large publishing houses. Conversely, the influence of engraved illustrations is clearly recognizable in a large body of illuminated work which seems quite deliberately to echo the clear, hard lines and sharp techniques of the engraver (Ill. 19).[7]

Although French book painting in the late fifteenth and early sixteenth centuries produced work of a high order of excellence, it seems never yet to have received the same degree of concentrated attention as the work of Flemish and Italian illuminators of the parallel period. The work of the Flemings has long proved particularly attractive because of its readily demonstrable relationship to the work of the well-documented panel painters of the time. Italian books, although subsidiary to monumental painting for the general history of the art of the period, have been worked on by students of the larger-scale work, as well as by historians of humanism. French illumination, with a few exceptions, does not enjoy an immediate and clear relationship with paintings on a more ambitious scale, because such paintings simply do not exist in sufficient quantity.[8] France lost much of her artistic heritage during political and religious crises, particularly during the ravages of the French Revolution, and the manuscripts are now of perhaps disproportionate importance for the history of her late medieval and Renaissance painting. A great deal of research still needs to be done before the several thousands of miniatures which the manuscripts contain yield up all the information which they have to offer.

Some sober reassessment of the contribution of the French illuminators to the overall development of the pictorial arts in Europe at this time is long overdue. Many monographs have been devoted to Fouquet, but his name means less to the general art-loving public than the names of Jan van Eyck or Hans Memling because his masterpieces lie between the pages of books rather than hang on the walls of churches and galleries. Were some of Fouquet's almost miraculously perfect landscapes or town scenes to be familiar on a larger scale, he would certainly rank with the most generally admired painters of any country in the world. The same is surely true of some individual images, such as the beautiful representation of the Virgin Mary from Bourdichon's Hours of Henry VII (Fig. 21e). Much has been written in the last forty years about the achievements of the Flemish manuscript illuminators who introduced illusionistic floral borders and the so-called "window aspect" into book painting from about 1480 onward,[9] but almost unknown are the Cloisters leaves by one of Fouquet's associates, the Master of Charles of France, painted about 1465, in which a most elaborate interplay of space and depth is already fully worked out with the utmost sophistication.[10]

Ill. 17 [ABOVE]. Master of Claude of France. *Visitation*, Book of Hours. London, British Library, Add. Ms. 35214, fols. 38v–39.

Ill. 18 [ABOVE RIGHT]. Master of Claude of France. *Spray of Pinks*, Book of Hours. London, British Library, Add. Ms. 35214, fol. 38.

Ill. 19 [BELOW]. French Master. *David and Bathsheba*, Book of Hours. London, British Library, Add. Ms. 21235, fols. 78v–79.

The picture presented here by only seven manuscripts covering a span of almost eighty years is of necessity a very simple one, confined to the Loire school and to the court to the exclusion of many interesting developments connected with the north, south, and east of the kingdom. A clear line of descent runs from Fouquet to the generation of Colombe, Bourdichon, and the Master of the Tilliot Hours, all of whom were probably in some degree his pupils. But although Fouquet's influence is to be seen in their work, the vast influence which they in their turn exercised over the next generation can only be mentioned here. The later painters, Godefroy le Batave and the masters in the 1520s Hours shop, appear here without preamble, although it seems to me that it is possible to draw a line of descent, albeit a somewhat tenuous one, from the work of the Master of the Tilliot Hours through that of the Master of Claude of France and ultimately to the little deluxe books of the 1520s. There is no place here for the painters of the so-called "Rouen school,"[11] or for those whose work is most closely connected with the work of printers and engravers, nor is there space to explore the relationship between some of the later illuminators and the enamel painters of Limoges.

The latest of the seven French manuscripts seen here was made during the 1520s, but this was by no means the end of the story of the illuminated manuscript in Renaissance France. The middle years of the sixteenth century saw the production of a whole series of ultra deluxe devotional books commissioned by members of the royal family and their immediate circle.[12] Among French refugees seeking asylum at the court of Henry VIII about 1540 was one Jean Mallard who had already made illuminated books for Francis I and who combined his skills as scribe and illuminator with a post as "orator in the French language" to the English king.[13] To him is due, among other items, a fine and original illuminated psalter which includes portraits of Henry in the character of King David.[14] One of the leading illuminators at the court of Pope Paul III was another Frenchman, Vincent Raymond.[15]

The techniques developed by generations of illuminators, less and less in general demand as printing expanded, were channeled into other related work. Mention is made in the discussion of Perréal (Cat. 22) of the close relationship between manuscript illumination and the development of the portrait miniature. Another, apparently particularly French, phenomenon was the development of the miniature flower "portrait." Flemish books of hours are renowned for the beautifully painted flower heads scattered over gold or colored grounds in their margins. French illuminators also adopted flowers for their border decoration, but they favored representations of entire (or almost entire) plants rather than single blossoms. Bourdichon's Hours of Anne of Brittany contains what amounts to an extensive flora, each specimen labeled with the appropriate name in French. The finest of the flower painters among the illuminators painted the flowers seen in the borders and on the versos of the miniatures in the British Library's little hours from the workshop of the Master of Claude of France (Ill. 18). These are the immediate precursors of the superb flower portraits of Jacques Le Moyne de Morgues, who is perhaps most famous for his illustrated account of the French expedition to Florida in 1564.[16] Expeditions to the New World offered yet another outlet for the techniques of the illuminators, for many of the finest maps and charts produced to record new territories discovered, and present them to past or potential backers, were drawn and painted upon vellum.[17]

NOTES

1. The most convenient recent introduction to this type of book is Harthan 1977.

2. Particularly useful are New York 1982, Pächt 1977, and, dealing with one clearly defined group of manuscripts, Reynaud 1977.

3. For references to the manuscripts owned by members of the Lallemant family, see Chenu 1946, and Orth 1980c. The Lallemants and their friends and neighbors in Bourges clearly modeled their behavior on that of their courtly contemporaries. They even founded their own "order of chivalry," the Order of the Round Table, statutes and an armorial of which are in the British Library, Harley Ms. 5301.

4. Warner 1907.

5. For a recent examination of Maître François's workshop, see Spencer 1974.

6. One may assume that useful drawings and, especially, engravings would have been deliberately collected by a workshop. For the influence of specific drawings upon one particular manuscript, see Cat. 25. It is worth mentioning the existence of a calligrapher's scrapbook (British Library, Add. Ms. 27869) which includes a mass of cuttings from printed sources. It was compiled by Francesco Alunno of Ferrara (d. 1556) when he was working in the Chancery of Venice.

7. Some manuscripts of this type are discussed in Backhouse 1966–67.

8. For a general survey, see Ring 1949a.

9. The subject was introduced by Pächt 1948.

10. New York, The Metropolitan Museum of Art, Cloisters Collection, 58.71a, b; New York 1982, no. 64.

11. Ritter/Lafond 1913.

12. This group is centered on the Hours of Henry II and the Dinteville Hours, Paris, Bibliothèque Nationale, Mss. lat. 1429 and 10558; see Leroquais 1927, I, pp. 276–79, and II, pp. 17–19.

13. Wallis 1981, pp. 10–11.

14. London, British Library, Royal Ms. 2 A XVI.

15. Dorez 1909.

16. Hulton 1977.

17. Wallis 1981 offers a useful recent survey of contemporary French cartography.

19 Hours of Etienne Chevalier

Detached leaf. *King David in Prayer*. Tours, circa 1452–61.
Additional Ms. 37421

MANUSCRIPT *Vellum, 19.7 × 15.2 cm, overall; miniature, 14.9 × 11.7 cm. The original leaf apparently laid down over a larger piece of vellum; strips on the left (.5 cm), right (.3 cm), and at top (.7 cm) not part of the manuscript.*

PROVENANCE *Etienne Chevalier (d. 1474); by descent through the Chevalier family to Nicolas Chevalier, Baron de Crissé (d. 1630); his nephew by marriage, the Seigneur de Longeuil; manuscript broken up during the eighteenth century; present leaf purchased by Samuel Rogers (d. 1855); his sale, Christie's, London, May 6, 1856, lot 981; John Campbell, 2nd Marquis of Breadalbane (d. 1862); Breadalbane sale, Christie's, London, June 4, 1886, lot 181; British Museum, Department of Prints and Drawings; transferred to the Department of Manuscripts, 1906.*

THIS detached miniature of *King David in Prayer* (Pl. XXIV) is the British Library's sole example of the work of Jean Fouquet, the great artistic genius whose work dominated the development of painting in France during the second half of the fifteenth century. It comes from the celebrated book of hours, now dismembered and scattered among eight collections in four different countries, which Fouquet illuminated for Etienne Chevalier (d. 1474), Treasurer of France, shortly after 1450.[1] Chevalier's device, EE linked by a knot, is enclosed in the initial letter.

Much has been written about Fouquet,[2] whose career was strongly influenced by the political situation of his time.[3] He was apparently born at Tours, in the Loire Valley, during the second decade of the fifteenth century, a period marked by the Battle of Agincourt (1415) and the subsequent Treaty of Troyes (1420) which resulted in the succession of an infant English prince to the throne of France. It was not until the middle of the century that the French claimant, Charles VII, crowned at Reims in 1429 under the protection of Joan of Arc, regained the greater part of his kingdom. Paris, principal center of the arts at the beginning of the century, was itself in English hands until after the death of the English regent, John, Duke of Bedford, in 1435. Charles eventually made his state entry into the city in 1437. His principal residence was at Bourges, some eighty miles upriver from Tours, a circumstance extremely influential in the development of the Loire school of painting, of which Fouquet was to become the leading personality.

Evidence for Fouquet's early career is scanty and largely inferential. We do however know, from more than one source, that he visited Rome during the 1440s and there painted a portrait of Pope Eugenius IV.[4] As the pope did

not return to Rome from a decade of exile in Florence until late in 1443 and as he died in February 1447, the portrait (known today only from a much later engraving)[5] must belong to the period 1444–46. The commission implies that Fouquet was already acknowledged as a portrait painter.[6] There are no records that reveal how long the artist remained in Italy, nor which of the several possible routes he took on his journey to Rome; but his subsequent work includes strong reflections of the experiences gained in the course of this excursion, during which he must have seen many masterpieces, both antique and contemporary, and probably made the acquaintance of some of the leading Italian painters of the day. By 1448 he had returned home to Tours, where he married and set up house.

The Hours of Etienne Chevalier was probably commissioned some four or five years after Fouquet's return to France. Its patron was one of the leading administrators at Charles VII's court, a member of a family which had risen to some prominence by providing several generations of servants to the crown.[7] Etienne Chevalier was born at Melun at the beginning of the fifteenth century. His grandfather Pierre had been *valet de chambre* to Charles V and his father, Jean, was "*notaire et secrétaire du roi*" in 1423. His own early career lay in the service of Arthur de Richemont, Constable of France, the one-time ally of the English regent, whose change of allegiance to Charles VII in 1425 was one of the landmarks on the road to the recovery of Charles' kingdom. By 1442 Chevalier had entered the royal service, where he held successive secretarial and financial positions. Sometime before 1447 he married Catherine, daughter of Dreux Budé, another of the royal secretaries.[8] During this period he had sufficient standing to be called upon to join the embassy sent to England to discuss peace terms in the summer of 1445. He was also one of the executors of Agnes Sorel, the king's mistress, who died in 1450. In March 1452 his career reached its zenith when he was appointed Treasurer of France.

No date appears on any of the surviving leaves of the Hours of Etienne Chevalier, but the book was probably ordered soon after its owner's appointment as treasurer. Although his personal device, the letters EE linked by a knot, appears on almost every page, both text and miniature, there is no direct reference in the book to his wife. This, together with the fact that he himself appears in the miniature of the *Entombment* dressed in black,[9] probably indicates a date after her death, which took place in the summer of 1452. Work on the manuscript's miniatures, which originally numbered well over fifty, was probably spread over several years, but must have been completed before Charles VII's death in July 1461, because he is rec-

Fig. 19a [RIGHT]. Jean
Fouquet. *Visitation*, Hours
of Etienne Chevalier. Chantilly, Musée Condé, de-
tached leaf.

Fig. 19b [FAR RIGHT]. Jean
Fouquet. *Christ Carrying the
Cross*, Hours of Etienne
Chevalier. Chantilly, Musée
Condé, detached leaf.

ognizably portrayed as the first of the Three Kings in the
Adoration of the Magi.[10] It has been argued that the second
and third Kings in this scene represent Charles' two sons,
the Dauphin Louis (later Louis XI) and Charles of
Guyenne, and that the book must therefore have been illuminated before Louis's serious quarrel with his father in
1456, but this proposal is more difficult to sustain.

The forty-seven surviving miniatures represent various
sections of the usual contents of a book of hours, and the
recent reappearance of two separate text leaves has made a
theoretical reconstruction of the original structure of the
manuscript possible.[11] As seen today, almost all the miniatures, none of which ever had surrounding marginal decoration, look like tiny individual paintings rather than book·
illustrations. This only serves to emphasize the brilliance of
Fouquet's compositional powers and technical achievement. He produces an apparently effortless realism,
whether in the portrayal of figures, of landscape, or of
architecture. The two miniatures chosen from among the
forty at Chantilly for illustration here (Figs. 19a, 19b) display contrasting settings. The *Visitation* takes place before
an elaborate portico within an enclosed courtyard opening
onto a garden.[12] An everyday touch is added by the inclusion of the two figures at the well. Christ carries his cross
along the banks of the Seine, with an enchanting distant
view of the river and of the Sainte-Chapelle, which housed
the relics of the Passion displayed to the people of Paris on
Good Friday.[13] Below the obliterated text panel, which has
been covered by a cutting from the decorations of some
other manuscript, a Roman soldier and the blacksmith's

wife prepare the nails for the Crucifixion in an apocryphal
scene culled from contemporary religious drama.

The British Library's *David* miniature[14] has suffered
until now from being seen, and often reproduced, within a
heavy, black-painted border which seems to have been
applied in the nineteenth century (Fig. 19c).[15] The removal
of this somewhat tasteless accretion (Pl. XXIV) immediately enhances appreciation of a magical landscape of water
and mountains, a formidable distant group of mounted and
heavily armed soldiery highlighted in liquid gold, and two
groups of brightly colored devils busily subjecting the
damned to the tortures of hell. King David, in fashionable
and costly Renaissance armor, kneels in supplication before

Fig. 19c. Jean Fouquet. *King David in Prayer*,
within the later black-painted border.

Pl. XXIV. Jean Fouquet. *King David in Prayer,* Hours of Etienne
Chevalier. Add. Ms. 37421, detached leaf.

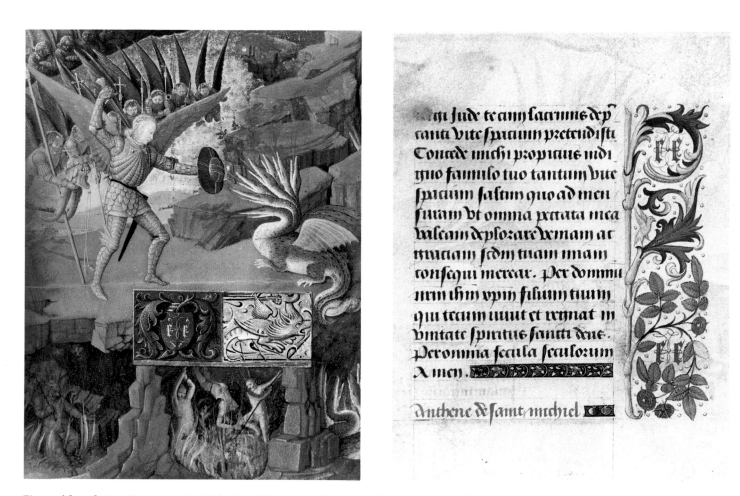

Fig. 19d [LEFT]. Jean Fouquet. *St. Michael and His Angels Fighting the Dragon*, Hours of Etienne Chevalier. Upton House, Bearsted Collection (National Trust), detached leaf.

Fig. 19e [RIGHT]. Text page with decorated border, other side of Fig. 19d.

the Almighty, an apparently beneficent figure enthroned among cherubim and seraphim. Of particular note is Fouquet's rendering of the foreshortened figure of a dead man in the center of the picture on the brink of the pit.

Only one other miniature from the manuscript is to be found in an English collection. This is the *St. Michael* (Fig. 19d),[16] now in the care of the National Trust at Upton House. The leaf is especially interesting because it is one of those on which the text side can be seen (Fig. 19e). Its distinctive marginal decoration, thought by some scholars to have been painted by Fouquet himself,[17] is common to all those text pages on leaves also bearing miniatures.

The Hours of Etienne Chevalier is Fouquet's masterpiece, but it is not his only surviving manuscript. His hand appears in other books of hours, one of which is now in the Pierpont Morgan Library, New York,[18] and contemporary documents tell us of further examples now lost.[19] He also painted narrative miniatures to illustrate a number of secular texts, outstanding among which are a *Grandes Chroniques de France* in Paris,[20] and a Boccaccio in Munich (Fig. 19f),[21] the latter commissioned by Laurent Girard, another royal financial officer at the court of Charles VII and Etienne Chevalier's son-in-law. These large manuscripts apparently show the work of subsidiary hands,

suggesting that Fouquet, as might be expected in an artist of his standing, had pupils and assistants.[22]

Fouquet's reputation as a painter of portraits has already been mentioned. Several fine drawings are also attributed to him, as well as the large altarpiece known as the *Pietà of Nouans*.[23] Records indicate that he produced "*certains tableaux*" for the Order of St. Michael in 1470, made up a design for a tomb for Louis XI in 1474, and worked on preparations for the state entry of the Portuguese King Alfonso V into Tours in 1476. However, although he clearly did work extensively for king and court, the only document in which he is actually named as "*peintre du roy*" dates from as late as 1475. He was dead before November 8, 1481, when mention is made of his widow.

The later history of the Hours of Etienne Chevalier is not a happy one. The book survived complete in the hands of Chevalier's descendants until the beginning of the seventeenth century. By the beginning of the eighteenth century it had disappeared, to emerge in fragments soon after the French Revolution.[24] Two conjoint leaves of the text, hitherto supposed to be entirely lost, were rediscovered as recently as 1980,[25] and it is not unrealistic to hope that further fragments, possibly even including missing miniatures, may still come to light.

Fig. 19f. Jean Fouquet. *Anointing of Saul*, in Boccaccio, LES CAS DE NOBLES HOMMES ET FEMMES. Munich, Bayerische Staatsbibliothek, Cod. gall. 6, fol. 46v.

BIBLIOGRAPHY Passavant 1833, pp. 87–88; Waagen 1837–39, p. 514; London (British Museum) 1912, pp. 38–39; Warner 1910, no. xxxv; Martin 1926, p. 42; London (British Museum) 1914–30, VI, pl. 12b; Cox 1931, p. 73, pl. 26; Millar 1933, no. 55; Perls 1940, pl. 37; Wescher 1947, pl. 20; Sterling/Schaefer 1971, no. 26; Schaefer/Hamel 1981, pp. 198–99.

NOTES

1. The largest part of the manuscript, forty illuminated leaves, is in the Musée Condé at Chantilly. Seven miniatures are in other collections: the present leaf in the British Library; Paris, Bibliothèque Nationale (one); Paris, Musée du Louvre, Cabinet des Dessins (two); Paris, Musée Marmottan, Wildenstein Collection (one); New York, The Metropolitan Museum of Art, Robert Lehman Collection (one); Upton House, Bearsted Collection, National Trust (one; Figs. 19d, 19e). The two detached leaves of text, which are referred to below, are now in private hands in Belgium. All the surviving miniatures are reproduced in color in Sterling/Schaefer 1971, to which references are given below.

2. The most convenient recent source, with an up-to-date bibliography and citation of all relevant literature, is Paris 1981.

3. For the political history of the period, see Vale 1974.

4. The evidence is given in detail in Durrieu 1908, pp. 82–84. Durrieu's work remains fundamental to the study of Fouquet's career.

5. Paris 1981, no. 2.

6. For discussion of Fouquet's early reputation as a painter of portraits, see Pächt 1974. Fouquet's sitters are listed in Paris 1981, pp. 5–38.

7. Lapeyre/Scheurer 1978 includes entries covering many of the royal servants mentioned here.

8. Ibid., pp. 67–68.

9. Sterling/Schaefer 1971, pl. 20.

10. Ibid., pl. 2.

11. The structure was worked out by Christopher de Hamel and published in Sotheby's, London, sale catalogue, July 14, 1981, lot 37, and in Schaefer/Hamel 1981.

12. Sterling/Schaefer 1971, pl. 7.

13. Ibid., pl. 16.

14. Ibid., pl. 26.

15. The heavy black paint is applied over the joins. There appears in fact to be a second sheet of vellum between the verso of the original leaf and its present card mount. The gold lines toward the edge of the leaf and around the edge of the actual miniature are painted over the black surface and therefore are not original. The small painted panel below the miniature, containing the words *"ne reminiscaris"* together with its accompanying sprays of leaves, is also an addition overlying the black paint. The original first line of the Penitential Psalms, inscribed on the blue panel below the miniature, should properly be followed by the words *tua corripias me*.

16. Sterling/Schaefer 1971, pl. 28.

17. The marginal decoration here, however, seems considerably bolder than that on the two text leaves recently recovered (see n. 11). The decoration in the Wildenstein and Lehman leaves is reproduced in Sotheby's, London, sale catalogue, December 18, 1946, lots 568, 569.

18. New York 1982, no. 42.

19. Paris 1981, pp. 4–5.

20. Paris, Bibliothèque Nationale, Ms. fr. 6465; reproduced in Omont 1906a.

21. Twenty-two of its miniatures are reproduced in color in Pleister 1965.

22. A large collection of reproductions of work by Fouquet, his followers, and related hands is to be found in Perls 1940.

23. Paris 1981, no. 13.

24. Exact details of what happened to the manuscript have not been determined. The forty miniatures now at Chantilly were purchased in Basel about 1803 by George Brentano of Frankfurt. He apparently acquired them from Peter Birmann (d. c. 1830), who also made up an album of miscellaneous detached leaves (see Sotheby's, London, sale catalogue, April 25, 1983, especially pp. 6–7 and lot 147) which includes fragments of decoration very similar to some of those used to cover over the text panels on Etienne Chevalier miniatures (cf. Fig. 19b). Birmann is known to have been in Paris frequently after June 1795, and Christopher de Hamel of Sotheby's suggests that he may have been responsible for breaking up the Chevalier Hours. Examination of the Chantilly leaves has revealed that their wooden frames were made in Paris by a framemaker active immediately after the French Revolution (see Ribault 1981, p. 200), and it is very likely that Samuel Rogers, the original owner of the British Library's leaf, acquired it in France on his first visit there in 1791. This cumulative evidence begins to suggest that the manuscript survived intact until the Revolution. Panels of apparently eighteenth-century decoration covering some of the text areas could connect the book with the Maurists, and it should be recalled that their library at Saint-Germain was a major casualty of the revolutionary period.

25. Schaefer/Hamel 1981, pp. 193–99.

20 Boethius, *De consolatione philosophiae*

Bourges, 1476. Harley Mss. 4335–4339

MANUSCRIPT *Vellum, 5 volumes (93, 80, 111, 98, and 82 fols., respectively); 18.5 × 13.5 cm. In each volume, the recto of the first leaf inscribed "Gabriel Hinselin 1616" and (in the hand of Humfrey Wanley, Harley's librarian) "24 die Januarii A.D. 1722/3." Hinselin's arms in vol. I, fols. 91 and 92 (colored) and vol. V, fol. 81 (colored); a seal with the same arms inside the front cover of each volume.*

BINDING *Brown morocco with gold fillets and remains of silk ties, c. 1723.*

PROVENANCE *Gabriel Hinselin, 1616; Charles David, bookseller, c. 1722; purchased in 1723 by Humfrey Wanley for Robert Harley, 1st Earl of Oxford; transferred to the British Museum on its foundation in 1753.*

D*E consolatione philosophiae* by Boethius, written in prison at Pavia shortly before its author, a Roman philosopher and statesman, was put to death as a traitor in A.D. 524 or 525, enjoyed an immense popularity during the whole of the Middle Ages and Renaissance. The original Latin text was many times translated into other languages and numerous commentaries appeared.[1] This particular copy, arranged for easy handling in a set of five small volumes, contains the French translation by Jean de Meun (better known as the continuator of the *Roman de la Rose*) addressed to Philip IV of France (d. 1314).[2] A colophon at the end of the fifth volume records that the copying of the book was completed on February 1, 1476, by a scribe signing himself Rousselli,[3] who is to be identified as André Rousseau, a bookseller associated with the University of Bourges, which had been founded by Louis XI as recently as 1463.[4] The five volumes contain among them a total of seven illustrations: one introducing Boethius' own prologue (Fig. 20a); one, the translator's preface (Pl. XXV); and one decorating the opening of each of the five books into which the treatise is divided (Figs. 20b, 20c).[5] These miniatures have been recognized on stylistic grounds as the work of Jean Colombe, the well-known Bourges illuminator who was active during the second half of the fifteenth century,[6] but there is no clue to the identity of the patron who ordered the manuscript.

The city of Bourges, like the city of Tours, was a center of great artistic activity during the fifteenth century. As the chief town of the duchy of Berry, it was associated at the beginning of the century with one of the greatest patrons of all time, Jean, duc de Berry, whose body lies in its cathedral, where he had built the Sainte-Chapelle as a mortuary chapel.[7] The completion of the duke's tomb was ordered about 1450 by his great-nephew, Charles VII, who had made Bourges virtually a capital during a quarter century of the English occupation of France, and whose courtiers and ministers, especially the treasurer Jacques Coeur (disgraced in 1451), provided much work for the artists and craftsmen of the town. Jean Colombe was born into a family prominent in the arts for several generations. His father, Philippe, was a sculptor whose activities are recorded during the first half of the century. His brother, Michel, also a sculptor, found favor with many influential patrons during the latter years of the century. He is especially known for such magnificent work as the tomb erected at Nantes between 1499 and 1507 by order of Louis XII's queen, Anne of Brittany, in honor of her parents, Duke Francis II of Brittany and Marguerite of Foix. A few years later, Margaret of Austria, Regent of the Netherlands, commissioned Michel Colombe to produce family tombs for the ducal mausoleum of Savoy at Brou. In the work on both these projects he was, at least for a time, associated with Jean Perréal.[8]

Knowledge of Jean Colombe's life and career, though gleaned from a variety of sources, is less detailed than information about his sculptor brother.[9] Jean is thought to have been born at Bourges about 1435. During his early professional years he is known to have been associated with a calligrapher named Clement Thibault. In 1464 he married and in 1467 he built himself a new house in Bourges in which, save for a few short periods, he lived for the remainder of his life. He probably died about 1493 and certainly before November 10, 1498. His style is most distinctive and has been recognized in a large number of manuscripts, many of them lavishly decorated, now scattered among collections all over the world. It is clear that he worked with a number of collaborators and assistants, including his own son, Philibert (d. 1505), and some of them, including a François Colombe (probably to be identified as a grandson), have left signatures or distinguishing marks on the pages of various manuscripts.[10]

Early on in his career, Colombe became noted as a producer of fine books of hours and in one instance his work appears beside that of Jean Fouquet.[11] Other examples are associated with the names of Jacques Coeur[12] and of Anne of Beaujeu, daughter of Louis XI and Charlotte of Savoy.[13] Queen Charlotte (d. 1484), a noted bibliophile, was one of Colombe's most important patrons and it was probably through her good offices that the artist was introduced into the service of Duke Charles I of Savoy, for whom he com-

Fig. 20a [ABOVE]. Jean Colombe. *Boethius in His Study*. Harley Ms. 4335, fol. 1.

Fig. 20b [TOP RIGHT]. Jean Colombe. *Boethius and Fortune*. Harley Ms. 4336, fol. 1v.

Fig. 20c [RIGHT]. Jean Colombe. *Boethius and Philosophy*. Harley Ms. 4337, fol. 2.

Fig. 20d. Jean Colombe. *Jesus and the Canaanite Woman,* Très Riches Heures of Jean, duc de Berry. Chantilly, Musée Condé, Ms. 65, fol. 164.

pleted two earlier. unfinished manuscripts, the splendid *Apocalypse* by Jean Bapteur and Perronet Lamy[14] and the famous Très Riches Heures of the duc de Berry, left incomplete when its original artists, the Limbourg brothers, succumbed to the plague in 1416.[15] No artist could remain uninfluenced by contact with the glorious painting in these two books, and some of Colombe's most successful miniatures were painted in this connection (Fig. 20d). Work on the *Apocalypse* dates from 1482, and an entry in the ducal accounts for 1485 apparently relates to the Très Riches Heures.[16] At much the same time, Colombe and his studio also produced one of their finest independent works, the immensely rich Hours of Louis of Laval, which contains 157 full-page miniatures and more than a thousand lesser illustrations.[17]

Colombe's work was by no means confined to the illus-

tration of books of hours and other religious texts. Some of his most spectacular creations appear in secular books designed for the libraries of well-to-do bibliophiles, and these include two copies of the *Romuléon* of Roberto della Porta,[18] and a fine copy of Josephus' *Jewish Antiquities*.[19] The most ambitious and exaggerated examples of his characteristic style are probably the very large illustrations in the *Histoire de la destruction de Troie*,[20] which is unfinished and must date from the very last years of his life. Much of the work on this manuscript was done by assistants,[21] but the sketches underlying these spectacular miniatures surely speak of the master himself. The scenes are set in wide and colorful landscapes or among massive and heavily sculpted architecture, usually seen in impossible perspectives. Vast crowds of "extras" are crammed into ridiculously small areas, sharing eagerly in the dramatic

Fig. 20e. Jean Colombe. *Achilles Meets Polyxena before the Tomb of Hector*, in HISTOIRE DE LA DESTRUCTION DE TROIE. Paris, Bibliothèque Nationale, Ms. nouv. acq. fr. 24920, fol. 27v.

Pl. xxv. Jean Colombe. *Jean de Meun Presenting His Translation to Philip IV of France*, in Boethius, DE CONSOLATIONE PHILOSOPHIAE. Harley Ms. 4335, fol. 10.

activities of the principal characters, who are shown decked out in extravagant costumes and with heavy-featured, often downright ugly, faces, exchanging theatrical gestures in the foreground (Fig. 20e). The manuscript has been slightly cropped at some time in its history, but there are traces of dark marbled grounds beyond the golden frames of the large miniatures, so the original impression must have been of a series of brightly colored panel paintings (or even tapestries) hung against darkened walls.

Beside the *Histoire de la destruction de Troie,* the Harley Boethius volumes seem small and modest examples of Jean Colombe's work. Closer examination reveals, however, that all the characteristic elements of his composition are to be seen in their miniatures. The interior scene of Jean de Meun presenting his translation to the king (Pl. xxv) shows up the erratic perspective and the unnaturally packed crowd of onlookers. A wonderfully ill-favored royal guard, with scornful expression and deliberately nonchalant stance, seems to cast his disapproval over the whole scene. This figure is repeated almost exactly in the *Troie* book (Fig. 20e), in the center of the composition. The frontispiece to Book II (Fig. 20b) includes a fine example of sculpted architecture and the frontispiece to Book III (Fig. 20c) is set in a delightful and characteristic, albeit somewhat less than naturalistic, Colombe landscape. The first miniature of the series, showing Boethius at work in his study (Fig. 20a), employs an unusual and remarkable device. Philosophy materializes not as the main subject of the miniature but as a figure in a picture hung on one of the study walls. The hook and chain by which the picture is suspended are quite clearly painted and the effect is further enhanced by the presence of a small window farther along the same wall. The frame of the window once again displays the inaccuracy of Colombe's ideas about perspective, but the embrasure is distinctly given depth in order to contrast with the adjacent picture and its protruding frame. This is the kind of spatial experiment which increasingly appealed to the decorators of the small, flat book pages at the end of the fifteenth century.

Although other members of the Colombe family were skilled exponents of the arts in other mediums, and although Jean Colombe himself reflects in his miniatures an awareness of architecture, sculpture, and panel painting, his own work seems to have been concentrated in the field of book decoration. He was not an artistic jack-of-all-trades like Fouquet, Bourdichon, and Perréal who, as court painters to the kings of France, were expected to turn their hands to whatever of a decorative nature might be required. Colombe seems to have made for himself a very successful career as a miniature painter and head of a substantial workshop in a center where patronage was not lacking, and his work was sufficiently appreciated to find copyists and imitators. The miniatures of the Harley Boethius were themselves adapted some twenty years after their first appearance in a Boethius manuscript made for a member of the Lallemant family of Bourges (Figs. 20f, 20g), who were to be important patrons of some of the illuminators of the early sixteenth century.[22]

Fig. 20f [TOP]. French Master. *Boethius in His Study*, in Boethius, DE CONSOLATIONE PHILOSOPHIAE. Paris, Bibliothèque Nationale, Ms. lat. 6643, fol. 1.

Fig. 20g [ABOVE]. French Master. *Boethius and Philosophy*, in Boethius, DE CONSOLATIONE PHILOSOPHIAE. Paris, Bibliothèque Nationale, Ms. lat. 6643, fol. 140.

BIBLIOGRAPHY London (British Museum) 1808–12, III, p. 137; Patch 1935, pls. 4–6; Saxl/Meier 1953, pp. 165–68; Wright 1972, pp. 125, 190, 443; Pächt 1974, p. 49 and n. 27; Schaefer 1977, pp. 137–50; Watson 1979, no. 808.

NOTES

1. Patch 1935.

2. For one of the most beautiful of all surviving copies of the *Roman de la Rose*, see Cat. 6.

3. Harley Ms. 4339, fol. 80v: "*Explicit . . . prima Mensis februarii. Anno domini Millesimo quadringentesimo septuagesimo sexto*," below which appears the name "*Roussellj*."

4. Rousseau wrote other manuscripts illuminated by Colombe and was also apparently the tenant of his house during one of the artist's absences in Savoy; see Schaefer 1977.

5. The three miniatures not illustrated here introduce Book I (Harley Ms. 4335, fol. 27; Patch 1935, pl. 6), Book IV (Harley Ms. 4338, fol. lv; ibid., pl. 5), and Book V (Harley Ms. 4339, fol. 2).

6. The connection was first recognized and published by Pächt 1974, p. 49 and n. 27.

7. Meiss 1967, pp. 35, 38–39.

8. Philippe, Michel, and Jean Colombe all receive useful entries in the *Dictionnaire* 1933–, IX, cols. 324–28. For Philippe, see also the first chapter of Pradel 1953.

9. Ibid., pp. 107–10. There is a useful summary in Longnon/Cazelles 1969, pp. 22–23. A full-scale study of Jean Colombe, which would incorporate the documents discovered by Jean-Yves Ribault and not as yet fully published, is a notable desideratum in the study of the period.

10. For members of the family, see Pradel 1953, pp. 109–11. Typical inscriptions are cited in Thomas 1973, p. 11.

11. New York 1982, no. 42. A typical Colombe book of hours is published by Schaefer 1973.

12. Munich, Bayerische Staatsbibliothek, Clm. 10103. The miniature of Jacques Coeur included in this manuscript cannot be a contemporary portrait of the treasurer, who fell from power in 1451. It may be in the nature of a memorial portrait made for a later member of his family.

13. New York 1982, no. 70.

14. Now in the library of the Escorial; see Gardet 1969.

15. Good color reproductions of Colombe's miniatures for the Très Riches Heures are included in Longnon/Cazelles 1969.

16. Ibid., p. 22.

17. Paris, Bibliothèque Nationale, Ms. lat. 920; Leroquais 1927, I, pp. 15–30, pls. LXXIII–LXXXV; see also Schaefer 1980, nos. 1–2, pp. 33–68. Louis of Laval-Châtillon, Grand Master of the Rivers and Forests of France, died in 1489.

18. Paris, Bibliothèque Nationale, Mss. fr. 364 and 265–267, respectively. The remarkable miniature of Hannibal crossing the Alps in a snowstorm from the latter copy is reproduced in Porcher 1960, p. 81.

19. Paris, Bibliothèque Nationale, Mss. fr. 405, 406.

20. Paris, Bibliothèque Nationale, Ms. nouv. acq. fr. 24920; Thomas 1973.

21. Colombe's assistants seem to have worked in styles very close to that of the head of the studio and it is not unreasonable to compare the practice to that of such later large-scale painters as Rubens or Van Dyck.

22. See Chenu 1946, and Orth 1980c.

21 Hours of Henry VII

Three detached leaves. *Job on His Dunghill, Pentecost, The Virgin Mary Receiving the Annunciation.* Tours, circa 1500.
Additional Ms. 35254, fols. T, U, V

MANUSCRIPT *Vellum, each leaf trimmed to approximately 24 × 17 cm.*

PROVENANCE *(?) Henry VII of England; John Malcolm of Poltalloch (d. 1893); bequeathed to the British Museum, Department of Prints and Drawings; transferred to the Department of Manuscripts, 1899.*

THESE three magnificent miniatures (Pl. XXVI, Figs. 21d, 21e), attributed on stylistic grounds to Jean Bourdichon of Tours, court painter successively to Louis XI, Charles VIII, Louis XII, and Francis I of France, come from a large-scale and richly decorated book of hours traditionally associated with the name of King Henry VII of England (d. 1509).[1] Henry is not popularly remembered as a great bibliophile, and only two of the manuscripts attributed to his ownership among those preserved in the British Library's Royal Collection are in the same class as the elaborate tomes ordered only a couple of decades earlier

by King Edward IV.[2] Nevertheless, he does have the distinction of being responsible for the appointment of the first royal librarian in England,[3] and his collection included deluxe work by the French printer Antoine Vérard.[4]

Surviving portions of the Hours of Henry VII, so far including eight miniatures, have gradually been identified in various public and private collections over the last ten years. At least a dozen more miniatures are still untraced and it is possible that some of them may come to light with a wider publication of the fragments already known. On the back of each miniature is a passage of text, accompanied by a distinctive panel of marginal decoration. This decoration, so far unparalleled in any other manuscript by Bourdichon's studio, connects the miniatures with a volume of miscellaneous and disordered text leaves in the Royal Collection (Fig. 21a). These text leaves are encased in a dark blue morocco binding attributable to a nineteenth-century British Museum binder, on the spine of which the name of Henry VII is inscribed. Many of the manuscripts in the Royal Collection have bindings labeled with the name of the king believed to have been their first owner, and the Henry VII inscription must certainly have

Fig. 21a [LEFT]. Jean Bourdichon. Text page with decorated border, in the Office of the Dead, Hours of Henry VII. London, British Library, Royal Ms. 2 D XL, fol. 22.

Fig. 21b [CENTER]. Jean Bourdichon. *Adoration of the Magi*, Hours of Henry VII. New York City, Collection B. H. Breslauer, detached leaf.

Fig. 21c [RIGHT]. Jean Bourdichon. *Presentation in the Temple*, Hours of Henry VII. New York City, Collection B. H. Breslauer, detached leaf.

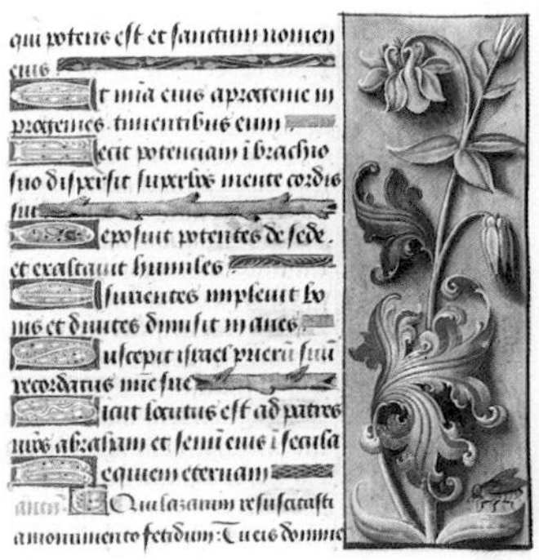

been copied from an earlier cover. There are no other signs of English royal ownership in the manuscript and the volume does not appear in the catalogue of the Royal Library drawn up in 1734, only twenty-three years before the collection was presented to the nation by George II.[5] However, the tradition of Henry's ownership was apparently strong and it is mentioned in descriptions of the book published before the date of the present binding.[6]

The British Library's three detached miniatures, *Job on His Dunghill* (Pl. xxvi), *Pentecost* (Fig. 21d), and *The Virgin Mary Receiving the Annunciation* (Fig. 21e), came into the British Museum with other loose miniatures, mostly Italian, from the collection of John Malcolm of Poltalloch, who also once owned the Sforza Hours (Cat. 15). We do not know where Malcolm acquired his miniatures,[7] and

the five other miniatures so far identified—*St. Luke,* the *Adoration of the Magi* (Fig. 21b), the *Presentation* (Fig. 21c), the *Flight into Egypt*, and *David and Bathsheba*—have equally obscure histories.[8] More helpful are two tiny fragments cut from text pages of the book, one in the Bagford Collection in the British Library,[9] the other in the Pepys Collection at Magdalene College, Cambridge.[10] Both these collections were formed during the late seventeenth century, which suggests that the manuscript was in England when it was broken up and that this took place shortly before 1700.

One other detached miniature has been tentatively connected with the Hours of Henry VII (Fig. 21f), suggesting an alternative, or perhaps merely earlier, royal owner. It shows Louis XII of France with four patrons—St.

Fig. 21d. Jean Bourdichon. *Pentecost*, fol. u.

Pl. XXVI. Jean Bourdichon. *Job on His Dunghill*, Hours of Henry VII. Add. Ms. 35254, fol. T, detached leaf.

Michael, Charlemagne, Louis IX, and St. Denis—and bears an inscription to the effect that it was painted when Louis was thirty-six years old.[11] As he was born on June 27, 1462, the miniature can be dated 1498–99. The composition is very similar to Bourdichon's miniature of Anne of Brittany and her patrons in his masterpiece, the Hours of Anne of Brittany.[12] The dimensions of the Louis XII leaf are apparently the same as those of the other detached leaves from the Hours of Henry VII. However, this leaf is at present lost to sight, and it is impossible to decide for certain, merely on the strength of rather old reproductions, whether or not it has some connection with the manuscript under discussion here.[13]

Jean Bourdichon was court painter to the kings of France from the early 1480s until his death, which took place sometime between June 1520 and July 1521.[14] He was, like Jean Fouquet, a native of Tours, where he had modest property, and his style is clearly influenced by that of the older artist, who was very probably his master. Bourdichon first appears in the French royal accounts about the time of Fouquet's death (c. 1481), undertaking work for which Fouquet himself might well have been responsible in earlier years. Like Fouquet, he was versatile. Written sources record many works now lost and indeed in their own time often ephemeral, including banners and heraldic devices for specific state occasions. He painted statues, provided illustrations, maps, and portraits, and is last heard of receiving payment for the decoration of tents for the meeting between Henry VIII of England and Francis I of France at the Field of the Cloth of Gold (1520). A series

Fig. 21e. Jean Bourdichon. *The Virgin Mary Receiving the Annunciation*, fol. v.

Fig. 21f [RIGHT]. Jean Bourdichon. *Louis XII of France with His Patrons*. Present whereabouts unknown.

Fig. 21g [FAR RIGHT]. Jean Bourdichon. *Adoration of the Magi*, Book of Hours. London, British Library, Harley Ms. 2877, fol. 55v.

of designs for English royal pavilions, possibly intended for the same occasion, provides a rare glimpse of the kind of work required of a court painter of the time.[15]

Because so much of his large-scale work was ephemeral, it is mainly as an illuminator that Bourdichon is recognized and assessed by modern scholarship, and this recognition and assessment are comparatively recent in date. It is less than a century since the document which identified him as the artist of the already famous Hours of Anne of Brittany was discovered, providing a touchstone for his personal style and permitting the attribution to him and to his workshop of a large number of manuscripts. It is clear from the variable quality of the work in these manuscripts that he had pupils, assistants, and imitators, and that the production of manuscripts, especially books of hours, was a flourishing business. Some of the books made for anonymous owners are of mediocre artistic quality, but the more ambitious works, usually commissioned by members of the royal family and their immediate circle, betray a master's touch, though the unevenness of the work does suggest that he was sometimes the director rather than the craftsman responsible for individual miniatures.

The Hours of Anne of Brittany, for which payment was authorized in 1508, remains Bourdichon's most famous work.[16] It is a true *tour de force*, containing forty-nine large miniatures, a series of calendar illustrations, and more than three hundred "portraits" of flowers and plants, each one labeled with its name in French. Less ambitious, but produced much earlier in his career, are the excellent miniatures in the Hours of Charles of Angoulême[17] and the Hours of Charles VIII.[18] A small-scale hours in the British Library's Harley collection (Fig. 21g), probably made during the 1490s and without identifying marks to connect it with a specific owner, may also be classed among the best of Bourdichon's work.[19] Finest of all are the miniatures in

the Hours of Frederick III of Aragon, who died in exile in Tours in 1504.[20] Conceived on a minute scale and painted on leaves of finest vellum, subsequently laid down onto the pages of the book and provided with elaborate marginal decoration, these little paintings show up the luminosity of the Bourdichon style at its very best.

The miniatures from the Hours of Henry VII are very close in scale, style, and design to the miniatures in the Hours of Anne of Brittany. Whoever the original owner may have been, the book cannot be far removed in date from the more celebrated manuscript. Its miniatures are conceived as small-scale pictures, framed in gold and hung against a dark surface. A preoccupation with half-length figures suggests some influence from contemporary Flemish illumination, as does the combination of real and imaginary plants in the decoration of the borders.[21] The overall impression is of a greater restraint than is seen in the French queen's extremely opulent manuscript, and this perhaps indicates a slightly earlier date for the British Library miniatures. These pages, especially the superb portrayal of the young Virgin Mary listening with humbly downcast eyes to the angel's message (Fig. 21e), deserve to be ranked with the very best French work of their period.

BIBLIOGRAPHY London (British Museum) 1901, p. 224; London (British Museum) 1914–30, VI, pl. 15a; MacGibbon 1933, pp. 104, 160; Millar 1933, no. 61; Backhouse 1973a, pp. 95–102; Backhouse 1979, pl. 65.

NOTES

1. Backhouse 1973a. Full details of the texts of the manuscript are given in this article. The three exhibited miniatures originally introduced the Office of the Dead, the Hours of the Holy Ghost, and Matins of the Hours of the Virgin.

2. A brief history of the royal manuscripts is given in the introduction to Warner/Gilson 1921, pp. xi–xxxii. The catalogue's index credits Henry VII with the direct ownership of about twenty volumes, but many of these were actually made long before his time. Only two volumes, Royal Ms. 16 F II (*Poèmes* by Charles d'Orléans) and Royal Ms. 19 C VIII (*Imaginacion de vraye noblesse*) really bear the stamp of a custom-made, deluxe, contemporary library book.

3. Warner/Gilson 1921, p. xiii.

4. Several printed volumes in the British Library, published in Paris by Antoine Vérard and richly illuminated, have the name of Henry VII substituted by hand for that of Charles VIII of France in their dedications. They include a copy of Boethius, *De consolatione philosophiae,* printed in 1494; reproduced in Backhouse 1979, pl. 70.

5. Casley 1734.

6. Dibdin 1817, p. clix; Humphreys 1859, p. clix.

7. The miniatures are not included among the illuminated leaves detailed in Appendix II of the second edition of Robinson 1876.

8. *St. Luke* is in Edinburgh, National Library of Scotland, Ms. 8999; see Edinburgh 1965, pl. 15, and Backhouse 1973a, pl. XLI. The *Adoration of the Magi,* once in private hands in England, was sold at Christie's, London, July 11, 1974, lot 6. The existence of the *Presentation* was called to my attention by H. P. Kraus of New York (letter, March 20, 1974). Both are now in the Collection of B. H. Breslauer in New York City. I am very grateful to Mr. Breslauer for permission to reproduce his photograph of it. For the *Flight into Egypt,* see Backhouse 1973a, pl. XXXVIII; it was also sold at Christie's, July 11, 1974, lot 7. The *David and Bathsheba,* sold at Sotheby's, London, July 8, 1974, lot 25, is reproduced in Backhouse 1973a, pl. XLII. These two leaves are also now in the same collection in New York.

9. Harley Ms. 5966, fol. 9; Wright 1972, p. 59.

10. James 1923, p. 115.

11. MacGibbon 1933, p. 104, first connected the Louis XII miniature with the three detached miniatures in the British Library.

12. Paris, Bibliothèque Nationale, Ms. lat. 9474, fol. 3; Harthan 1977, pl. 127.

13. The miniature was once in the collection of William Beckford of Fonthill; it was sold from Lord Taunton's collection, Sotheby's, London, July 14, 1920, lot 67 (ill.). It is also reproduced in Laborde 1923, pl. VII, from which our illustration is taken.

14. The outline of Bourdichon's life and career given here is based mainly on information in MacGibbon 1933, who publishes the texts of thirty-five documents relating to the painter; see also, Limousin 1954, for a large number of reproductions of works by and relating to Bourdichon.

15. British Library, Cotton Ms. Augustus III, fols. 11, 18, 19; fol. 18 is reproduced in color in Marks/Payne 1978, no. 67. The artist is unidentified.

16. Leroquais 1927, I, pp. 298–305. All the miniatures in the manuscript are reproduced, on a reduced scale, in black and white, in Omont 1906b; thirty-one of them appear in color in Mâle 1946.

17. Paris, Bibliothèque Nationale, Ms. lat. 1173; Leroquais 1927, I, pp. 104–08, pl. XCIII.

18. Paris, Bibliothèque Nationale, Ms. lat. 1370; ibid., pp. 189–92, pls. XCVI–XCVIII.

19. Millar 1914–20, pp. 32–35, pls. 40, 41, 43, 45; Limousin 1954, p. 71, figs. 106–09.

20. Paris, Bibliothèque Nationale, Ms. lat. 10532; Leroquais 1927, I, pp. 328–32, pls. CX–CXIV.

21. The Master of the Hortulus Animae, the Master of James IV of Scotland, and the Master of the Prayer Books of c. 1500 all display a taste for half-length figures. The design of the borders in the Hours of Henry VII is also related to Flemish work, in which a similar mixture of naturalistic flowers and conventionalized foliage frequently appears. These borders are cautiously described as "in Flemish style" in Warner/Gilson 1921, p. 62, and the miniatures themselves as Flemish in London (British Museum) 1901, p. 224.

22 Pierre Sala, *Emblesmes et devises d'amour*

Lyons, circa 1500. Stowe Ms. 955

MANUSCRIPT *Purple-stained vellum, 21 original leaves; 13 × 10 cm. A transcript of the poems, on paper and probably dating from the eighteenth century, inserted into the binding after the original text. An extract from an unidentified early-nineteenth-century catalogue, laid down at the end of the book (fol. 35), identifies one previous owner as Field Marshal Junot, Duke of Abrantes.*

BINDING *Remains of original binding of dark olive velvet, with traces of silk ties.*

CARRYING CASE *Wood covered with leather, colored with gold, green, and red paint and carved with a design of flowers and foliage and the initials M and P; four metal rings on each side.*

PROVENANCE *Marguerite Bullioud, later the wife of Pierre Sala; (?) Eléonore de Guilhens, Sala's great-niece; Field Marshal Andoche Alexandre Junot, Duke of Abrantes (d. 1813); Richard Temple-Nugent-Brydges-Chandos, 1st Duke of Buckingham and Chandos (d. 1839); Stowe Collection; purchased by Bertram, 4th Earl of Ashburnham, 1849; bought by the British Government, 1883, and transferred to the British Museum.*

PIERRE Sala's little book of love poems is the most personal, indeed the most intimate, of all the French Renaissance manuscripts in the collections of the British Library. Sala, described in a later inscription (fol. 17v) as "*mestre dotel de ches le roy*," was associated for most of his life with the city of Lyons, where he was born into a respectable bourgeois family, probably not long before 1457.[1] He entered the royal service perhaps as early as 1480, during the reign of Louis XI, and over the next three or four decades held various positions, including that of *panetier* to Charles VIII's infant son, the Dauphin Charles Orland (1492–1495). The manuscript, which was probably made about 1500, was designed as a gift to the poet's ladylove, whose name was Marguerite Bullioud. In a lengthy preamble addressed to her, Sala confesses that he has desired to love, serve, and honor her since their childhood and tells her that the words and pictures of his gift are certain to keep him always in her memory.[2] A wooden carrying case for the little volume is covered with decorated leather colored green, red, and gold and is fitted with rings so that it could be hung at the girdle of Marguerite's dress (Fig. 22a).[3] Both manuscript and case are lavishly adorned with the initials of Pierre and Marguerite, frequently formed from combinations of what appears to be a pair of dividers.

Marguerite Bullioud was, like Sala himself, a native of Lyons. Her sister, Sibylle, was a favorite among Anne of Brittany's maids of honor and her brother, Symphorien, was bishop successively of Glandève, Bazas, and Soissons, and also served as Louis XII's legate to Pope Julius II. Marguerite's first husband, Antoine Buatier, the king's treasurer, died before December 9, 1506 and eventually, more than a decade later, she did finally marry Sala, when both were in late middle life.[4] The devotion expressed in the preamble to the poems was no doubt already of long standing when the poems were offered, and Pierre Sala probably saw himself in the guise of a troubadour of old, faithfully honoring his unattainable lady.

The manuscript is largely written in gold ink on vellum stained a reddish purple, imitating splendid books of a far earlier period.[5] Most of the poems are inscribed on placards "hung" against the surface of the page, and some of the written surfaces are colored white or gold, necessitating the use of a dark-red ink matching the vellum color. The preamble (fols. 1–4v) is followed by a sequence of twelve four-line poems accompanied by lively emblematic miniatures (fols. 5v–16; Figs. 21b–e). The poems are in French with the exception of the third (fol. 7v), which is in Spanish. The miniatures, which are of fine although not outstanding quality, have been associated with the work of an anonymous artist known as the Master of the Clubfeet, who designed woodcut illustrations for books printed in Lyons in the 1490s.[6] At the end of the manuscript (fol. 17) is a miniature which ranks with the finest masterpieces of the period, a portrait of Pierre Sala himself, attributed to

Fig. 22a. Carrying case of Stowe Ms. 955.

Jean Perréal, otherwise known as Jean de Paris (Pl. XXVII), and accompanied, above and below, by the motto *"Lesses le venir."* The facing page is inscribed, in mirror writing, *"Reguardez en pytye / votre loyal amy / qui na Jour ne demy / Bien pour votre amytye."*[7]

Jean Perréal's name was honored by contemporary French writers celebrating the great painters of the late fifteenth and early sixteenth centuries.[8] Concrete identification of his work has, however, been a matter of intense controversy, though his life and career are very well documented.[9] He seems to have been born about 1455 and became court painter successively to Charles VIII, Louis XII, and Francis I. For most of his life he was closely associated with the city of Lyons, where several times between 1485 and 1517 he provided schemes for the pageantry at state entries, and also on numerous occasions supervised building works and fortifications. He visited Italy in 1499, probably in the entourage of Louis XII, and was there again in 1502 and 1509. In 1501–02 he made designs for the tombs of Anne of Brittany's parents, sculpted by Michel Colombe for the cathedral of Nantes,[10] and was again associated with Colombe between 1509 and 1512 when he worked on the tombs ordered for Brou by Margaret of Austria. In 1514 he organized the funeral of Anne of Brittany and made her funeral effigy,[11] and subsequently joined the embassy sent to England by Louis XII to arrange for his marriage to Henry VIII's younger sister, Princess Mary. There he was charged with painting a portrait of the bride and with overseeing the French fashions for her trousseau.[12] His latter years were spent mainly in Lyons, where he died, after a long and varied career, in 1530.

The paintings for which Perréal was so highly regarded in his own time are not clearly identified and have exercised the imagination of generations of scholars. Many

Fig. 22b [LEFT]. Lyons Master. *Pierre Sala Presents His Heart to a Marguerite*, fols. 5v–6.

Fig. 22c [BOTTOM LEFT]. Lyons Master. *Blind Man's Buff*, fols. 6v–7.

writers have agreed that the miniature of Pierre Sala should be attributed to him, because it is known that the two men were closely acquainted,[13] but only comparatively recently has another single miniature come to light which, as an illustration for a book composed by Perréal himself, can logically be judged his work.[14] This provides a firmer foundation for the further attribution to him of a number of outstanding portraits and portrait drawings, establishing him as a vital force in the development of a form of painting which was to have a distinguished history in France during the remainder of the sixteenth century.

Pierre Sala, the subject of our miniature, is almost equally well documented. He was by inclination a poet and an antiquarian, with a considerable body of written work to his credit. He returned to live in Lyons early in the reign of Francis I, but retained the royal favor and was visited at his home by Francis in 1522. Much of his writing dates

from these later years of retirement in Lyons,[15] and many of the surviving manuscripts were apparently made, like the love poems, for presentation to friends and patrons, often being written out by Sala himself.[16] Two volumes, very like the Stowe manuscript in design though on a slightly larger scale, are illustrated collections of animal fables made for Francis I's mother, Louise of Savoy (Fig. 22f).[17]

The love poems addressed to Marguerite seem from the costumes shown in their illustrations to date from about 1500. Sala is portrayed, perhaps a little flatteringly, as a fairly young man. Perréal's miniature is of considerable interest and importance for the history of the portrait miniature as a separate art form, a development of early-sixteenth-century painting which was in time to become particularly fashionable in England with the work of Holbein and Hilliard. It is widely appreciated that the tech-

Fig. 22d [LEFT]. Lyons Master. *A Wise Man and a Fool, Each Painting a Likeness of the Other*, fols. 9v–9*.

Fig. 22e [BOTTOM LEFT]. Lyons Master. *A Man Chopping down the Tree that Supports Him*, fols. 14v–15.

Pl. XXVII. Jean Perréal. *Portrait of Pierre Sala*, in Pierre Sala, EMBLESMES ET DEVISES D'AMOUR. Stowe Ms. 955, fols. 16v–17.

Fig. 22f [LEFT]. Lyons Master. *The Fable of the Horse and the Donkey*, in a collection of animal fables. London, British Library, Add. Ms. 59677, fols. 16v–17.

Fig. 22g [RIGHT]. Lyons Master. *Valtan Presenting Charles VIII with a Copy of His Commentary*, in Pierre Louis de Valtan, COMMENTARY ON THE APOSTLES' CREED. London, British Library, Add. Ms. 35320, fol. 2v.

niques adopted by the early portrait miniature painters were basically those of contemporary manuscript illuminators.[18] Portraits within manuscripts already had a long history. In the sense of representations rather than likenesses, they had been a feature of book illustration for many centuries. True likenesses are found with increasing frequency from the late fourteenth century onward, the many recognizable miniatures of Charles V and his brother Jean de Berry providing excellent and early examples.[19] Some of the portrait faces in fifteenth-century miniatures are so good that one suspects they may have been contributed by specialists in the field. The portrait head of John, Duke of Bedford, in the Bedford Hours is a possible example.[20] Another, very nearly contemporary with Sala's manuscript, is the portrait head of Pierre Louis de Valtan in the miniature which shows him presenting Charles VIII with a copy of his work on the Apostles' Creed (Fig. 22g).[21] The Sala manuscript provides specific evidence of the practice in its first miniature, where the poet is depicted symbolically placing his heart within the petals of an out-size marguerite (Fig. 22b). All the details of the little scene are complete except for the poet's face, which is represented only by a very crude ink outline. It seems clear that the painter of the likeness at the end of the manuscript was expected to provide a small-scale version of it to complete the miniature but never did so.[22]

The Perréal likeness of Sala is, however, to be distinguished from other, earlier portraits in manuscripts because of a clear difference in intention. The portraits mentioned in the preceding paragraph appear within the context of devotional or presentation miniatures, or are occasionally provided as memorials to the dead.[23] The Sala is a straightforward portrait of a living person, deliberately designed to keep that person continually before the eye of the lady for whom it was painted. Who first took the step which detached such a portrait from between the covers of a book and translated it into a separate work of art, we do not know.[24] There does seem very good reason to regard the line of development of the portrait miniature in France as playing a vitally significant role in the history of the portrait miniature as a whole.[25]

BIBLIOGRAPHY London (British Museum) 1895–96, I, pp. 638–39; Parry 1908–09; Durrieu 1919, p. 152; Blum/Lauer 1930, pl. 69(iii); Millar 1933, no. 65; Fabia 1934, pp. 64–69; Perls 1935; Sterling 1938, p. 143, fig. 182; Goldblatt 1949, pp. 97–98; Ring 1949a, no. 331; Ring 1950, pp. 258–59; Huillet d'Istria 1952; Muir 1958, pp. 10–11; Sterling 1963, p. 10 and n. 14.

NOTES

1. For full details of Sala's life and career, see Fabia 1934.

2. The text of the manuscript is printed in Parry 1908–09.

3. For comparable leatherwork, see Gall 1965, especially pls. 77, 105, 108.

4. Marguerite Bullioud's life and connections are outlined in Fabia 1934, pp. 37–41.

5. The use of gold or silver ink on purple-dyed vellum for anything from a single page to an entire book was a feature of particularly fine copies of biblical texts from Early Christian times into the early Middle Ages. An outstanding example is the Vienna Genesis, written and illuminated in the sixth century (Vienna, Österreichische Nationalbibliothek, Cod. theol. gr. 31). The

practice was sometimes extended to other important texts, such as the English Newminster Charter of 966 (British Library, Cotton Ms. Vespasian A VIII). The idea was revived in Renaissance Italy (for an example, see Salmi 1957, pl. xliii) and it was probably from an Italian source that Sala adopted it.

6. Huillet d'Istria 1952.

7. The motto has only very recently been discerned, as the result of an idle examination of the leaf under oblique light. It appears in extended form, on the pastedown inside the front cover of the volume, as *"Lessez le venir a la trappe."* This may perhaps be loosely translated as "Let him fall into the snare." The verses opposite the miniature (fol. 16v) may be rendered as "Look with pity on your loyal friend, who for your love knows not a day, or even half a day, of peace." Both sentiments are in full accord with the general feeling of old-fashioned romance implicit in the entire volume. I am very grateful to my colleague, T. A. J. Burnett, for his help with Sala's texts.

8. A famous verse by Jean Lemaire de Belges, in which Perréal's name appears in company with those of Leonardo, Gentile Bellini, Perugino, and Jean Hey, occurs in the *Plainte du désiré sur la mort de Louis de Luxembourg . . .* 1503, published in Lyons in 1509.

9. Perréal's career is outlined and the earlier part of the immense bibliography is cited in Audin/Vial 1918–19, II, pp. 100–03; and Thieme/Becker 1907–50, XXXVI, pp. 433–35.

10. See Cat. 20, n. 8.

11. The funeral of Anne of Brittany was commemorated in a number of illuminated descriptive volumes made for various members of the court circle; see Pächt 1977, pp. 16–19, for a survey of surviving copies.

12. Detailed inventories of Mary's trousseau survive, the finest being a contemporary fair copy purchased by the British Library in 1978 and numbered Egerton Ms. 3800. Roughly two-thirds of her gowns are described as being in the French fashion. About a third were English, and a few followed the fashion of Milan.

13. Sala dedicated a copy of his *Livre d'amitié* (Paris, Bibliothèque Nationale, Ms. lat. 14942) to Perréal. A second copy of the same work (Lyons, Bibliothèque de la Ville, Ms. 853) is dedicated to Claude Laurencin, husband of Marguerite Bullioud's sister, Sibylle; see Guigue 1884.

14. Sterling 1963. The miniature, a frontispiece long missing from Perréal's *La Complainte de nature à l'alchimiste errant* (Paris, Bibliothèque Sainte-Geneviève, Ms. 3220), is now in the Wildenstein Collection at the Musée Marmottan in Paris.

15. Pierre Sala's house, *"la Maison de l'Antiquaille,"* and its surroundings are depicted in two of his manuscripts: Vienna, Österreichische Nationalbibliothek, Cod. 2618, fol. 1, reproduced in Pächt 1977, pl. 331; and Paris, Bibliothèque Nationale, Ms. fr. 10420, fol. 1v, reproduced in Fabia 1934, opposite p. 292.

16. A recent list of the manuscripts of Sala's works is given in Muir 1958, pp. 10–11. Manuscript "C" of *Tristan,* formerly Ms. 3637 in the library of the famous nineteenth-century collector Sir Thomas Phillipps, is now in the Bodmer Collection in Geneva. To Muir's list may be added a second volume of animal fables, now British Library, Add. Ms. 59677 (Fig. 22f); and two further copies of the *Epistre* to Cardinal François de Tournon, one in the British Library, Add. Ms. 17377, and the other Cod. 2618 in Vienna, cited in n. 15 above. The British Library's Add. Ms. 59677 includes a colophon implying that Sala was himself the scribe, and it seems likely that this is true of many of his manu-

scripts, including the present one, which includes numerous corrections attributable to the author.

17. An allusion in the text to Francis I's absence in Spain dates the collection of *Fables* to the period of his captivity in Madrid, September 1525 to March 1526, at which time Louise as Regent was holding court in Lyons.

18. For recent work on the technical aspects of portrait miniature painting, see the first chapter in Murdoch/Murrell/Noon/Strong 1981.

19. Sherman 1969, and Meiss 1967, pp. 68–94.

20. British Library, Add. Ms. 18850, fol. 256v.

21. Pierre Louis de Valtan, a Catalan by birth, was archdeacon of Angers and served Louis XII as an envoy to Spain in 1500. During Charles VIII's reign he held several posts in the royal service and was also the author of other religious commentaries. He was bishop of Rieux between 1501 and 1518. The British Library manuscript of his commentary on the Creed must date from before the death of Charles VIII in 1498. A second and slightly more elaborate copy of the same work, made for presentation to Isabella of Castile at the time of the embassy in 1500, was in the Huth Collection; sold at Sotheby's, London, July 10, 1919, lot 7656.

22. Another early-sixteenth-century miniature including a portrait head is worthy of note: the portrait of Louis de Chandio riding in a triumphal car in François du Moulin's *Le fort Chandio* (Paris, Bibliothèque Nationale, Ms. fr. 1194, fols. 6–7, reproduced in Couderc 1910, pl. clv). The head is certainly the work of a specialist and is very close to those of the heroes of Marignano in Book II of the *Commentaires de la guerre gallique* in Paris (Bibliothèque Nationale, Ms. fr. 13429; see Cat. 24), which can be attributed to Clouet. Beneath the miniature is a note by du Moulin: "Pardonnez au paintre que a ici mys leffigie de Loys de Chandio Car il na heu le loysir de myeulx faire. Aussi ce nest que sur papier que ne peut souffrir bonne paincture." This is in itself a most interesting comment on the miniaturist's view of his raw materials—vellum remained the usual support for independent miniature portraits until late in the seventeenth century. I am most grateful to Myra Orth for sharing with me her notes and comments on this manuscript.

23. Portraits which may be regarded as memorials include that of Louis of Anjou (Paris, Bibliothèque Nationale, Ms. lat. 1156A, fol. 61); reproduced in Couderc 1910, pl. lxviii.

24. An astonishing array of miniature portraits, approaching the scope of a Victorian family album, was kept between the covers of a book by Catherine de' Medici, Queen of France. The host manuscript is a small book of hours (Paris, Bibliothèque Nationale, Ms. lat. nouv. acq. 82) originally made for Francis I. Portraits of Francis himself and of his immediate family were apparently painted into it during his own reign; additions extend to the reign of Henry III (1574–89). The present binding, which bears the initials of Henry II and Catherine, is provided with rings so that it could be hung from a girdle; see Leroquais 1927, II, pp. 230–34 and pl. cxxiii.

25. For further stages in this immensely complex story, where much work remains to be done, see in particular Mellen 1971. The present entry does not discuss the relationship between the development of the portrait miniature and the fashion for commemorative medals, although a specific instance of such a relationship, in an Italian context, is discussed in Cat. 14.

23 Tilliot Hours

Use of Rome; Loire school, circa 1500. Yates Thompson Ms. 5

MANUSCRIPT *Vellum, 126 leaves; 18.5 × 11.5 cm. Ownership inscription, dated 1710, by Jean Bénigne Lucotte du Tilliot on fol. 1; note concerning acquisition of the manuscript at the Tilliot sale on previous, unnumbered leaf.*

BINDING *Sealskin, with 2 metal clasps; nineteenth century. Yates Thompson bookplate on inside front cover.*

PROVENANCE *Jean Bénigne Lucotte, Seigneur du Tilliot, 1710; Frédéric Spitzer; Spitzer sale, Chevallier, Paris, June 14, 1895, lot 3017; purchased by Henry Yates Thompson; presented to the British Museum in 1941 by the executors of Mrs. Yates Thompson, in accordance with her wishes.*

THE miniatures in the Tilliot Hours (Pls. XXVII, XXIX, Figs. 23a, 23c, 23d) were produced by an illuminator who ranks with Colombe and Bourdichon among the leading members of the Loire school and is a worthy follower of Fouquet, whose influence is implicit in all his work. An increasing number of manuscripts, largely luxury books of hours such as the present one, is gradually being associated with his style and it is clear that we are dealing with an important and popular artist who attracted a significant clientele.[1] The study of this material has not, however, enjoyed the same impetus as the study of the work of other members of the Loire school, largely because no scholar has so far managed to connect it convincingly with a particular name.

Familiarity is said to breed contempt, and it is all too easy to forget how very slight may be the evidence upon which the identification of the work of a named artist of this period rests. Both Fouquet and Colombe have the unusual advantage of being named in notes written into manuscripts on which they worked. These notes, made not long after the work had been completed and within a circle where reliable information was available,[2] provide a solid foundation upon which further evidence, both documentary and stylistic, can be built up to form the comparatively detailed biographical and critical structure available today. The identification of Bourdichon rests upon the quite fortuitous survival of the document recording payments to him in connection with the Hours of Anne

Fig. 23a [RIGHT]. Loire Master. *The Nativity*, fol. 41v.

Fig. 23b [FAR RIGHT]. Loire Master. *The Nativity*, Great Book of Hours of Henry VIII. New York, The Pierpont Morgan Library, Heinemann Collection, H.8, fol. 51v.

175

of Brittany,[3] and the identification of Perréal still depends largely on the supposition that he is likely to have painted the frontispiece for his own book.[4] The artist of the Tilliot Hours has as yet offered no clue at all. It is suggested that he may have been Jean Poyet, a painter who worked for Anne of Brittany in the mid-1490s.[5] Poyet is described as living in Tours and was probably the son of Mathurin Poyet, an exact contemporary of Fouquet and, like him, styled *peintre du roy* in 1475.[6] However, no documentary evidence which would extend Jean Poyet's career into the sixteenth century has yet come to light[7] and, while this may very well be due to the fact that relevant archives have simply not survived the intervening centuries, the attribution to him of the fine body of work which includes the Tilliot Hours should at best be regarded as "not proven."

The manuscripts themselves seem certainly to range in date over a period which includes the early years of the sixteenth century. The Tilliot Hours itself was at one time thought to have been made as late as 1530, though this view is now long superseded.[8] Closely dated work in the style of the group does in fact exist in the two copies of Pierre Louis de Valtan's commentary on the Apostles' Creed (Fig. 22g), which were made as presentation volumes, one before 1498 (Fig. 23e) and the other in 1500.[9] The miniatures of the Apostles in these two manuscripts bear a marked resemblance to the miniatures in the Tilliot Hours and its relatives. A fine Missal of Tours Use, apparently made for Guillaume Lallemant, canon and archdeacon at Tours and canon in his own hometown of Bourges, includes miniatures by a second hand, which is

Fig. 23c [LEFT]. Loire Master. *The Journey of the Magi* and *The Adoration of the Magi*, fol. 48v.

Fig. 23d [RIGHT]. Loire Master. *Job on His Dunghill, Visited by His Friends*, fol. 75v.

Pl. XXVIII [LEFT]. Loire Master. *Circumcision*, Tilliot Hours. Yates Thompson Ms. 5, fol. 45.

Pl. XXIX [RIGHT]. Loire Master. *Parable of Dives and Lazarus*, Tilliot Hours. Yates Thompson Ms. 5, fol. 70v.

Fig. 23e [TOP LEFT]. Loire Master. *St. Bartholomew*, in Pierre Louis de Valtan, COMMENTARY ON THE APOSTLES' CREED. London, British Library, Add. Ms. 35320, fol. 20v.

Fig. 23f [LEFT]. Loire Master. *Raising of Lazarus*, Lallemant Hours. London, British Library, Add. Ms. 39641, fol. 19v.

Fig. 23g [ABOVE]. Loire Master. *St. Matthew* and *The Journey of the Magi*, Great Book of Hours of Henry VIII. New York, The Pierpont Morgan Library, Heinemann Collection, H.8, fol. 10v.

found elsewhere decorating an hours printed for Guillaume Eustace about 1497.[10] The group also includes another manuscript made for the Lallemant family, an extremely attractive book of hours of which one fragment is in the British Library (Fig. 23f),[11] which suggests that the style seen in the Tilliot Hours is to be associated as much with Bourges as with Tours.

The Tilliot Hours contains thirteen full-page miniatures and thirty small ones, the majority of the latter devoted to illustrating the Suffrages of the Saints toward the end of the book. Eight of the large miniatures introduce the eight hours of the Little Office of the Virgin and these, with the exception of the last (fol. 60), which depicts the death of the Virgin, are all of subjects from the Christmas story.[12] Each is divided into two registers, the area above the text panel being devoted to the main subject and the smaller panel below containing a subsidiary scene. The lesser scenes are mainly the more human and homely ones, perhaps, like Fouquet's blacksmith's wife (Fig. 19b), reflecting episodes from contemporary religious drama.[13] Thus the *Nativity* (Fig. 23a) is accompanied by a smaller miniature showing Mary and Joseph being turned away from the main door of the inn.[14] The *Circumcision* (Pl. XXVIII), which is itself a fairly uncommon scene, has below it a picture of the Holy Child, accompanied by his parents, being carried from the stable on the way to the ceremony. For the theme of the Adoration of the Magi the arrangement is reversed. The Three Kings kneel before the Virgin and Child below the text panel, and the larger space is given up to their journey (Fig. 23c).[15]

Two miniatures are devoted to the Office of the Dead. The first (Pl. XXIX) depicts the parable of Dives and Lazarus in the setting of a contemporary cityscape, its buildings those of late-fifteenth-century Touraine. Lazarus, approaching the rich man's table, sounds the wooden clappers of the unclean. In the second (Fig. 23d), Job on his dunghill is visited by his friends, while the lesser panel shows his defenseless figure belabored by scaly demons. The three remaining large miniatures introduce the Passion narrative, the Hours of the Cross, and the Penitential Psalms.[16]

All the miniatures in the Tilliot Hours seem to be the work of a single hand. The manuscript's closest relative, the superb so-called "Great Book of Hours of Henry VIII" (Figs. 23b, 23g), also seems from available reproductions to be all of a piece and probably attributable to the same illuminator.[17] The growing number of other manuscripts associated with the group includes several styles, some of which may be due to the development of the central artist and some to the involvement of associates.[18] In the various attempts which have been made over the years to link these books with other work of the time, many known artists have been cited. The Henry VIII Hours was once attributed to Bourdichon.[19] Henry Yates Thompson, although his printed catalogue gave a date as late as 1530, came closer to the truth in a personal note, where he related the Tilliot Hours to the Diurnal of René of Lorraine, a connection which deserves to be much

more vigorously investigated.[20] External influences visibly include Fouquet and probably also Colombe while, as in the case of Bourdichon, there seem to be quite distinct traces of familiarity with contemporary Flemish manuscript work.[21] The manuscripts of the Tilliot Hours group also include miniatures by artists quite distinct from the central hand. One of these, whose work is found in the Lallemant Missal, has already been mentioned.[22] Another appears in the Hours of Mary, Queen of France, in the Bibliothèque Municipale of Lyons.[23] The miniature in question, which accompanies devotions to St. Jerome, seems to be an addition to the original scheme of this book, but details of the composition, and especially of its landscape, reveal strong influence from the manuscript's earlier artist. As the *St. Jerome* miniature and its accompanying floral border are very closely related to illuminations of the Master of Claude of France and his group, the folio provides an important link between fashionable workshops of the two centuries.[24]

Absence of a name for the illuminator responsible for this fine body of works means that his achievement is assessed almost entirely in relation to manuscripts identified on stylistic grounds. It is not possible to search written records for references to ceremonial or lost, large-scale works which he may have carried out. The picture has, however, been enlarged recently by recognition of the connection between the miniatures and a series of fine drawings of Old Testament subjects which are clearly in the same style.[25] There is no way of telling for what kind of work these drawings were intended, but they do indicate that the artist, like Fouquet, Bourdichon, and Perréal, was probably more than just a book painter.

The identity of the original owner of the Tilliot Hours is as obscure as the identity of its illuminator. The calendar, Litany, and Memorials include names which suggest a connection with central France and especially with Lyons, and these probably reflect the local preoccupations of the patron.[26] The name which the manuscript now bears is that of its owner in the early eighteenth century, Jean Bénigne Lucotte, Seigneur du Tilliot (1668–1750), a celebrated collector of *objets d'art* and a devoted antiquarian.[27]

BIBLIOGRAPHY James 1898, pp. 88–93; Thompson 1907–18, VII, pls. XXXVI, XXXVII; Turner 1965, pl. XLIX; New York 1982, p. 87.

NOTES

1. A list of manuscripts associated with this illuminator is given in New York 1982, no. 112.

2. The notes were provided by François Robertet, secretary to Duke Pierre of Bourbon, and have been frequently cited; see Wescher 1947, p. 22.

3. Printed in MacGibbon 1933, p. 144.

4. See Cat. 22, n. 14.

5. Interest in Poyet as the possible illuminator of these manuscripts is of fairly recent date, though the nineteenth century thought him the artist of the Hours of Anne of Brittany. An interesting note on him appears in Bradley 1887–89, III, pp. 93–94, incorporating the document relating to his work for the queen. François Avril and Nicole Reynaud have each brought together a large file of material on this group of manuscripts and I am extremely grateful to them both for sharing their views with me.

6. Wescher 1947, p. 55. Jean Poyet is classed beside Fouquet in Pelegrin's *De artificiale perspectiva,* published in Toul in 1501; see MacGibbon 1933, p. 122.

7. I am grateful to Nicole Reynaud for information on this point.

8. James 1898, no. 19, pp. 88–93. Yates Thompson's collection was never allowed to exceed a total of one hundred volumes, so in later years each acquisition was balanced by a sale. The 1530 date made this manuscript the latest item in the first catalogue and it says much for its quality that it was never discarded in favor of a better book. In Turner 1965, no. XLIX, a date about 1525 is suggested.

9. Cat. 22, n. 21.

10. New York, The Pierpont Morgan Library, M.495; New York 1982, no. 112.

11. Chenu 1946. Two miniatures from the Lallemant Boethius manuscript (Paris, Bibliothèque Nationale, Ms. lat. 6643) are reproduced here (Figs. 20f, 20g). The Boethius in particular appears to look forward to manuscripts of the second decade of the sixteenth century, the period of the Master of Claude of France, mentioned further below.

12. A full description of the manuscript's contents is given by James 1898.

13. See Cat. 19.

14. The scene of Mary and Joseph turned away from the inn is used several times in Flemish illumination and may here reflect familiarity with Flemish manuscripts; see Pächt 1948, pls. 21a, 29a, 29b.

15. It seems quite likely that the scene of the Magi's journey was inspired by the miniature of the same subject in the Très Riches Heures (reproduced in Longnon/Cazelles 1969, pl. 48), probably through the medium of Jean Colombe, who would have been familiar with it through his own work on the earlier manuscript. The same scene is used, in variant form, in the margin surrounding the Gospel extract from Matthew in the Great Book of Hours of Henry VIII (Fig. 23g).

16. Fols. 13, 40, and 99v, respectively.

17. New York, The Pierpont Morgan Library, Heinemann Collection, H.8; New York 1982, no. 113. This magnificent book, a comparatively recent addition to the Morgan Library, is not yet known to me at firsthand. It was reproduced in *Description* 1923.

18. Comparison between the Lallemant Missal in New York (reproduced in New York 1982, no. 112) and the book of hours in the Teyler Foundation in Haarlem (Byvanck 1931, pls. X–XIII) sufficiently makes this point.

19. The attribution to Bourdichon, reflected in the title of the edition cited in n. 17, was supported by a supposed connection between the manuscript and an entry in Francis I's royal accounts concerning a payment made to Bourdichon in 1518; see *Description* 1923, pp. 12–13.

20. The handwritten note is in his personal copy of the James 1898 catalogue, now in the reference library of the Department of Manuscripts, British Library. René of Lorraine's manuscripts (Paris, Bibliothèque de l'Arsenal, Ms. 601; Paris, Bibliothèque du Petit-Palais, Ms. 42; and Paris, Bibliothèque Nationale, Ms. lat. 10491) are described and illustrated in Leroquais 1934, II, pp. 437–40 and III, pp. 216–21 and 345–47. The scripts of these volumes are closely related to the script of the Tilliot Hours, and that of the Bibliothèque Nationale volume has been identified (Reynaud 1977, pp. 55–57) as the work of François Elzine, a Provençal scribe. However, this form of script, a sort of gothicized roman hand, seems to have been very fashionable in France, particularly during the final decade of the fifteenth century.

21. See n. 14 above.

22. New York 1982, no. 112, cited in n. 10 above.

23. Ms. 1558, published by Perrat 1926, pp. 4–15. The manuscript was given by Mary to her brother in 1530, and it is quite possible that she herself acquired it during her short sojourn in France in 1514–15 as wife and then widow of Louis XII.

24. Sterling 1975; New York 1982, nos. 127, 128.

25. One of these drawings was sold at Sotheby's, London, July 7, 1966, lot 94. Two more are in the Department of Prints and Drawings in the British Museum and were included in the museum's exhibition *The Art of Drawing* in 1972, nos. 106 and 107. Their connection with the manuscripts has only recently been recognized, and the two British Museum subjects will be included in a more extensive examination of Yates Thompson Ms. 5, to appear in a future issue of the *British Library Journal.*

26. Of particular significance are the names of St. Irenaeus and St. Annemundus, the former placed at the head of the martyrs in the Litany.

27. According to a later note at the beginning of the manuscript, he acquired it from a gentleman of the French court when he was in attendance there on the duc de Berry. Another manuscript formerly owned by Tilliot is in the Spencer Collection of the New York Public Library; see Ricci 1935–40, II, p. 1339.

24 François du Moulin and Albert Pigghe,
Les Commentaires de la guerre gallique
Paris or Blois, 1519. Harley Ms. 6205

MANUSCRIPT *Vellum, 76 folios and 1 blank; 24.7 × 12.4 cm. 12 grisaille miniatures the same width as the text but of heights varying from 4 to 10.5 cm, framed by gold bands. All dated 1519, and all but 2 (fols. 5v and 23) signed G. On fol. 3 a round grisaille portrait of Francis I (4.5 cm) above a medallion of Caesar (3 cm; Fig. 24a); large map of France (46 × 46 cm; Fig. 24e) originally folded and bound in at the very beginning of the book. Roman book hand. Text dialogue punctuated by headings in gold, blue, and red; marginal remarks in a small roman script.*

BINDING *Red morocco with closed fleur-de-lis crowns, traces of red and green silk ties. Apparently seventeenth century in date, this binding defies precise localization.*

PROVENANCE *Christophe Justel (d. 1649), conseiller et secrétaire du Roi (Louis XIII); Henri Justel (d. 1693), who took the codex to England in 1681; Robert Harley (d. 1724); entered the British Museum, 1758.*

THE Harley *Commentaires de la guerre gallique* is the first of three volumes made to flatter the imperial ambitions of Francis I. Of the three, it has the earliest secure provenance. The second volume, dated August 1519, is in the Bibliothèque Nationale in Paris; the third, dated November 1520, is in the Musée Condé at Chantilly. All three were illuminated by Godefroy le Batave and written by François du Moulin, a Franciscan long close to the royal family, who had worked with Godefroy on earlier manuscripts.[1] It is usually thought that Albert Pigghe, a Dutch humanist and specialist in astronomy, was responsible for the text, but he may have been involved only with the maps in the Chantilly volume, as the inscription suggests.[2] It seems improbable that Pigghe could have grasped the French vernacular or that he would have produced the allusive and sometimes ludicrous convolutions apparent in the text of these books.

The *Commentaires* is a landmark in the art of the book in France. In this intricately planned work, the page composition, the undecorated wide margins, and the relationship between text and illustration are uncommonly well controlled. Even the book hand, a tall and full roman, is unusual in France at this time. One is immediately reminded of Italian and French humanist printing—unillustrated, of course—and the *Hypnerotomachia Poliphili* published by Aldus Manutius in 1499.

The Harley volume is chiefly concerned with the parallels between Caesar and Francis I as military heroes and

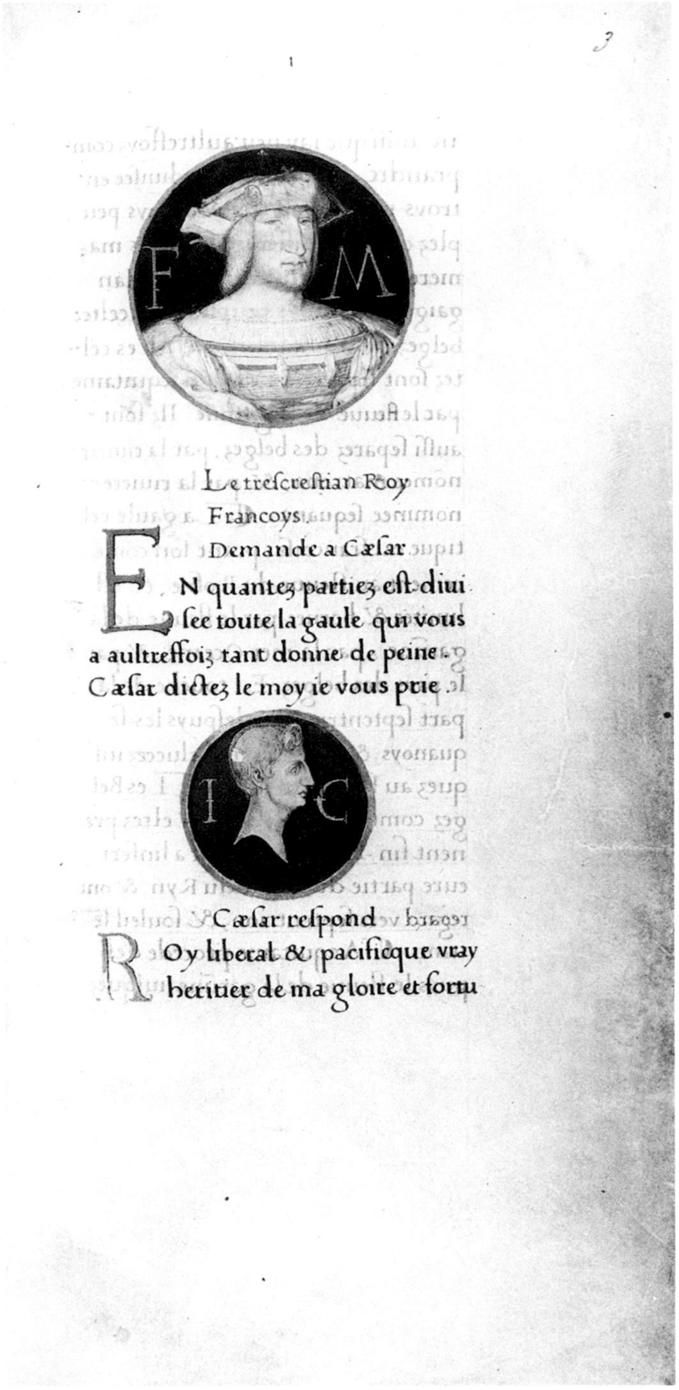

Fig. 24a. Godefroy le Batave. *Portraits of Francis I and Caesar*, fol. 3.

mez/retirerent les hõmez champe-
ſtrez auecquez eulx/pour ſe fortifier.
Touteffoiz ce pandant Orgetorix
mourut, Et diſoyent les ſouycez,
que luymeſmez ſeſtoit occis, affin
de neſtre puny par iuſtice.

Le Roy demande.
La mort de Orgetorix fut elle
cauſe de garder les ſouycez

Fig. 24b. Godefroy le Batave. *Swiss Dancing as Their Villages Burn*, fol. 9v.

meeting in the forest of Cognac, recounts the Breton campaign and is bracketed by some events of the Field of the Cloth of Gold (June 1520), where Francis I and Henry VIII met.[3]

The *Commentaires* is a richly illuminated work. The three volumes together contain forty-seven major narrative miniatures, portraits of the heroes of Marignano, medallions of the twelve Caesars, artillery of antiquity, and a total of three maps.[4] These three volumes follow, very roughly, the first three books of Caesar's *Gallic Wars*, but they are in no sense a translation from the Latin. The text is a further simplification of the fifteenth-century Burgundian *Lives of the Caesars*.[5] Godefroy's work can in many ways be related to the Burgundian tradition of grisaille illuminations in these same Caesar manuscripts. But in the sixteenth century, the miniatures Godefroy so imaginatively painted in color-flecked grisaille evoked, by their monochrome technique, the Italian Renaissance vision of antiquity. Without moving from the royal library, Godefroy could have consulted several works from looted Italian collections for examples of an Italian grisaille "antique" style of manuscript decoration of Paduan or Venetian origin.[6] The self-conscious Italianism of the *Commentaires* is evident from the small-scale, precious, personal, and often witty aesthetic so typical of the best Renaissance decorative metalwork and jewelry. It is this overall effect which conveys the unmistakable Italianate flavor of Godefroy's miniatures in both religious and secular manuscripts. There is nothing comparable in French art in 1519.

The costuming in the reception scene (Pl. xxx) illus-

conquerors of the Swiss. The emphasis is on the Battle of Marignano (1515) through which Francis reasserted his rights to the duchy of Milan. While work on this volume may have been started in 1518, the miniatures are dated 1519. The text gives the date of the meeting described between Caesar and Francis at Saint-Germain-en-Laye as the last day of April 1519, a date reiterated in the text of the second volume. This second volume concentrates on the French campaign and is prefaced by a curious section concocted by du Moulin: it introduces Francis to the responsibilities of emperorship through a dialogue with Caesar in the forest of Fontainebleau. Although Charles V, grandson of Maximilian I, was elected emperor in June 1519, production of the Paris volume continued through August 1519. The third volume, at Chantilly, which begins with a

Fig. 24c. Antwerp Master. *Judgment of Solomon*, drawing. London, British Museum, Department of Prints and Drawings.

Fig. 24d. Godefroy le Batave. *Caesar Dismounts*, fol. 36v.

Le cheual de
cæfar ne fe lef.
foit ramaiç che-
uaucher qua fon
maiftre. & auoit
les deux piets
de dauant, cō-
me vng hõme.

L e R oy demande.
C e pandant que vous eftieç en cefte
meflee, vous gens que vous auyeç au
plus ault de la petite montaigne, vous
ayderent ilç [illegible] au befoing.
Cæfar refpond
S ans leur ayde ieuffe heu beaucoup –

It is obvious from Godefroy's miniatures that he was trained in Antwerp, despite a declared Dutch nationality. Godefroy shows his debt to Flemish art in many details. His landscape style, best seen in the *Swiss Dancing as Their Villages Burn* (Fig. 24b), is very close to the earliest Flemish master of the Errera Album (Brussels, Musées Royaux des Beaux-Arts), a collection of sixteenth-century Flemish landscape drawings.[8] Godefroy often employs details of a large Flemish drawing, the *Judgment of Solomon* (Fig. 24c), which the 1520s Hours Workshop also used.[9] For example, for the reception of the French ambassadors (Pl. xxx), he borrows the entire left side of the drawing. He also makes frequent use of the right-hand repoussoir figures.

The narrative compositions in the *Commentaires* fall into a few convenient categories: battles, forest scenes, and audiences. Indoor scenes are set in Caesar's various throne rooms, where he is represented receiving ambassadors or hearing pleas. The arrangement of these scenes derives from the traditional judgment scenes in Flemish art, such as Dieric Bouts' *Justice* panels for the Town Hall of Louvain (1470–75; now Brussels, Musées Royaux des Beaux-Arts). The subjects in the *Commentaires* emphasize the humane and just treatment of ambassadors and hostages appropriate to the enlightened imperial conqueror. This was both flattering to Francis and intended to be educational.

The battle scenes are in marked stylistic contrast to the French tradition of the genre. In a miniature depicting Caesar dismounting to help his ambushed troops (Fig. 24d), the tangle of soldiers, clanging lances and armor, and tumbling rocks is stated by the sketchiest of artistic means, conveying the idea of the battle with a minimum of detail. In the foreground, Caesar's famous horse, decked in blue-and-gold parade armor, seems to have sprouted too many legs and his master has one arm too few.[10] The Alpine pass in the background recalls the terrain Francis and his men passed through in 1515 on the way to the Battle of Marignano.

The splendid vellum map of France originally bound in the front of the Harley manuscript (Fig. 24e) derives directly from the newly revised Ptolemy, printed in Strasbourg in 1513.[11] The idea of including maps with the *Commentaires* came from the 1513 Venetian edition of the Latin text of the *Commentaires* printed by Aldus Manutius, but du Moulin warns about the inaccuracy of the Italian maps and recommends the version he includes in his manuscript.[12] The Chantilly maps of Brittany and Aquitaine are smaller, with more delicate pictorial detail.

BIBLIOGRAPHY London (British Museum) 1808–12, III, p. 342; Laborde 1850–55, II, pp. 891–913, especially pp. 896–99; Noirmont 1894b; Morison 1924, figs. A, B (illustrating fols. 42v, 43); Millar 1933, p. 42; Wright 1972, p. 208; Orth 1976.

trates Godefroy's approach to historical accuracy. The Romans are clad in "antique" armor and imaginative costumes, while the French are dressed as fifteenth-century courtiers, for which a miniature in the *Livre de Tournois* by the Master of René of Anjou served as a model.[7] The contrast, as with the portrait and medal on the opening page, is that between *à la moderne* and *à l'antique* (Fig. 24a). For the latter type, Godefroy's scenes of antiquity are almost as far from being historically and archaeologically correct as those of the fifteenth century, but he evokes classical antiquity through exotic and inventive costuming.

Le Roy demande.
Les francoys furent ilʒ bien ayseʒ de
vouſtre victoire.

Cæſar reſpond.
Il fault dire quil en furent bien ayſeʒ,
Car ilʒ vindrent incontinant me feſti-
uer, & ſe reſiouyr auecqueʒ moy de
ma victoire. Et diſoient quil entẽdoiẽt

Pl. xxx. Godefroy le Batave. *Caesar Receiving the Homage of the Gallic
Ambassadors*, in François du Moulin and Albert Pigghe, Les Commentaires de la guerre gallique. Harley Ms. 6205, fol. 43.

Fig. 24e. Godefroy le Batave. *Map of France*,
fol. 1 (now detached).

Albert Pigghe of Campen (d. 1542) came to Paris briefly from
Louvain (via Cologne), perhaps encouraged by Erasmus, who
was also in Louvain and who had just declined an invitation to the
French court. Pigghe published several books in Paris: *Adversus
prognosticatorum vulgus* (Paris, Estienne, 1519; the copy at Harvard
University, Houghton Library, bears French script annotations in
the margins in the same hand as the *Commentaires*); *De aequinoc-
tiorum solsticiorumque inventione* (Paris, Resch, 1520), dedicated to
du Moulin. Pigghe's introduction to Beneventari's *Adversus
novam* (Paris, Colines, 1522) marks his departure for Rome,
where the Dutch Pope Adrian VI was gathering compatriots
around him.

Professor M. A. Screech has kindly informed me that Pigghe
was primarily important as a figure in the controversy over free
will in the 1520s; see further, *Lexikon* 1957–67, VIII, p. 502. One
reason for Godefroy's being characterized as *batavus* (i.e., Dutch)
in the inscription must be related to Pigghe's and Erasmus' common origins in the northern Netherlands.

NOTES

1. François du Moulin (d. c. 1526), Abbot of Saint-Mesmin and,
by October 1519, Grand Aumônier of France, composed three
other royal manuscripts which he had Godefroy illuminate: Paris,
Bibliothèque Nationale, Ms. fr. 2088 (1516), Ms. fr. 24955
(1517), and Ms. fr. 1890 (c. 1517). On du Moulin, see Orth 1982.
On Godefroy, see Laborde 1850–55 and 1855. See also Orth 1976,
chap. 3.

2. The inscription naming Godefroy as artist, Pigghe as maker,
and du Moulin as director appears in a cartouche on both maps
bound in the Chantilly volume (a matching cartouche specifies
that the source of the maps was Ptolemy). The inscription does
not say that Pigghe is the author of the *Commentaires*: "Albertus
pichius auxilio godofredi pictoris batavi faciebat. Praecipiente
francisco molinio mense nouembris, Anno sesquimillesimo vig-
esimo" (Albert Pigghe made this with the help of Godefroy the
Dutchman as painter, supervised by Francis Du Moulin in the
month of November 1520). The maps have been trimmed. Traces
of Pigghe's name can also be seen on the upper border, painted
over in black.

It seems astonishing that all the manuscript scholars who
flocked to a Parisian dealer in 1850 to view volume III never
noticed the inscription (see Laborde 1850–55, p. 908). It was
"discovered" by the duc d'Aumale in 1892; see Noirmont 1894b.
Volume III was in England at the duc d'Aumale's luxurious
Twickenham exile (Orleans House) from 1855 to about 1889. A
copy of Harley Ms. 6205 was made in England for the duke; it is
now at Chantilly, Musée Condé, Ms. 765.

Godefroy signed his name in full in both the Chantilly *Commentaires* (fol. 52) and in the later *Triomphes de Pétrarque* (Paris,
Bibliothèque de l'Arsenal, Ms. 6480, fol. 108v). The reference to
Godefroy as *"le Batave"* is the convention of French art historians.
Despite the signatures and Laborde's excellent account, Renouvier 1857, p. 511, and Bernard 1865, pp. 202–22, attributed
the miniatures to Geofroy Tory. Durrieu 1922 compiled an au-
thoritative list of Godefroy's oeuvre.

3. From the time of the publication of all three volumes in a
semi-facsimile in 1894 (the text is typeset) their renown spread;
see Noirmont 1894a. The book was printed in thirty-one copies.
The introduction contains roughly the same material as Noirmont 1894b.

For reproductions of the Paris volume, see Blum/Lauer 1930,
pls. 84 (I), 89; for Chantilly, see Meurgey 1930, pl. CXXX. Aspects
of the *Commentaires* are discussed in Walbe 1974, pp. 39–41. See
also the review of this published dissertation by Büttner 1978, pp.
296–303.

4. Much of the disagreement over attributions in the Paris volume centers around the Clouet portraits of the heroes of Marignano, the so-called "Preux," which are not our concern here. The
quite different portrait of Francis I in the Harley manuscript
(doubtless by Godefroy) clearly derives from the same Clouet
prototype as the Chantilly portrait of the young king. Wescher
1976, p. 17, mentions the Harley portrait in an analysis that agrees
with the view presented here.

The squabble over the interpretation of Godefroy's signatures
and his portraits began with Bouchot 1892, pp. 14, 16; it continued with, among others, Mély 1907 and Mély 1913, pp. 112,
362–74; more recently, Mellen 1971. For the clearest *état de la
question*, see Paris 1970, pp. 14–15.

5. Reference here is specifically to two Burgundian tomes that
Godefroy and du Moulin could have seen at Blois: an *Histoire
universelle* (now Paris, Bibliothèque Nationale, Ms. fr. 279) and
Les Faictz de Jules César (now Paris, Bibliothèque Nationale, Ms.
fr. 64). Comparison of the text of fols. 28v–29 of the *Histoire* with
fols. 28–30v of the Harley manuscript, and fol. 296 of the *Faictz*
with fol 50v of the Harley, yields interesting similarities. Other
pertinent Burgundian Caesar manuscripts, originally made for
Louis of Bruges, are Paris, Bibliothèque Nationale, Mss. fr.
20312 bis, and fr. 40. For a history of Caesar manuscripts in
general, see Brown 1981.

6. See Armstrong 1981. A number of the manuscripts she discusses are from the Aragon library, which was taken to France;

see Marinis 1947–52, pp. 201ff. The French also plundered the Visconti-Sforza Library at Pavia; see Pellegrin 1955.

7. The original is Paris, Bibliothèque Nationale, Ms. fr. 2695, fol. 3v. At least two copies were then at Blois (Paris, Bibliothèque Nationale, Mss. fr. 2692 and 2693); see Delaissé 1969. On Netherlandish historicism, see Van de Waal 1952, pp. 46–49.

8. The stylistic relationship between Godefroy and the Flemish master confirms a date for this unknown follower of Patinir; Dunbar 1972, pp. 64–65. I am indebted to Mr. Dunbar for photographs and advice. Like Patinir, Godefroy also uses a *kakker* as a signature in one miniature of the Paris volume (fol. 37v).

9. Popham 1932, no. 2; on the 1520s Hours Workshop, see also Cat. 25.

10. The traditional *Lives of the Caesars,* repeating Suetonius, stated that Caesar's horse would be mounted only by his master and that his two front feet were "human."

11. *Claudii Ptolemei in geographiae opus,* Strasbourg, Schott, 1513. I am indebted to Mr. Claude Pognon for identifying the source of the map of France.

12. Fol. 3v: "*ne vous fiez pas en la Charte myse au commencement des Commentaires de Caesar imprimé à venise par Aldus Pius car elle est en aulcuns lieux defectueuse*" (Do not rely on the map put at the beginning of the Commentaries of Caesar printed at Venice by Aldus Pius because it is wrong in several places). The Harley map of France is also referred to in the text of the Paris volume, fol. 22.

25 Book of Hours

Use of Rome; France (Paris?), circa 1525–30. Additional Ms. 35318

MANUSCRIPT *Vellum, 124 leaves; 14 × 8.6 cm. 15 full-page miniatures, 1 half-page miniature, 3 small miniatures. Beginning on fol. 1 with the calendar, each text page is bordered with a flat gold fillet (6 × 10 cm), terminating in a knot below. The 15 large miniatures framed in sober architectural borders; on the facing pages of text, 11 surrounding borders of stylized fauna and flora on a stippled gold ground and 4 borders with antique motifs in gold on a blue background. Of the 213 floriated initials, the larger ones are blue and gold with floral tendrils; the smaller ones, black and gold. Line ends are black and gold "logs." The text is written in a fine upright roman hand.*

BINDING *Red morocco; nineteenth century.*

PROVENANCE *Baron Ferdinand Rothschild Bequest, 1899.*

T HIS book of hours in the British Library belongs to a group of at least fourteen manuscripts which come from the same French (probably Parisian) workshop.[1] The books of hours within this group show, by similarities of book hand, decoration, size, and, above all, duplication of the main illuminations, a common genesis both in time and place. Those few manuscripts that are dated range from 1524 to about 1528;[2] the others can be dated stylistically during the decade of the 1520s. It has long been noted that these hours relate closely to the printed hours published in Paris by Geofroy Tory in exactly these same years. It is probable that these miniaturists designed his woodcuts.[3]

Political events of the 1520s did not favor art patronage in France. Both the Italian wars and the growing Reform movement drained the country's energies and its treasury. Hence, the period is not rich in panel paintings, with the significant exception of a group of Burgundian works.[4] The hours miniatures discussed here allow us to document artistic development within a small circle of artists who may best have realized the artistic potential of their era. The miniatures reflect a complex variety of influences from both Flanders and Italy, while following in composition and iconography the middle road so often, and so rightly, attributed to French art in the early years of the sixteenth century.

The 1520s Hours Workshop manuscripts, to which the hours in the British Library belongs, are distinguished by a marked reliance on Dürer and the Antwerp Mannerists, overlaid with a figure and drapery style which strongly

recalls Italian prototypes. Of the group of manuscripts from the workshop (cited in n. 1), the hours in the British Library is most closely related to Morgan M.452 and the so-called "Hours of Anne of Austria," although they are not by the same hand. Within the 1520s group these three are the most Italianate in style, a quality they share with the woodcuts in an hours published by Geofroy Tory in 1529. The *privilège* for these printed hours dates from 1526, which suggests an early date for their execution.[5] Thus the miniatures, too, may not be as late as generally supposed.

The miniatures in the hours in the British Library (Fig. 25a, Pls. XXXI, XXXII, Figs. 25b, 25d) all seem to be by one

Fig. 25a. 1520s Hours Workshop. *Adoration of the Magi*, fol. 51v.

Pl. xxxi. 1520s Hours Workshop. *Annunciation to the Shepherds*, Book of Hours. Add.
Ms. 35318, fols. 47v–48.

Pl. XXXII. 1520s Hours Workshop. *Agony in the Garden*, Book of Hours. Add. Ms.
35318, fols. 17v–18.

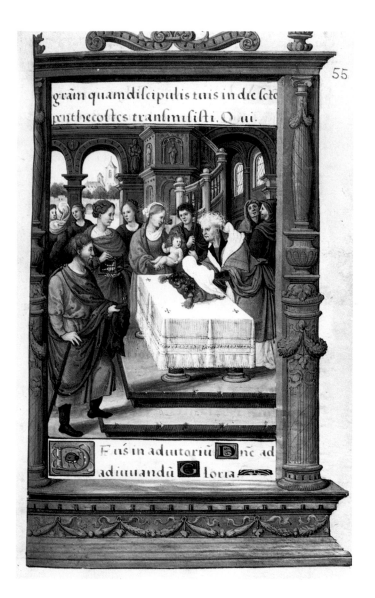

miniatures painted in the 1520s Hours Workshop and by Godefroy le Batave as well. The *serpentinata* pose of the shepherd is similar to a standing figure in that same drawing. The Rosenwald Hours shepherds are much the same, while the central figure is a more literal copy of the one in the *Judgment* drawing. The relationship to the Antwerp drawing is puzzling in the context of manuscript illumination, since the style that the miniaturists imitate is unknown in Flemish manuscripts. In other manuscripts in the 1520s group, the Flemish borrowings are frequent and easily traced. In fact, so thoroughly Flemish are the models and the style of the miniatures in the Rosenwald Hours— one of the earliest of the group—that one can easily suppose they were painted by a recent emigrant from Flanders. Godefroy le Batave (see Cat. 24) was Netherlandish, as was the court portraitist Jean Clouet. Franco-Flemish artists had a long history in France, particularly in manuscript painting—one thinks immediately of the duc de Berry and the Limbourgs. The other manuscripts in the 1520s group are less obviously Flemish, yet they often rely on the same Antwerp drawings for models.

However strong the Flemish influence may have been, the illuminators in the 1520s group did not ignore Dürer, who provided them with a much-utilized set of workshop models. For example, the *Adoration of the Magi* (Fig. 25a) in many of the 1520s Hours illuminations is directly derived (in reverse) from Dürer's 1511 woodcut (Bartsch 3).[7] The *Presentation* (Fig. 25b), too, comes from Dürer, via the earlier Rosenwald miniature. The Antwerp drawing of the *Judgment of Solomon* mentioned above is also the basis of a *Presentation* composition common to several manuscripts in this hours group.[8]

Quite different in stylistic orientation is the use of a famous Italian engraving, Marcantonio Raimondi's *Judgment of Paris* (Fig. 25c) in the British Library miniature of *Job on His Dunghill* (Fig. 25d) and in the *Annunciation to the Shepherds* (Pl. xxxi) discussed above. The figure of Job comes from the river god at the right in the engraving, and the pointing shepherd is borrowed from the goddess in the center. A second Italian High Renaissance example seems to have been employed in the same *Job on His Dunghill* for the two standing men: the central figure in Raphael's *Death of Ananias* from the Sistine tapestry series was the model for the man pointing down in the Job miniature, and the figure just above Ananias, bending down toward him and pointing rearward, seems to have determined the center figure in the illumination.[9] Job as a subject is not uncommon in French manuscripts—one thinks of Fouquet's miniature in the Hours of Etienne Chevalier, or Bourdichon's (Pl. xxvi). Bernaert van Orley's Job Altarpiece of 1521 in Brussels (where Raphael's tapestry cartoon remained) also may have had some influence on our miniaturists.

hand. Miniatures identical in every respect appear in Morgan M.452: *Annunciation, Crucifixion, Pentecost, Annunciation to the Shepherds, Adoration of the Magi, Presentation in the Temple, Flight into Egypt, Coronation of the Virgin, Penitent David, Job on His Dunghill,* and the *Trinity.* Many of the architectural borders are repeated in the Hours of Anne of Austria and similar ones are used in Smith-Lesouëf 42. Single figures recur in the other hours manuscripts: Mary in the *Flight into Egypt* is the same in Walters Ms. 449; the Doheny *Penitent David* and *Adoration of the Magi* are very close, but not identical, to the British Library and Morgan miniatures. Both the British Library book of hours and the Morgan hours have the same dimensions. It would be instructive to study them side by side.

The sinuous postures of the figures in these miniatures come directly from Antwerp painting of the period. The *Annunciation to the Shepherds* makes this clear (Pl. xxxi). The twisted figure on the ground derives from a large Antwerp Mannerist drawing, the *Judgment of Solomon* (Fig. 24c),[6] which inexplicably is the source for a large variety of

Fig. 25c [TOP]. Marcantonio Raimondi. *Judgment of Paris*, engraving.

Fig. 25d [ABOVE]. 1520s Hours Workshop. *Job Mocked*, fol. 83.

Color plays a vital role in linking these manuscripts. There is a distinctive color range and finesse of painting which is, next to the persistent duplications, the most convincing element in establishing the identity of the workshop. The majority of the hues is kept in a light range of values, almost chalky, yet high in intensity. Among these colors, certain fuchsia pinks and bright acid greens are unusual in French manuscript painting in these years. Set in the foreground of the miniatures, against deep, pale-blue landscapes à la Patinir, are figures robed in brilliant orange, deep raspberry reds, and enamel blue. Gold is used in profusion in the frames and borders.

Far from being eclipsed by the stylistic peculiarities of the school of Fontainebleau, the style initiated by the 1520s Workshop, as well as its compositional models, landscape backgrounds, and even a few figures, continued through the middle of the century. Details changed—obelisks replaced windmills, strapwork frames replaced the more sober architectural ones—but the technique and color range remained essentially the same.[10]

BIBLIOGRAPHY London (British Museum) 1901, p. 256; London (British Museum) 1914–30, VI, p. 14 and pl. 15c; Millar 1933, pl. LXIII; Orth 1976, chap. 5; Orth 1980b, nn. 2, 32; New York 1982, pp. 102, 104.

NOTES

1. Ten, including the British Library codex, are books of hours (Use of Rome, unless otherwise indicated): Paris, Bibliothèque Nationale, Ms. nouv. acq. lat. 3090, the so-called "Hours of Anne of Austria" (Solente 1960, p. 34); Ms. Smith-Lesouëf 42 (Leroquais 1943, pp. 41–44, pls. 29–34, 46); Paris, Petit Palais, Dutuit Collection, Ms. 37 (Dutuit 1899, p. 18); Washington, D.C., Library of Congress, Rosenwald Collection, Ms. 10 (Washington, D.C. [Library of Congress] 1977, no. 14); Camarillo, Calif., St. John's Seminary, Estelle Doheny Collection (Camarillo 1955, p. 8 and pl. III); Cambridge, Fitzwilliam Museum, Ms. 134 (James 1895, p. 315); New York, Alexandre P. Rosenberg Collection, Ms. 9 (New York 1982, no. 131); New York, The Pierpont Morgan Library, M.452, Use of Paris (ibid., no. 132); Baltimore, Walters Art Gallery, Ms. 449, Use of Toulouse (ibid., no. 130). Also: London, Victoria and Albert Museum, *Epistles*, Ms. 1721–1921; Malibu, Calif., The J. Paul Getty Museum, *Epistles*, Ms. Ludwig I 15 (Euw/Plotzek 1979–82, I, pp. 134–39); Paris, Bibliothèque Nationale, Ms. fr. 5715 (Etienne le Blanc, *Les Gestes de Blanche de Castille*, 1526); and a Peace Treaty sent to Henry VIII in 1527, London, P.R.O. E30/1109 (Orth 1980a). Other examples are cited by John Plummer in New York 1982, p. 104. In that catalogue, too, Plummer (pp. xii–xiii, 103) presents excellent arguments, based on textual analysis, in favor of locating the workshop at Tours. The workshop participated in at least two royal commissions (*Les Gestes* and the Peace Treaty) and perhaps others, encouraged by Tourangeau humanists at court. However, the connection of the workshop to Tory and Parisian printing discussed in my article (Orth 1980b) should also be taken into consideration. I should like to retain Paris as a working hypothesis.

2. The Rosenwald Hours is dated 1524; Walters Art Gallery, Ms. 449 has an Easter calendar which begins in 1524; that in the Doheny Hours begins 1528.

3. Orth 1980b.

4. Laclotte 1967. On the preceding period, see Sterling 1963, pp. 2–15.

5. The *privilège* constituted permission to publish and granted to the publisher certain legal monopolies over the contents of the book; see Orth 1980b, p. 46, n. 10; three of the 1529 woodcuts are there reproduced (figs. 3, 8, 10).

6. Popham 1932, no. 2. The Rosenwald *Annunciation to the Shepherds* is illustrated in *Lessing J. Rosenwald Collection* 1977, p. 6.

7. See also the Adorations in the Doheny Hours (Orth 1980b, fig. 12), the Hours of Anne of Austria, and Smith-Lesouëf 42. The complex interchange of motifs in these manuscripts is typified by the *Adoration,* identical in the British Library and Morgan hours. They use the black King from the Doheny Hours which, in turn, supplies one other King to the Hours of Anne of Austria. The Hours of Anne of Austria uses the same Virgin (in reverse) from the British Library composition.

8. For example, Walters Ms. 449, Fitzwilliam Ms. 134, and Dutuit Ms. 37. The latter two reproduce a painting now in Nancy; see Orth 1980b, n. 35, and figs. 15, 16. On the *Presentation* and Dürer, using the Hours of Anne of Austria and Smith-Lesouëf manuscripts as examples, see Büttner 1980, p. 22.

9. There are similar Job miniatures (reversed) by the 1520s Hours Workshop in Fitzwilliam Ms. 134 (identical to the Rosenberg Ms. 9 miniature of Job, as well as to that in Dutuit Ms. 37) and Smith-Lesouëf 42; see Orth 1980b, p. 43, figs. 9, 11, and nn. 33, 34, for further details.

10. Miniatures in French manuscripts of the 1540s and 1550s frequently demonstrate the persistence of the same workshop models. For example, in an hours for Claude of Guise (Paris, Bibliothèque de l'Arsenal, Ms. 654) the same models were used for the *Agony in the Garden* and the *Crucifixion*. A detached miniature in the Louvre, Cabinet des Dessins, uses the same *Crucifixion* background as that in the British Library hours, while it takes its figure of Christ from that in the Doheny and Anne of Austria hours. The figure of Job in the Hours of Henry II (Paris, Bibliothèque Nationale, Ms. lat. 1429) is the same as that in Fitzwilliam Ms. 134 (see n. 9). The Dutuit manuscript includes several fine miniatures with Fontainebleau-style frames which must date in the 1540s. They are close in style to several in the Hours of Anne de Montmorency (Chantilly, Musée Condé, Ms. 1943), dated 1549, specifically the *Sacrifice of Isaac* and *Jonah Preaching to the Ninevites*. The same hand may be responsible for the detached leaf from a choir book, cited by Plummer in New York 1982, p. 104 (which he was kind enough to discuss with me). All of these miniatures are strikingly close in color, drawing, drapery, and technique to the artist of the Hours of Anne of Austria. The mid-century miniatures are a subject worthy of independent study.

Genealogical Table of the Ruling Houses of Europe

YORK
(England)

CASTILE AND ARAGON
(Spain, Naples, and Sicily)

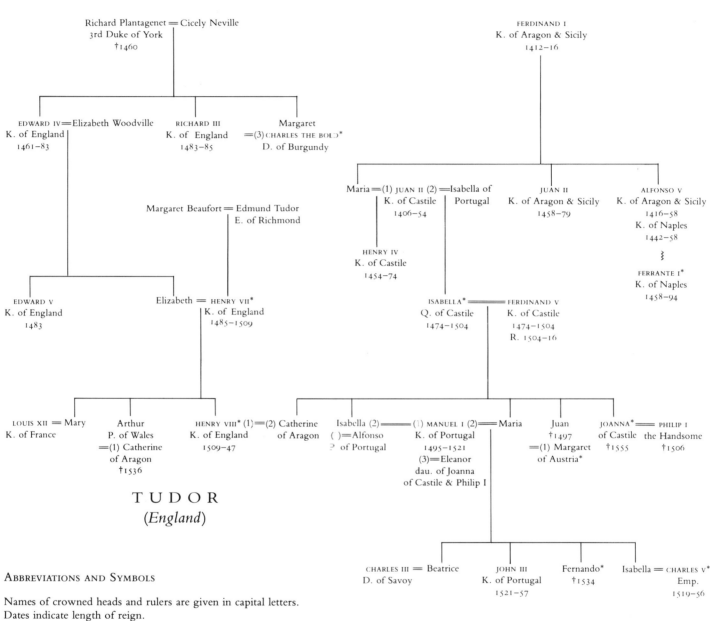

TUDOR
(England)

ABBREVIATIONS AND SYMBOLS

Names of crowned heads and rulers are given in capital letters.
Dates indicate length of reign.
Not all spouses are cited.
Not all issue are cited; issue are not listed in order of birth.
(1) (2) (3) indicate first, second, or third marriage.

=	married	C.	Count
†	date of death	D.	Duke
⸨	illegitimate	Dss.	Duchess
*	patrons or owners of manuscripts in exhibition	dau.	daughter
		E.	Earl
		Emp.	Emperor
		K.	King
		P.	Prince
		Q.	Queen
		R.	Regent

Continued overleaf

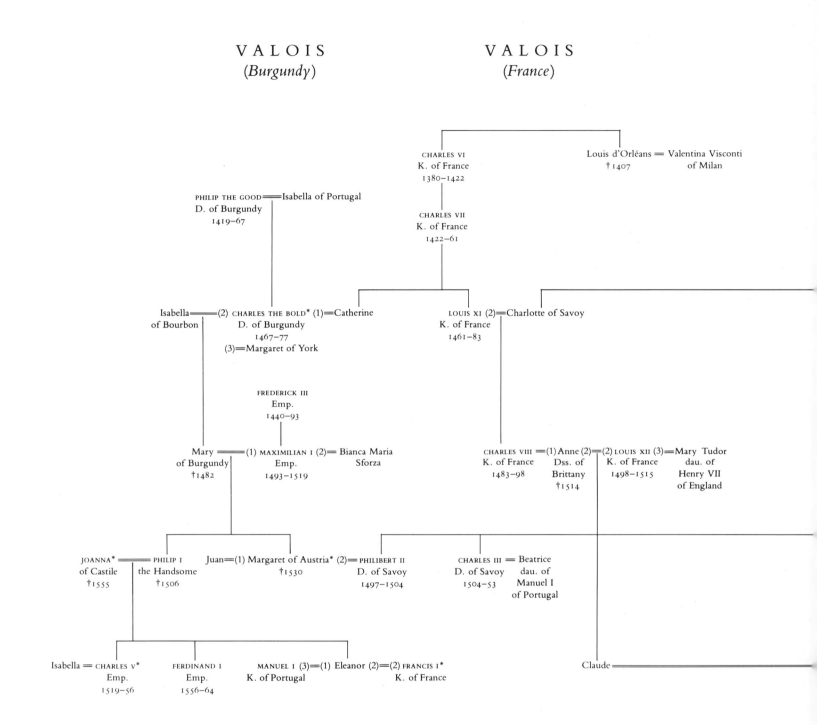

VALOIS
(Burgundy)

VALOIS
(France)

HAPSBURG EMPIRE

Continued from overleaf

SAVOY

MILAN

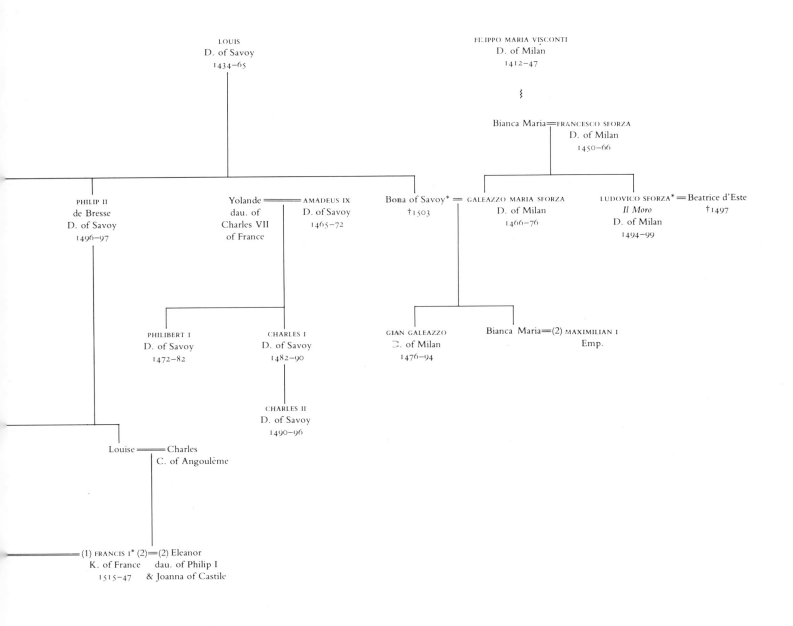

LOUIS
D. of Savoy
1434–65

FILIPPO MARIA VISCONTI
D. of Milan
1412–47

Bianca Maria═FRANCESCO SFORZA
D. of Milan
1450–66

PHILIP II
de Bresse
D. of Savoy
1496–97

Yolande ═══════ AMADEUS IX
dau. of   D. of Savoy
Charles VII   1465–72
of France

Bona of Savoy* ═ GALEAZZO MARIA SFORZA
†1503   D. of Milan
                       1466–76

LUDOVICO SFORZA* ═ Beatrice d'Este
Il Moro   †1497
D. of Milan
1494–99

PHILIBERT I
D. of Savoy
1472–82

CHARLES I
D. of Savoy
1482–90

GIAN GALEAZZO
D. of Milan
1476–94

Bianca Maria═(2) MAXIMILIAN I
Emp.

CHARLES II
D. of Savoy
1490–96

Louise ═══ Charles
C. of Angoulême

═ (1) FRANCIS I* (2)═(2) Eleanor
K. of France   dau. of Philip I
1515–47   & Joanna of Castile

Bibliography

Aguiar, António de. "Acerca de António de Holanda, um dos autores da Genealogia de D. Manuel Pereira, 3° Conde da Feira." *Arquivo do Distrito de Aveiro*, 25 (1959), pp. 117–45.

————. *A Genealogia iluminada do Infante Dom Fernando por Antonio de Holanda e Simão Bening: estudo histórico e crítico*. Lisbon, 1962.

Alexander, J. J. G. *The Master of Mary of Burgundy: A Book of Hours for Engelbert of Nassau: The Bodleian Library, Oxford*. New York, 1970.

————. *Italian Renaissance Illuminations*. New York, 1977.

————. *The Decorated Letter*. New York, 1978.

————. *Wallace Collection: Catalogue of Illuminated Manuscript Cuttings*. London, 1980.

Alexander, J. J. G., and A. C. de la Mare. *The Italian Manuscripts in the Library of Major J. R. Abbey*. London, 1969.

Alvin, Louis Joseph. "Les Grandes Armoiries du duc Charles de Bourgogne, gravées vers 1467." *Bulletin de l'Académie Royale de Belgique*, 4 (1859), pp. 5–27, 144.

Ancona, Paolo d'. *La Miniature italienne du Xe au XVIe siècle*. Paris and Brussels, 1925.

Ancona, Paolo d', and Erardo Aeschlimann. *Dictionnaire des miniaturistes du moyen âge et de la renaissance dans les différentes contrées de l'Europe*. 2nd ed. Milan, 1949.

Andrés, Gregorio de. *Catálogo de los códices griegos desaparecidos de la Real Biblioteca de El Escorial*. Madrid, 1968.

Armstrong, Lilian. *Renaissance Miniature Painters and Classical Imagery: The Master of the Putti and His Venetian Workshop*. London, 1981.

Audin, Marius, and Eugène Vial. *Dictionnaire des artistes et ouvriers d'art du Lyonnais*. 2 vols. Paris, 1918–19.

Backhouse, Janet. "Two Books of Hours of Francis I." *British Museum Quarterly*, 31 (1966–67), pp. 90–95.

————. 1973a. "Bourdichon's 'Hours of Henry VII.'" *British Museum Quarterly*, 37 (1973), pp. 95–102.

————. 1973b. Review of *The Master of Mary of Burgundy* by J. J. G. Alexander. *Burlington Magazine*, 115 (1973), pp. 684–85.

————. *The Illuminated Manuscript*. Oxford, 1979.

Baltimore Museum of Art. *Two Thousand Years of Calligraphy*. Compiled by Dorothy E. Miner, Victor I. Carlson, P. W. Filby. Exhibition catalogue. 1965.

Baltimore, Walters Art Gallery. *The History of Bookbinding, 525–1950 A.D.* Foreword by Dorothy E. Miner. Exhibition catalogue. 1957.

Bartsch, A. *Le Peintre-Graveur*. 21 vols. Vienna, 1803–21.

Baumgarten, Sandor. "Saint Etienne et sa 'Descendance' vus par Simon Bening." *Acta Historiae Artium*, 18 (1972), pp. 137–41.

————. "Présence de la Hongrie." *Acta Historiae Artium*, 21 (1975), pp. 83–85.

Baxandall, Michael. *Painting and Experience in Fifteenth Century Italy*. Oxford, 1972.

Bellonci, Maria, and Niny Garavaglia. *L'Opera completa del Mantegna*. Milan, 1967.

Berkovits, Ilona. *Illuminated Manuscripts from the Library of Matthias Corvinus*. Budapest, 1964.

Berlin, Staatliche Museen Preussischer Kulturbesitz, Berlin-Dahlem. *Zimelien: Abendländische Handschriften des Mittelalters aus den Sammlungen der Stiftung Preussischer Kulturbesitz Berlin*. Compiled by Tilo Brandis et. al. Exhibition catalogue. 1975.

Berlin, Staatsbibliothek. *Das christliche Gebetbuch im Mittelalter*. Exhibition catalogue. 1980.

Bern, Bernisches Historisches Museum. *Die Burgunderbeute und Werke burgundischer Hofkunst*. Exhibition catalogue. 1969.

Bernard, Auguste Joseph. *Geofroy Tory*. 2nd ed. Paris, 1865.

Berry, William. *Encyclopedia Heraldica*. 3 vols. London [1828].

Biermann, Alfons. "Das verschollene Stundenbuch Kardinal Albrechts von Brandenburg." *Mainzer Zeitschrift*, 63–64 (1968–69), pp. 47–66.

————. "Die Miniaturenhandschriften des Kardinals Albrecht von Brandenburg (1514–1545)." *Aachener Kunstblätter des Museumsvereins*, 46 (1975), pp. 15–310.

Biryukova, Nina Y. *The Hermitage, Leningrad: Gothic and Renaissance Tapestries*. London, 1966.

Blomfield, Reginald, and F. I. Thomas. *The Formal Garden in England*. 3rd ed. London, 1892.

Blum, André, and Philippe Lauer. *La Miniature française au XVe et au XVI siècles*. Paris and Brussels, 1930.

Bober, Phyllis Pray. *Drawings after the Antique by Amico Aspertini: Sketchbooks in the British Museum*. London, 1957.

Bologna, Ferdinando. *Napoli e le rotte mediterranee della pittura: Da Alfonso il Magnanimo a Ferdinando il Cattolico*. Naples, 1977.

Bouchot, Henri. *Les Clouet et Corneille de Lyon d'après des documents inédits*. Paris, 1892.

Bourdillon, Francis William. *The Early Editions of the Roman de la Rose*. London, 1906.

Bradley, John William. *A Dictionary of Miniaturists, Illuminators, Calligraphers, and Copyists. . . .* 3 vols. London, 1887–89.

————. *The Life and Works of Giorgio Giulio Clovio, Miniaturist, with Notices of His Contemporaries and of the Art of Book Decoration in the Sixteenth Century*. London, 1891.

Brown, Virginia. "Portraits of Julius Caesar in Latin Manuscripts of the *Commentaries*." *Viator*, 12 (1981), pp. 319–53.

Bruck, Robert. *Die Malereien in den Handschriften des Königreichs Sachsen*. Dresden, 1906.

Bruges, Groeningemuseum. *Anonieme Vlaamse Primitieven: Zuidnederlandse Meesters met Noodnamen van de 15de en het Begin van de 16de Eeuw*. Exhibition catalogue. 1969.

————. *Chefs d'oeuvre de Prague 1450–1750: Trois siècles de peinture flamande et hollandaise*. Compiled by Jaromir Sip, Jarmila Vackova. Exhibition catalogue. 1974.

————, Gruuthusemuseum. *Vlaamse Kunst op Perkament: Handschriften en miniaturen te Brugge van 12de tot de 16de Eeuw*. Compiled by N. Geirnaert et al. Exhibition catalogue. 1981.

Brussels, Bibliothèque Royale de Belgique. *Le Siècle d'or flamande: Le Mécénat de Philippe le Bon*. Compiled by L. M. J. Delaissé. Exhibition catalogue. 1959.

————. 1967a. *La Librairie de Philippe le Bon*. Compiled by Georges Dogaer, Marguerite Debae. Exhibition catalogue. 1967.

————. 1967b. *Margaretha van York en haar tijd*. Exhibition catalogue. 1967.

Büttner, F. O. "Zur französischen Buchmalerei um 1500: Bemerkungen." *Scriptorium*, 32 (1978), pp. 290–303.

————. "Fortwirkung in Abwandlung. Zur Verwendung von Vorlagen bei einigen Darstellungen von zwei Szenen aus der Kindheit Christi: Anbetung der Könige und Darbringung im Tempel." In *Relations artistiques entre les Pays-Bas et l'Italie à la renaissance: Etudes dédiées à Suzanne Sulzberger*. Etudes d'art publiées par l'Institut historique belge de Rome, IV. Brussels and Rome, 1980, pp. 15–42.

Byvanck, A. W. *Les Principaux Manuscrits à peintures de la Bibliothèque Royale des Pays-Bas et du Musée Meermanno-Westreenianum à la Haye*. Société française de Reproductions de Manuscrits à Peintures. Paris, 1924.

————. "Les Principaux Manuscrits à peintures conservés dans les collections publiques du royaume des Pays-Bas." *Bulletin de la Société française de Reproductions de Manuscrits à Peintures*, 15 (1931), pp. 5–115.

Cahn, Walter, and James H. Marrow. "Medieval and Renaissance Manuscripts at Yale: A Selection." *Yale University Library Gazette*, 52 (1978), pp. 173–284.

Camarillo, Calif., St. John's Seminary. *Catalogue of Books and Manuscripts in the Estelle Doheny Collection*. 3 vols. Los Angeles, 1940–1955.

Cambridge, Harvard University, Houghton Library. *Late Medieval and Renaissance Illuminated Manuscripts, 1350–1525, in the Houghton Library*. Compiled by Roger S. Wieck. Exhibition catalogue. 1983.

Canuti, Fiorenzo. *Il Perugino*. 2 vols. Siena, 1931.

Cartellieri, Otto. *Am Hofe der Herzöge von Burgund: Kulturhistorische Bilder*. Basel, 1926.

Casier, Joseph, and Paul Bergmans. *L'Art ancien dans les Flandres*. 3 vols. Brussels and Paris, 1914–22.

Casley, David. *A Catalogue of the Manuscripts of the King's Library, An Appendix to the Catalogue of the Cottonian Library; together with an Account of Books Burnt or Damaged by a Late Fire: One Hundred and Fifty Specimens of the Manner of Writing in Different Ages, from the Third to the Fifteenth Century, in Copper-plates: and some Observations upon Mss., in a preface*. London, 1734.

Chambers, D. S. *Patrons and Artists in the Italian Renaissance*. London, 1970.

Chenu, Paul. "Sur un essai de reconstitution d'un manuscrit aux armes de Lallemant (de Bourges), XVe S., et sur ses rapports avec un manuscrit de la Consolation de Boèce." Académie des Inscriptions et Belles-Lettres. Fondation Eugène Piot. *Monuments et Mémoires*, 41 (1946), pp. 103–22.

Cionini-Visani, Maria, and Grgo Gamulin. *Giorgio Clovio: Miniaturist of the Renaissance*. New York, 1980.

Cleveland Museum of Art. *Treasures from Medieval France*. Compiled by William D. Wixom. Exhibition catalogue. 1967.

————. *Catalogue of Paintings*. III, *European Paintings of the 16th, 17th, and 18th Centuries*. 1982.

Coggiola, Giulio. *Le Bréviaire Grimani de la Bibliothèque S. Marc à Venise: Recherches d'histoire et d'art*. Leiden, 1908–10.

Cologne, Kunsthalle. *Die Parler und der Schöne Stil 1350–1400: Europäische Kunst unter den Luxemburgern*. 3 vols. Exhibition catalogue. 1978.

Corstanje, Charles van, et al. *Vita Sancta Coletae (1381–1447)*. Leiden, 1982.

Couderc, Camille. *Album de portraits d'après les collections du Département des Manuscrits [Bibliothèque nationale]*. Paris, 1910.

Courcelle-Ladmirant, Jeanne. "Le Bréviaire flamand dit 'La Flora' de la Bibliothèque Nationale de Naples." *Bulletin de l'Institut historique belge de Rome*, 20 (1939), pp. 223–33.

Cox, Trenchard. *Jehan Foucquet: Native of Tours*. London, 1931.

Csapodi, Csaba, and Klára Csapodi-Gárdonyi. *Bibliotheca Corviniana: The Library of King Matthias Corvinus of Hungary*. New York and Washington, D.C., 1969.

Dacos, Nicole. *La Découverte de la Domus Aurea et la formation des grotesques à la Renaissance*. Studies of the Warburg Institute, 31. London, 1969.

Davies, Martin. *National Gallery Catalogues: The Earlier Italian Schools*. London, 1961.

Dehaisnes, Chrétien. *Recherches sur le retable de Saint-Bertin et sur Simon Marmion*. Lille and Valenciennes, 1892.

Delaissé, L. M. J. *Medieval Miniatures from the Department of Manuscripts . . . the Royal Library of Belgium*. New York, 1965.

————. *A Century of Dutch Manuscript Illumination*. Berkeley and Los Angeles, 1968.

————. "Les Copies flamandes du 'Livre des Tournois' de René d'Anjou." *Scriptorium*, 33 (1969), pp. 187–98.

Delisle, Léopold. *Les Grandes Heures de la reine Anne de Bretagne et l'atelier de Jean Bourdichon*. Paris, 1913.

Demuynck, Paul. "Het Getijdenboek voor een Lid van de Familie Louthe: Bijdrage tot de Studie van de Gents-Brugse Miniatuurkunst tijdens de Tweede Helft der Vijftiende Eeuw." Master's thesis, Université Catholique de Louvain, 1979.

de Schryver. *See* Schryver

A Description of the Great Book of Hours of Henry VIII, Illuminated by Jean Bourdichon of Tours. 1923.

Destrée, Joseph. "Recherches sur les enlumineurs flamands." *Bulletin des Commissions royales d'Art et d'Archéologie*, 30 (1891), pp. 263–98; 31 (1892), pp. 186–231; 37 (1898), 80–137.

————. *Hugo van der Goes*. Brussels and Paris, 1914.

————. "Un Livre d'heures peint par Simon Marmion." *Annuaire de la Société des Bibliophiles et Iconophiles de Belgique* (1918), pp. 131–37.

————. *Les Heures de Notre-Dame dites de Hennessy: Étude sur un manuscrit de la Bibliothèque royale de Belgique*. Brussels, 1923.

Detroit Institute of Arts. *Flanders in the Fifteenth Century: Art and Civilization*. Exhibition catalogue. 1960.

de Vos. *See* Vos

de Winter. *See* Winter

Dhanens, Elisabeth. *Hubert and Jan van Eyck*. New York, 1980.

Dibdin, Thomas F. *The Bibliographical Decameron*. 3 vols. London, 1817.

The Dictionary of National Biography. Oxford, 1917–.

Dictionnaire de biographie française. Paris, 1933–.

Dogaer, Georges. "Ein Wappenbuch des Ordens vom Goldenen Vliess—Ms. Brüssel, Bibliothèque royale, IV, 84." *Alte und Moderne Kunst*, 60–61 (1962), pp. 2–4.

————. "Des anciens livres des statuts manuscrits de l'Ordre de la Toison d'Or." *Publications de Centre Européen d'Etudes Burgondo-Médianes*, 5 (1963), pp. 65–70.

————. "Miniature flamande vers 1475–1485: A propos de trois ouvrages récents." *Scriptorium*, 26 (1972), pp. 97–104.

————. "Margaretha van York, bibliofiele." In *Koninklijke Kring voor Oudheidkunde: Letteren en Kunst*. Brussels, 1975, pp. 99–111.

————. "L'Ecole Ganto-Brugeoise: Une Fausse Appelation." In *Miscellanea codicologia F. Masai dicata*. Ghent, 1979, pp. 511–18.

Dolfi, Pompeo Scipione. *Cronologia delle famiglie nobili di Bologna*. Bologna, 1670.

Dominguez Rodríguez, Ana. *Libros de Horas del siglo XV en la Biblioteca Nacional*. Madrid, 1979.

Dorez, Léon. "Les Manuscrits à peintures du Musée Britannique." Review of *Illuminated Manuscripts in the British Museum*, Series I–IV, by George Frederic Warner. *Revue des Bibliothèques*, 13 (1903), pp. 159–60.

———. *Les Manuscrits à peintures de la Bibliothèque de Lord Leicester à Holkham Hall, Norfolk*. . . . Paris, 1908.

———. *Le Psautier de Paul III: Reproduction des peintures et des initiales du manuscrit latin 8880 de la Bibliothèque nationale, précédée d'un essai sur le peintre et le copiste du psautier*. Paris, 1909.

dos Santos. *See* Santos

Doutrepont, Georges. *La Littérature française à la cour des Ducs de Bourgogne*. Paris, 1909.

Dunbar, Burton L. "Some Observations on the 'Errera Sketchbook' in Brussels." *Bulletin des Musées royaux des Beaux-Arts de Belgique*, 21 (1972), pp. 53–82.

Durrieu, Paul. "Alexandre Bening et les peintres du Bréviaire Grimani." *Gazette des Beaux-Arts*, 5 (1891), pp 353–67; 6 (1891), pp. 55–69.

———. *Les Antiquités judaïques et le peintre Jean Foucquet*. Paris, 1908.

———. "L'Enlumineur flamand Simon Bening." Académie des Inscriptions et Belles-Lettres. *Comptes rendus des séances*, 1910, pp. 162–69.

———. "Les Relations de Lionardo da Vinci avec le peintre français Jean Perréal." *Etudes Italiennes*, 1 (1919), p. 152.

———. *Dominus illuminatio mea: Les Vingt Rondeaux dédiés au roi François Ier* [Facsimile of Bibliothèque Nationale, Ms. fr. 2088]. Paris, 1922.

———. *La Miniature flamande au temps de la cour de Bourgogne* (1415–1530). 2nd ed. Paris and Brussels, 1927.

Dutuit, Eugène. *La Collection Dutuit: Livres et manuscrits*. Paris, 1899.

Duverger, Jozef. "Gerard Horenbault, 1465?–1540, Hofschilder van Margareta van Oostenrijk." *De Kunst. Maandblad voor Oude en Jonge Kunst*, I (1930), pp. 81–90.

Edinburgh, National Library of Scotland. *Notable Accessions since 1925: A Book of Illustrations*. Edinburgh, 1965.

Edwards, Edward. *Memoirs of Libraries: Including a Handbook of Library Economy*. 2 vols. London, 1859.

Elliott, J. H. *Imperial Spain 1469–1716*. New York, 1963; 2nd ed. 1977.

Ettro, F. J. van. "De oudste afbeelding van het Wapen van Zeeland." *De nederlandsche Leeuw*, 93 (1976), cols. 368–72.

Euw, Anton von, and Joachim M. Plotzek. *Die Handschriften der Sammlung Ludwig*. 2 vols. Cologne, 1979–82.

Evans, Mark. "An Illusionistic Device in the Hours of Etienne Chevalier." *Scriptorium*, 35 (1981), pp. 81–83.

Fabia, Philippe. *Pierre Sala: Sa vie et son oeuvre, avec la légende et l'histoire de l'antiquaille*. Lyons, 1934.

Fairbairn, James. *Book of Crests of the Families of Great Britain and Ireland*. 2 vols. London, 1905.

Fairbank, Alfred J., and Berthold Wolpe. *Renaissance Handwriting: An Anthology of Italic Scripts*. London, 1960.

Farquhar, James Douglas. "Identity in an Anonymous Age: Bruges Manuscript Illuminators and their Signs." *Viator*, 11 (1980), pp. 371–83.

Fava, Domenico, and Mario Salmi. *I manoscritti miniati della Biblioteca Estense di Modena*. 2 vols. Florence, 1950–73.

Figanière, Frederico Francisco de la. *Catalogo dos manuscriptos portuguezes existentes no Museu brittanico*. Lisbon, 1853.

Fleming, Vincent John. *The Roman de la Rose: A Study in Allegory and Iconography*. Princeton, 1969.

Flower, Robin. "Margaret of Austria and the Sforza Book." *British Museum Quarterly*, 10 (1935–36), pp. 100–02.

Fossi Todorow, Maria. *I disegni del Pisanello e della sua cerchia*. Florence, 1966.

Friedländer, Max J. *Early Netherlandish Painting*. Trans. by Heinz Norden. 14 vols. New York and Washington, D.C., 1967–76.

Frizzoni, Gustavo, ed. *Marcantonio Michiel. Notizia d'opera di disegno da Jacopo Morelli*. Bologna, 1884. Reprint. Bologna, 1976.

Gagnebin, Bernard. "L'Enluminure de Charlemagne à François Ier: Les Manuscrits à peintures de la Bibliothèque publique et universitaire de Genève." *Genava*, 24 (1976), pp. 5–200.

Gall, Günter. *Leda im europäischen Kunsthandwerk: Ein Handbuch für Sammler und Liebhaber*. Braunschweig, 1965.

Gardet, Clément. *De la peinture du moyen âge en Savoie*. III, *L'Apocalypse figurée des ducs de Savoie (Ms. Escurial E. Vitr. V)*. Annecy, 1969.

Gaspar, Camille. *The Breviary of the Mayer van den Bergh Museum at Antwerp*. Brussels and New York, 1932.

———. *Le Calendrier des Heures de Hennessy*. 2 vols. Brussels, 1943.

Gasparrini Leporace, Tullia. *Il Calendario del Breviario Grimani*. Milan, 1954.

Ghent, Bijlokemuseum. *Gent: Duizend Jaar Kunst en Kultur*. Exhibition catalogue. 1975.

Ghirardacci, Cherubino. *Historia di Bologna*. Ed. by L. A. Muratori. Raccolta degli storici italiana, XXXIII. Bologna, 1929–31.

Gibson, Walter S. *Bruegel*. New York and Toronto, 1977.

Góis, Damião de. *Crónica do Felicíssimo Rei D. Manuel*. Lisbon, 1619. Reprint. Coimbra, 1953.

Goldblatt, Maurice Henry. "Jean Perréal: Thirty-five Portraits Identified." *Connoisseur*, 123 (1949), pp. 94–98.

Goloubew, Victor. *Die Skizzenbücher Jacopo Bellinis*. 2 vols. Brussels, 1908–12.

Goris, J.-A., and G. Marlier. *Albrecht Dürer: Diary of His Journey to the Netherlands 1520–1521*. Greenwich, Conn., 1971.

Guicciardini, Lodovico. *Descrittione di tutti i paesi altrimenti detti germania inferiere*. Antwerp, 1581.

Guigue, Georges. *Le Livre d'amitié dédié à Jehan de Paris par l'escuyer Pierre Sala*. Lyons, 1884.

Guillaume, Gustave. *Histoire de l'organisation militaire sous les ducs de Bourgogne*. Académie royale des Sciences, des Lettres et des Beaux-Arts. *Mémoires*, XXII. Brussels, 1848.

The Hague, Rijksmuseum Meermanno-Westreenianum, Museum van het Boek. *Verluchte Handschriften uit eigen Bezit: 1300–1550*. Exhibition catalogue. 1979.

Hahnloser, Hans Robert. *Villard de Honnecourt: Kritische Gesamtausgabe des Bauhüttenbuches ms. fr. 19093 der Pariser Nationalbibliothek*. 2nd ed. Graz, 1972.

Harthan, John P. *The Book of Hours: Illuminated Pages from the World's Most Precious Manuscripts*. New York, 1977.

Hassall, W. O. *The Holkham Library: Illuminations and Illustrations in the Manuscript Library of the Earl of Leicester*. Oxford, 1970.

Herbert, J. A. *Illuminated Manuscripts*. London, 1911. Reprint. Bath, 1972.

Hermann, H. J. *Die illuminierten Handschriften in Tirol*. Beschreibendes Verzeichnis der illuminierten Handschriften in Österreich, I. Ed. by Franz Wickhoff. Leipzig, 1905.

Heydenreich, Ludwig H., and Wolfgang Lotz. *Architecture in Italy 1400–1600*. Baltimore, 1974.

Hilger, Wolfgang. *Das ältere Gebetbuch Maximilians I.* Codices selecti, XXXIX. Graz, 1973.

Hill, George Francis, and Graham Pollard. *Renaissance Medals from the Samuel H. Kress Collection at the National Gallery of Art.* London, 1967.

Hind, Arthur M. *An Introduction to a History of Woodcut.* 2 vols. London, 1935.

_____. *Early Italian Engraving.* 7 vols. London, 1938–48.

Hindman, Sandra. "The Case of Simon Marmion; Attributions and Documents." *Zeitschrift für Kunstgeschichte,* 40 (1977), pp. 185–204.

_____. "Pieter Bruegel's *Children's Games,* Folly, and Chance." *Art Bulletin,* 63 (1981), pp. 447–75.

Hoffmann, Edith Warren. "Simon Marmion Reconsidered." *Scriptorium,* 23 (1969), pp. 243–71.

_____. "Simon Marmion or the 'Master of the Altarpiece of Saint-Bertin': A Problem in Attribution." *Scriptorium,* 27 (1973), pp. 263–90.

Hollstein, F. W. H. *Dutch and Flemish Etchings, Engravings, and Woodcuts, ca.* 1450–1700. 24 vols. Amsterdam, 1949–.

Horodyski, Bogden. "Birago, Miniaturiste des Sforza." *Scriptorium,* 10 (1956), pp. 251–55.

Huillet d'Istria, Madeleine. "Au sujet d'articles récents sur Jean Perréal, le Maître aux Pieds-bots." *Gazette des Beaux-Arts,* 40 (1952), pp. 57–63.

Hulin de Loo, Georges. "Quelques notes de voyage. II, Une oeuvre authentique de Simon Bening." *Académie Royale de Belgique. Bulletin de la Classe des Beaux-Arts,* 7 (1925), pp. 100–06.

_____. 1939a. "Comment j'ai retrouvé Horenbaut." *Annuaire des Musées royaux des Beaux-Arts de Belgique,* 2 (1939), pp. 3–21.

_____. 1939b. "La Vignette chez les enlumineurs gantois entre 1475 et 1500." *Académie Royale de Belgique. Bulletin de la Classe des Beaux-Arts,* 21 (1939), pp. 158–80.

Hulst, Roger A. d'. *Flemish Tapestries from the Fifteenth to the Eighteenth Century.* New York, 1967.

Hulton, Paul. *The Work of Jacques Le Moyne de Morgues.* London, 1977.

Humphreys, Henry Noel. *The Illuminated Books of the Middle Ages.* London, 1859.

The Huth Library: A Catalogue of the Printed Books, Manuscripts, Autograph Letters, and Engravings Collected by Henry Huth. . . . 5 vols. London, 1880.

Ionescu, Teodor. *Muzeul Brukenthal: Galeria de Artă Plastică.* Sibiu, Romania, 1964.

Ithaca, N.Y., Cornell University. *A Medieval Treasury.* Compiled by Robert G. Calkins. Exhibition catalogue. 1968.

James, Montague Rhodes. *A Descriptive Catalogue of Manuscripts in the Fitzwilliam Museum.* Cambridge, 1895.

_____. *A Descriptive Catalogue of Fifty Manuscripts from the Collection of Henry Yates Thompson.* Cambridge, 1898.

_____. *A Descriptive Catalogue of the Second Series of Fifty Manuscripts in the Collection of Henry Yates Thompson.* Cambridge, 1902.

_____. *Biblioteca Pepysiana: A Descriptive Catalogue of the Library of Samuel Pepys.* III, *Medieval Manuscripts.* London, 1923.

Janson, H. W. *The Sculpture of Donatello.* 2 vols. Princeton, 1957.

Kaemmerer, Ludwig Joachim Karl, and H. G. Ströhl. *Ahnenreihen aus dem Stammbaum des portugiesischen Königshauses: Miniaturenfolge in der Bibliothek des British Museum.* 2 vols. Stuttgart [1903].

Kenyon, Frederic George. *Catalogue of Fifty Manuscripts and Printed Books Bequeathed to the British Museum by Alfred H. Huth.* London, 1912.

Knaus, Hermann. "Handschriften der Grafen von Nassau-Breda." *Archiv für Geschichte des Buchwesens,* 3 (1960), cols. 567–80.

Koch, Robert. *Joachim Patinir.* Princeton, 1968.

Köster, Kurt. "Religiöse Medaillen und Wallfahrts-Devotionalien in der flämischen Buchmalerei des 15. und frühen 16. Jahrhunderts." In *Buch und Welt: Festschrift für Gustav Hofmann.* Ed. by Hans Striedl and Joachim Wieder. Weisbaden, 1965, pp. 459–504.

Kren, Thomas. "A Book of Hours in the Beinecke Library (Ms. 287) and an Atelier from the Ghent-Bruges School." Master's thesis, Yale University, New Haven, 1974.

Kuhn, Alfred. "Die Illustrationen des Rosenromans." *Jahrbuch der Kunsthistorischen Sammlungen des Allerhöchsten Kaiserhauses,* 31 (1913–14), pp. 1–66.

Kunert, S. de. "Un Padovano ignoto ed un suo memoriale de' primi anni del cinquecento." *Bollettino del Museo Civico di Padova,* 10 (1907), pp. 64–73.

Kupfer-Tarasulo, Marcia. 1979a. "Innovation and Copy in the Stein Quadriptych of Simon Bening." *Zeitschrift für Kunstgeschichte,* 42 (1979), pp. 274–98.

_____. 1979b. "A Rosary Psalter Illuminated by Simon Bening." *Quaerendo,* 10 (1979), pp. 209–26.

Laborde, Alexandre de. *La Mort chevauchant un boeuf: Origine de cette illustration de l'office des morts dans certains livres d'heures de la fin du XVe siècle.* Paris, 1923.

Laborde, Léon de. *La Renaissance des arts à la cour de France: Etudes sur le seizième siècle.* 2 vols. Paris, 1850–55.

_____. "Godefroy, peintre de François I." *Revue Universelle des Arts,* 1 (1855), pp. 5–18.

Laclotte, Michel. "Quelques tableaux bourguignons du XVIe siècle." In *Studies in Renaissance and Baroque Art Presented to Anthony Blunt on His Sixtieth Birthday.* London, 1967, pp. 83–85.

Laloire, Edouard. "Le Livre d'heures de Philippe de Clèves et de la Marck, Seigneur de Ravestein." *Les Arts Anciens de Flandre,* 1 (1905–06), pp. 172–87.

Langlois, Ernest. *Les Manuscrits du Roman de la Rose: Description et classement.* Travaux et Mémoires de l'Université de Lille, n.s., I, Droit Lettres, VII. Paris and Lille, 1910.

Lapeyre, André, and Rémy Scheurer. *Les Notaires et secrétaires du roi sous les règnes de Louis XI, Charles VIII et Louis XII (1461–1515): Notices personnelles et genealogies.* 2 vols. Paris, 1978.

Lázaro, José. "Le Manuscrit du British Museum intitulé 'Isabella Book' ou Bréviaire d'Isabelle la Catholique." In *Actes du Congrès d'Histoire de l'Art.* Paris, 1924, IV, pp. 138–39.

_____. "Un supuesto breviario de Isabel la Católica." In *Comunicación al Congreso de historia del arte celebrado en Paris en 1921.* Madrid, 1928, pp. 12–26.

Lehrs, Max. *Geschichte und kritischer Katalog der deutschen, niederländischen, und französischen Kupferstichs im 15. Jahrhunderts.* 9 vols. Vienna, 1908–34.

Leidinger, Georg. *Flämischer Kalendar. Miniaturen aus Handschriften der Königlichen Hof- und Staatsbibliothek München.* Munich, 1913.

_____. *Flämischer Kalendar des XVI Jahrhunderts gemalt vom Meister des "Hortulus animae."* Munich, 1936.

Leroquais, Victor. *Les Livres d'heures: Manuscrits de la Bibliothèque nationale.* 3 vols. Paris, 1927.

_____. *Les Bréviaires Manuscrits des Bibliothèques publiques de France.* 5 vols. Paris, 1934.

————. *Les Livres d'heures: Manuscrits de la Bibliothèque nationale. Supplément*. Mâcon, 1943.

Levi d'Ancona, Mirella. *Miniatura e miniatori a Firenze dal XIV al XVI secolo: Documenti per la storia della miniatura*. Florence, 1962.

Lexikon für Theologie und Kirche. 2nd ed. 10 vols. Freiburg, 1957–67.

Lieftinck, Gerard I. 1964a. *Manuscrits datés conservés dans les Pays-Bas: Catalogue paléographique des manuscrits en écriture latine portant des indications de date*. 2 vols. Amsterdam, 1964.

————. 1964b. "De Meester van Maria van Bourgondië en Rooclooster bij Brussel." *Bulletin van de Koninklijke Nederlandsche Oudheidkunde Bond*, 17 (1964), cols. 254–92.

————. *Boekverluchters uit de Omgeving van Maria van Bourgondië, c. 1475–c. 1485*. With a contribution by Dr. David Rogers, Oxford, and an English translation of the introduction by Mrs. Jane Sandberg-Lowe. 2 vols. Brussels, 1969.

Limentani Virdis, Caterina. *Codici miniati fiamminghi e olandesi nelle biblioteche dell' Italia nord-orientale*. Vicenza, 1981.

Limousin, Raymond. *Jean Bourdichon, peintre et enlumineur: Son atelier et son école*. Lyons, 1954.

London, British Library, *A Royal Heritage*. Exhibition catalogue. 1977.

London, British Museum. *A Catalogue of the Harleian Manuscripts in the British Museum*. 4 vols. London, 1808–12.

————. *Catalogue of Additions to the Manuscripts in the British Museum in the Years 1841–1845*. London, 1850.

————. *Catalogue of Additions to the Manuscripts in the British Museum in the Years 1848–1853*. London, 1868.

————. *Catalogue of Additions to the Manuscripts in the British Museum in the Years 1888–1893*. London, 1894.

————. *Catalogue of Additions to the Manuscripts in the British Museum in the Years 1894–1899*. London, 1901.

————. *Catalogue of Additions to the Manuscripts in the British Museum in the Years 1900–1905*. London, 1907.

————. *Catalogue of Additions to the Manuscripts in the British Museum in the Years 1906–1910*. London, 1912.

————. *Catalogue of Additions to the Manuscripts in the British Museum in the Years 1911–1915*. London, 1925.

————. *Catalogue of Additions to the Manuscripts 1936–1945*. 2 vols. London, 1970.

————. *Catalogue of Books Printed in the XVth Century Now in the British Museum*. VI. London, 1930.

————. *Catalogue of the Stowe Manuscripts in the British Museum*. 2 vols. London, 1895–96.

————. *Miniatures and Borders from a Flemish Horae, British Museum Add. ms. 24098, Early Sixteenth Century: Reproduced in Honour of Sir George Warner*. London, 1911.

————. *Schools of Illumination: Reproductions from Manuscripts in the British Museum*. 6 vols. London, 1914–30.

London, Burlington Fine Arts Club. *Exhibition of Illuminated Manuscripts*. Exhibition catalogue. 1908.

London, Palaeographical Society. *Facsimiles of Manuscripts and Inscriptions*. 1st series. 3 vols. London, 1873–83.

————. *Facsimiles of Manuscripts and Inscriptions*. 2nd series. 2 vols. London, 1884–94.

————. *Facsimiles of Ancient Manuscripts*. London, 1903.

London, Royal Academy of Arts. *Flemish Art 1300–1700*. Exhibition catalogue. 1953.

London, Victoria and Albert Museum. *Catalogue of Miniatures, Leaves, and Cuttings from Illuminated Manuscripts*. London, 1923.

————. *Splendours of the Gonzaga*. Compiled by David Chambers and Jane Martineau. Exhibition catalogue. 1981.

Longhi, Roberto. *Officina Ferrarese*. 2nd ed. Florence, 1956.

Longnon, Jean, and Raymond Cazelles. *The Très Riches Heures of Jean, Duke of Berry, Musée Condé, Chantilly*. New York, 1969.

Loomis, Roger Sherman, and Laura Hibbard Loomis. *Arthurian Legends in Medieval Art*. New York, 1938.

Luria, Maxwell. *A Reader's Guide to the Roman de la Rose*. Hamden, Conn., 1982.

MacGibbon, David. *Jean Bourdichon: A Court Painter of the Fifteenth Century*. Glasgow, 1933.

Malaguzzi Valeri, F. *La Corte di Ludovico il Moro: La Vita privata e l'arte a Milano nella seconda metà del quattrocento*. 4 vols. Milan, 1913–23.

Mâle, Émile. *Les Heures d'Anne de Bretagne: Bibliothèque nationale (manuscrit latin 9474)*. Paris, 1946.

Malibu, Calif., The J. Paul Getty Museum. *Master Drawings from the Woodner Collection*. Compiled by George Goldner. Exhibition catalogue. 1983.

Manchester, Whitworth Art Gallery. *Medieval and Early Renaissance Treasures in the North West*. Compiled by J. J. G. Alexander. Exhibition catalogue. 1976.

Mander, Carel van. *Het Schilder-Boeck waerin voor eerst de leerlustighe Iueght den grondt der edel vry Schilderconst in Verscheyden deelen wort voorghedraghen*. Haarlem, 1604.

Mann, Nicholas. "Petrarch Manuscripts in the British Isles." *Italia Medioevale e Umanistica*, 18 (1975), pp. 139–527.

Mantua, Biblioteca Communale. *Mostra dei codici Gonzagheschi: La Biblioteca dei Gonzaga da Luigi I ad Isabella, 1328–1540*. Compiled by U. Meroni. Exhibition catalogue. 1966.

Mariani Canova, G. *La Miniatura veneta del Rinascimento 1450–1500*. Venice [1969].

Marinis, Tammaro de. *La Biblioteca napoletana dei re d'Aragona*. 4 vols. Milan, 1947–52.

————. *La Legatura artistica in Italia nei secoli XV e XVI: Notizie ed elenchi*. 3 vols. Florence, 1960.

————. *La Biblioteca napoletana dei re d'aragona. Supplemento*. 2 vols. Verona, 1969.

Marks, Richard, and Ann Payne. *British Heraldry from Its Origins to c. 1800*. London, 1978.

Marle, Raimond van. *The Development of the Italian Schools of Painting*. 19 vols. The Hague, 1923–38.

Marrow, James H. *Passion Iconography in Northern European Art of the Late Middle Ages and Early Renaissance: A Study of the Transformation of Sacred Metaphor into Descriptive Narrative*. Kortrijk, Belg., 1979.

————. "In desen spiegell: A New Form of *Memento Mori* in Fifteenth-Century Netherlandish Art." In *Essays in Northern European Art Presented to Egbert Haverkamp-Begemann on His Sixtieth Birthday*. Ed. by Anne-Marie Logan. Doornspijk, Netherlands, 1983, pp. 154–63.

————. "Simon Bening in 1521: A Group of Dated Manuscripts." In *Liber Amicorum Herman Liebaers*. Brussels [1984].

Martin, Henri. *Les Fouquet de Chantilly: Livre d'heures d'Etienne Chevalier*. Paris, 1926.

McFarlane, Kenneth Bruce. *Hans Memling*. Oxford, 1971.

Meiss, Millard. *Andrea Mantegna as Illuminator: An Episode in Renaissance Art, Humanism, and Diplomacy*. New York, 1957.

————. *French Painting in the Time of Jean de Berry: The Late Fourteenth Century and the Patronage of the Duke*. 2 vols. London, 1967.

————. *French Painting in the Time of Jean de Berry: The Limbourgs and Their Contemporaries*. 2 vols. New York, 1974.

Meiss, Millard, and Elizabeth H. Beatson. *The Belles Heures of Jean, Duke of Berry*. New York, 1974.

Meiss, Millard, and Edith W. Kirsch. *The Visconti Hours, National Library, Florence.* New York and London, 1972.

Mellen, Peter. *Jean Clouet: Catalogue raisonné des dessins, miniatures et peintures.* Paris, 1971.

Mély, Fernand de. "Jean Clouet ou Godefroy le Batave?" *Gazette des Beaux-Arts,* 37 (1907), pp. 403–17.

———. *Les Primitifs et leurs signatures: Les Miniaturistes.* Paris, 1913.

Messina, Museo Regionale. *Antonello da Messina.* Exhibition catalogue. 1981.

Meurgey, Jacques Pierre. *Les Principaux Manuscrits à peintures du Musée Condé à Chantilly.* Société française de Reproductions de Manuscrits à Peintures. Paris, 1930.

Milan, Palazzo Reale. *Arte lombarda dai Visconti agli Sforza: L'Arte manifestazioni milanesi e la cassa di risparmio delle provincie lombarde.* Exhibition catalogue. 1958.

Millar, Eric George. "Les Manuscrits à peintures des bibliothèques de Londres." *Bulletin de la Société française de Reproductions de Manuscrits à Peintures,* 4 (1914–20), pp. 83–149.

———. *Reproductions from Illuminated Manuscripts* [in the British Museum]. Series IV. London, 1928.

———. *Souvenir de l'exposition de manuscrits français à peintures organisée à la Grenville Library (British Museum).* Société française de Reproductions de Manuscrits à Peintures. Paris, 1933.

Miller, Edward. *Prince of the Librarians: The Life and Times of Antonio Panizzi of the British Museum.* Athens, Ohio, 1967.

———. *That Noble Cabinet: A History of the British Museum.* London, 1973.

Mittelalterliche Miniaturen. See Munich, Jacques Rosenthal

Mongan, Agnes. "A *Pietà* by Simon Marmion." *Bulletin of the Fogg Museum of Art,* 9 (1942), pp. 114–20.

Morison, Stanley. "Towards an Ideal Type." *Fleuron,* no. 2 (1924), pp. 57–75.

Muir, L., ed. *Pierre Sala: Tristan, roman d'aventures du XVIe siècle.* Geneva, 1958.

Munby, Alan Noel Latimer. *Connoisseurs and Medieval Miniatures, 1750–1859.* Oxford, 1972.

Munich, Jacques Rosenthal. *Mittelalterliche Miniaturen.* Exhibition catalogue. 1931.

Murdoch, John, J. Murrell, P. J. Noon, and R. Strong. *The English Miniature.* New Haven, 1981.

New York, The Pierpont Morgan Library. *The Last Flowering: French Painting in Manuscripts, 1420–1530.* Compiled by John Plummer and Gregory Clark. Exhibition catalogue. 1982.

Noirmont, J. A. E. Dunoyer de. 1894a. *Commentaires de la Guerre Gallique.* Paris, 1894.

———. 1894b. "L'Histoire d'un livre." *Revue Britannique,* 6 (1894), pp. 5–33.

Nuremberg, Germanisches Nationalmuseum. *Albrecht Dürer 1471–1971.* Exhibition catalogue. 1971.

Omont, Henri Auguste. 1906a. *Les Grandes Chroniques de France enluminées par Jean Foucquet: Reproduction des 51 miniatures du manuscrit français 6465 de la Bibliothèque nationale.* Paris, 1906.

———. 1906b. *Heures d'Anne de Bretagne: Reproduction réduite des 63 peintures du manuscrit latin 9474 de la Bibliothèque nationale.* Paris, 1906.

Onghena, M. J. "Enkele Gegevens en Opmerkingen Betreffende Twee Zestiende Eeuwse Handschriften van het Gulden Vlies." In *Miscellanea Jozef Duverger: Bijdragen tot de Kunstgeschiedenis der Nederlanden.* Ghent, 1968, I, pp. 187–215.

Orth, Myra Dickman. "Progressive Tendencies in French Manuscript Illumination, 1515–1530: Godefroy le Batave and the 1520's Hours Workshop." Ph.D. diss., New York University, Institute of Fine Arts, 1976.

———. 1980a. "A French Illuminated Treaty of 1527." *Burlington Magazine,* 122 (1980), pp. 125–26.

———. 1980b. "Geofroy Tory et l'enluminure: Deux livres d'heures de la collection Doheny." *Revue de l'Art,* 50 (1980), pp. 40–47.

———. 1980c. "Two Books of Hours for Jean Lallemant Le Jeune." *Journal of the Walters Art Gallery,* 38 (1980), pp. 70–92.

———. "Francis Du Moulin and the *Journal* of Louise of Savoy." *Sixteenth Century Journal,* 13 (1982), pp. 55–66.

Pächt, Otto. *The Master of Mary of Burgundy.* London [1948].

———. "René d'Anjou—Studien I." *Jahrbuch der Kunsthistorischen Sammlungen in Wien,* 33 (1973), pp. 85–126.

———. "Die Autorschaft des Gonella-Bildnisses." *Jahrbuch der Kunsthistorischen Sammlungen in Wien,* 34 (1974), pp. 39–88.

———. "Die niederländischen Stundenbücher des Lord Hastings." In *Litterae textuales. Miniatures, Scripts, Collections: Essays Presented to G. I. Lieftinck.* Ed. by J. P. Gumbert and M. J. M. de Haan. Amsterdam, 1976, IV, pp. 29–32.

———. *Die illuminierten Handschriften und Inkunabeln der Österreichischen Nationalbibliothek.* II, *Französische Schule.* Vienna, 1977.

———. "La Terre de Flandres." *Pantheon,* 36 (1978), pp. 3–16.

———. "Simon Marmion myt der handt." *Revue de l'Art,* 46 (1979), pp. 7–15.

———. "Dévotion du roi René pour sainte Marie-Madeleine et le sanctuaire de Saint-Maximin." *Chronique Méridionale: Arts du Moyen Age et de la Renaissance,* 1981, pp. 15–28.

Pächt, Otto, and J. J. G. Alexander. *Illuminated Manuscripts in the Bodleian Library, Oxford.* 3 vols. Oxford, 1966–73.

Panofsky, Erwin. *Early Netherlandish Painting: Its Origins and Character.* 2 vols. Cambridge, Mass., 1953.

Paris, Bibliothèque Nationale. *Les Clouet et la cour des rois de France de François Ier à Henri IV.* Ed. by Jean Adhémar. Exhibition catalogue. 1970.

Paris, Musée du Louvre. *Jean Fouquet: Catalogue.* Les Dossiers du Département des Peintures, 22. Compiled by Nicole Reynaud. Exhibition catalogue. 1981.

Parry, G. A. "'Les Enigmes de l'amour' de Pierre Sala." *Revue de Philologie Française,* 22–23 (1908–09), pp. 214–20.

Passavant, J. D. *Kunstreise durch England und Belgien.* Frankfurt, 1833.

Patch, Howard Rollin. *The Tradition of Boethius: A Study of His Importance in Medieval Culture.* New York, 1935.

Pellegrin, Elisabeth. *La Bibliothèque des Visconti et des Sforza, ducs de Milan au XVe Siècle.* Paris, 1955.

Perls, Klaus. "Le Maître du Charles VIII." *L'Amour de l'Art* (1935), pp. 95–99.

———. *Jean Fouquet.* London and New York, 1940.

Perrat, Charles. *Un Livre d'heures de Marie, reine de France, et d'Henri VIII d'Angleterre.* Documents paléographiques, typographiques, iconographiques de la Bibliothèque de Lyon, 6. Lyons, 1926.

Pinchart, Alexandre Joseph. *Archives des arts, sciences et lettres, Documents inédits,* series 1. 3 vols. Ghent, 1860–61.

Pleister, Werner, ed. *Giovanni Boccaccio: Die neun Bücher vom Glück und vom Unglück berühmter Männer und Frauen.* Munich, 1965.

Pompilio, Mario, and Angela Ottino della Chiesa. *L'Opera completa di Leonardo pittore.* Milan, 1967.

Popham, A. E. *Catalogue of Drawings by Dutch and Flemish Artists Preserved in the Department of Prints and Drawings in the British*

Museum. V, *Dutch and Flemish Drawings of the XV and XVI Centuries.* London, 1932.

Popham, A. E., and Philip Pouncey. *Italian Drawings in the Department of Prints and Drawings in the British Museum. The Fourteenth and Fifteenth Centuries.* 2 vols. London, 1950.

Porcher, Jean. *Medieval French Miniatures.* New York, 1960.

Pradel, Pierre. *Michel Colombe, le dernier imagier gothique.* Paris, 1953.

Preston, Raymond. *Chaucer.* London and New York, 1952.

Quaritch, Bernard, Ltd. *Facsimiles of Illustrations in Biblical and Liturgical Manuscripts Executed in Various Countries During the XI–XVI Centuries, Now in the Possession of Bernard Quaritch.* London, 1892.

————. *Description of a Very Beautiful Book of Hours Illuminated probably by Hans Memling and Gerard David.* London, 1905.

Reinach, Salomon. "Un Manuscrit de la bibliothèque de Philippe le Bon à Saint-Pétersbourg." Académie des Inscriptions et Belles-Lettres. Fondation Eugène Piot. *Monuments et Mémoires,* 11 (1904), pp. 7–82.

Renouvier, Jules. "Les Estampes de Geofroy Tory et sa marque de graveur." *Revue Universelle des Arts,* 5 (1857), pp. 510–19.

Reynaud, Nicole. "Georges Trubert, enlumineur du roi René et de René II de Lorraine." *Revue de l'Art,* 35 (1977) pp. 41–63.

Ribault, Jean-Yves. "L'Encadreur des enluminures du Musée Condé: Le Menuisier Basset." *Gazette des Beaux-Arts,* 98 (1981), p. 200.

Ricci, Seymour de. *Census of Medieval and Renaissance Manuscripts in the United States and Canada.* 3 vols. New York, 1935–40.

Ring, Grete. 1949a. *A Century of French Painting, 1400–1500.* London, 1949.

————. 1949b. Review of *The Master of Mary of Burgundy* by Otto Pächt. *Burlington Magazine,* 91 (1949), pp. 86–87.

————. "An Attempt to Reconstruct Perréal." *Burlington Magazine,* 92 (1950), pp. 255–60.

Ringbom, Sixten. *Icon to Narrative: The Rise of the Dramatic Close-up in Fifteenth-Century Devotional Painting.* Åbo, 1965.

Ritter, Georges, and Jean Lafond. *Manuscrits à peintures de l'école de Rouen: Livres d'heures normands.* Rouen and Paris, 1913.

Robertson, Giles. *Giovanni Bellini.* Oxford, 1968.

Robinson, John Charles. *Descriptive Catalogue of the Drawings by the Old Masters, Forming the Collection of John Malcolm of Poltalloch, Esq.* 2nd ed. London, 1876.

————. "The Sforza Book of Hours." *Bibliographica,* 1 (1895), pp. 428–36.

Rodríguez Villa, A. "Don Francisco de Rojas, embajador de los Reyes Católicos." *Boletín de la Real Academia de la Historia,* 28 (1896), pp. 180–203.

Ryder, Alan F. *The Kingdom of Naples under Alfonso the Magnanimous: The Making of a Modern State.* Oxford, 1976.

Salmi, Mario. *Italian Miniatures.* Rev. ed. New York, 1957.

————. *The Grimani Breviary: Reproduced from the Illuminated Manuscript Belonging to the Biblioteca Marciana, Venice.* Woodstock, N.Y., 1974.

Santos, Reynaldo dos. "Les Principaux Manuscrits à peintures conservés en Portugal." *Bulletin de la Société française de Reproductions de Manuscrits à Peintures,* 14 (1930), pp. 5–32.

————. "Un Exemplaire de Vasari annoté par Francisco de Olanda." *Studi Vasariani* (1950), pp. 91–92.

Saxl, Fritz, and Hans Meier. *Verzeichnis astrologischer und mythologischer illustrierte Handschriften des lateinischen Mittelalters.* III,

Handschriften in englischen Bibliotheken. Ed. by Harry Bober. Heidelberg, 1953.

Schaefer, Claude. "Un Livre d'heures illustré par Jean Columbe à la Bibliothèque Laurentienne à Florence." *Gazette des Beaux-Arts,* 82 (1973), pp. 287–96.

————. "Les Débuts de l'atelier de Jean Colombe: Jean Colombe et André Rousseau, prêtre, libraire, et 'escrivain.'" *Gazette des Beaux-Arts,* 90 (1977), pp. 137–50.

————. "Nouvelles observations au sujet des Heures de Louis de Laval." *Arts de l'Ouest,* 1–2 (1980), pp. 33–68.

Schaefer, Claude, and Christopher de Hamel. "Du nouveau sur les Heures d'Etienne Chevalier illustrées par Fouquet." *Gazette des Beaux-Arts,* 98 (1981), pp. 193–99.

Schleinitz, Otto von. "Die Sforza-Werke in British Museum." *Zeitschrift für Bücherfreunde,* 5 (1901), pp. 130–41.

Schloss Schallaburg, Niederösterreichisches Landesmuseums. *Matthias Corvinus und die Renaissance in Ungarn 1458–1541.* Exhibition catalogue. 1982.

Schöne, Wolfgang. "Über einige altniederländische Bilder vor allem in Spanien." *Jahrbuch der Preussischen Kunstsammlungen,* 58 (1937), pp. 153–81.

Schryver, Antoine de. 1969a. *Gebetbuch Karls des Kühnen vel potius Stundenbuch der Maria von Burgund: Codex Vindobonensis 1857 der Österreichischen Nationalbibliothek.* With a codicological introduction by Franz Unterkircher. Graz, 1969.

————. 1969b. "Nicolas Spierinc calligraphe et enlumineur des Ordonnances des États de l'hôtel de Charles le Téméraire." *Scriptorium,* 23 (1969), pp. 434–58.

Schwarz, Heinrich. "The Mirror of the Artist and the Mirror of the Devout." In *Studies in the History of Art Dedicated to William E. Suida.* London, 1959, pp. 90–105.

Schweinsfert, Eberhard Freiherr Schenk zu. "Das Gebetbuch für Graf Engelbert II von Nassau und seine Meister." *Nassauische Annalen,* 88 (1975), pp. 139–57.

Scillia, Diane Graybowski. "Gerard David and Manuscript Illumination in the Low Countries, 1480–1509." Ph.D. diss., Case Western Reserve University, Cleveland, 1975.

Scott, Kathleen L. *The Caxton Master and His Patrons.* Cambridge, 1976.

Scott, Margaret. *The History of Dress: Late-Gothic Europe, 1400–1500.* London and Atlantic Highlands, N.J., 1980.

Segurado, Jorge. *Francisco d'Ollanda.* Lisbon, 1970.

————. "Damião de Goes." *Belas Artes,* 28–29 (1975), pp. 133–84.

Shaw, Henry. *Dresses and Decorations of the Middle Ages.* London, 1843.

Shearman, John. *Mannerism.* Baltimore, 1967.

Sherman, Claire Richter. *The Portraits of Charles V of France (1338–1380).* New York, 1969.

Sieveking, A. Forbes. "The Medieval Garden as Pictured in the 'Roman de la Rose.'" *Country Life,* 14 (1903), pp. 916–20.

Smith, Robert C. *The Art of Portugal 1500–1800.* New York, 1968.

Snyder, James. "The Early Haarlem School of Painting, Part III: The Problem of Geertgen tot Sint Jans and Jan Mostaert." *Art Bulletin,* 53 (1971), pp. 445–58.

Solente, Suzanne. *Bibliothèque nationale: Nouvelles acquisitions latines et françaises de la Département des Manuscrits pendant les années 1951–1957. Inventaire sommaire.* Paris, 1960.

Spencer, Eleanor P. "Dom Louis de Busco's Psalter." In *Gatherings in Honor of Dorothy E. Miner.* Ed. by Ursula E. McCracken, Lilian M. C. Randall, Richard H. Randall, Jr. Baltimore, 1974, pp. 227–40.

Sterling, Charles. *La Peinture francaise: Les primitifs*. Paris, 1938.

———. "Une Peinture certaine de Perréal enfin retrouvée." *L'Oeil*, nos. 103–104 (1963), pp. 2–15, 64–65.

———. *The Master of Claude, Queen of France: A Newly Defined Miniaturist*. New York, 1975.

———. "Un Nouveau Tableau de Simon Marmion." *Revue d'Art Canadienne/Canadian Art Review*, 8 (1981), pp. 3–18.

Sterling, Charles, and Claude Schaefer. *The Hours of Etienne Chevalier, Jean Fouquet, Musée Condé, Chantilly*. New York, 1971.

Stirling-Maxwell, William. *The Chief Victories of the Emperor Charles V: Designed by Martin Heemskerck in M.D.LV. and Now Illustrated with Portraits, Prints, and Notes*. London and Edinburgh, 1870.

Tagliente, Giovanni Antonio. *Lo Presente Libro insegna la vera arte de lo excelléte scriuere. . . .* Venice, 1524.

Thieme, U., and F. Becker. *Allgemeines Lexikon der bildenden Künstler*. 37 vols. Leipzig, 1907–50.

Thomas, Marcel. *Histoire de la destruction de Troye la grant*. Paris, 1973.

Thompson, Henry Yates. *A Descriptive Catalogue of Twenty Illuminated Manuscripts, Nos. LXXV to XCIV (Replacing Twenty Discarded from the Original Hundred) in the Collection of Henry Yates Thompson*. Cambridge, 1907.

———. *Illustrations of One Hundred Manuscripts in the Library of Henry Yates Thompson*. 7 vols. London, 1907–18.

Thorpe, James. *Book of Hours: Illuminations by Simon Marmion* [in the Huntington Library]. San Marino, Calif. [1977].

Tolnay, Charles de. "Studien zu den Gemälden Pieter Bruegels der Ältere." *Jahrbuch der Kunsthistorischen Sammlungen in Wien*, 8 (1934), pp. 105–35.

Torresan, Paolo. "Libri d'ore franco-fiamminghi del XV e XVI secoli conservati nelle Biblioteche del Veneto." *Arte Illustrada*, 7 (1974), pp. 73–81.

Tosetti Grandi, P. (a). "Lorenzo Costa miniatore." In *Atti del II convegno di storia della miniatura italiana: La Miniatura italiana tra gotico e rinascimento*. [Cortona.] In press.

———. (b). "Lorenzo Costa." In *Dizionario biografico degli Italiani*. In press.

Trenkler, Ernst. *Rothschild-Gebetbuch Codex Vindobonensis seria nova 2844 des Österreichischen Nationalbibliothek*. Codices selecti, LXVII. Graz, 1979.

Turner, Derek H. *Reproductions from Illuminated Manuscripts* [in the British Museum]. Series V. London, 1965.

———. *Illuminated Manuscripts Exhibited in the Grenville Library* [in the British Museum]. London, 1967.

———. *The Hastings Hours*. London [1983].

Tuve, Rosemond. *Allegorical Imagery: Some Medieval Books and Their Posterity*. Princeton, 1966.

Unterkircher, Franz. *Inventar der illuminierten Handschriften, Inkunabeln und Frühdrucke der Österreichischen Nationalbibliothek*. Vienna, 1957–59.

Vale, M. G. A. *Charles VII*. Berkeley and Los Angeles, 1974.

Van Buren, Anne. "The Master of Mary of Burgundy and His Colleagues: The State of Research and Questions of Method." *Zeitschrift für Kunstgeschichte*, 38 (1975), pp. 286–309.

Van de Waal, H. *Drie Eeuwen vaderlandsche Geschied-Uitbeelding 1500–1800: Een iconologische Studie*. 2 vols. The Hague, 1952.

Van de Walle de Ghelcke, T. "Gerard David." Master's thesis, Université Catholique de Louvain, 1949.

———. "Y a-t-il Gerard David miniaturiste?" In *Album English. Studien over de Kerkelijke en Kunstgeschiedenis van West-Vlaanderen, opgedragen aan Z. E. H. Michiels English*. Bruges, 1952, pp. 399–422.

Vasari, Giorgio. *The Lives of the Painters, Sculptors and Architects*. Trans. by A. B. Hinds. 4 vols. London, 1927.

Vatican City, Biblioteca Vaticana. *Libri manoscritti e stampati del Belgio nella Biblioteca Vaticana, Secoli IX–XVII*. Exhibition catalogue. 1979.

Vaughn, Richard. *Charles the Bold: The Last Valois Duke of Burgundy*. London, 1973.

Vespasiano da Bisticci. *The Vespasiano Memoirs*. Ed. and trans. by William George Waters and Emily Waters. London, 1926.

Vienna, Österreichische Nationalbibliothek. *Manuscrits et livres imprimés concernant l'histoire des Pays-Bas*. Exhibition catalogue. 1962.

Voelkle, William M., ed. *The Pierpont Morgan Library. Masterpieces of Medieval Painting: The Art of Illumination*. Chicago, 1980.

Voronova, T. *Les Grandes Chroniques de France: Enluminures du XVe siècle*. Les Trésors des Musées de l'URSS. Leningrad, 1980.

Vos, Dirk de. *Catalogus Schilderijen: 15de en 16de eeuw*. Bruges, 1979.

Waagen, Gustav Friedrich. *Kunstwerke und Künstler in England und Paris*. 3 vols. Berlin, 1837–39.

———. *Treasures of Art in Great Britain*. 3 vols. London, 1854.

Walbe, B. *Studien zur Entwicklung des allegorischen Porträts in Frankreich von seinen Anfängen bis zur Regierungszeit Heinrichs II*. Frankfurt-am-Main, 1974.

Wallis, Helen. *The Maps and Text of The Boke of Idrography Presented by Jean Rotz to Henry VIII now in the British Library*. Oxford, 1981.

Ward, Henry Leigh Douglas. *Catalogue of Romances in the Department of Manuscripts in the British Museum*. 3 vols. London, 1883–1910.

Wardrop, James. "Arrighi Revived." *Signature*, 1 (1939), pp. 26–46.

———. "Pierantonio Sallando and Girolamo Pagliarolo: Scribes to Giovanni II Bentivoglio." *Signature*, 2 (1946), pp. 4–30.

———. *The Script of Humanism: Some Aspects of Humanistic Script, 1460–1560*. Oxford, 1963.

Warner, George Frederic. *Miniatures and Borders from the Book of Hours of Bona Sforza, Duchess of Milan, in the British Museum*. London, 1894.

———. *Illuminated Manuscripts in the British Museum. Miniatures, Borders, and Initials, Reproduced in Gold and Colours*. Series I–IV. London, 1903.

———. *Valerius Maximus. Miniatures of the School of Jean Fouquet*. London, 1907.

———. *Reproductions from Illuminated Manuscripts* [in the British Museum]. Series I–III. 2nd ed. 3 vols. London, 1910.

———. *Descriptive Catalogue of Illuminated Manuscripts in the Library of C. W. Dyson Perrins*. 2 vols. Oxford, 1920.

Warner, George Frederic, and Julius P. Gilson. *Catalogue of Western Manuscripts in the Old Royal and King's Collections* [in the British Museum]. 4 vols. London, 1921.

Washington, D.C., United States Library of Congress. *The Lessing J. Rosenwald Collection: A Catalog of the Gifts . . . to the Library of Congress, 1943 to 1975*. Washington, D.C., 1977.

Watson, Andrew G. *Catalogue of Dated and Datable Manuscripts, c. 700–1600, in the Department of Manuscripts, The British Library*. 2 vols. London, 1979.

Waywell, G. B. "A Roman Grave Altar Rediscovered." *American Journal of Archaeology*, 86 (1982), pp. 238–42.

Weale, W. H. James, "Gérard David," *Le Beffroi*, 1 (1863), pp. 223–34.

———. "Gérard David II. 1: Oeuvres attribuées." *Gazette des Beaux-Arts*, 21 (1866), pp. 489–501.

———. "Les Enlumineurs de Bruges." *Le Beffroi*, 4 (1872–73), pp. 111–19, 233–37.

———. *Gerard David: Painter and Illuminator*. London, 1895.

———. Review of *Ahnenreihen aus dem Stammbaum des portugiesischen Königshauses, Miniaturenfolge in der Bibliothek des British Museum* by Ludwig Kaemmerer and H. G. Ströhl. *Burlington Magazine*, 3 (1903), pp. 321–24.

Weinberger, Martin. *Michelangelo, the Sculptor*. 2 vols. New York, 1967.

Wescher, Paul. "Sanders and Simon Bening and Gerard Horenbout." *Art Quarterly*, 9 (1946), pp. 191–211.

———. *Jean Fouquet and His Time*. New York, 1947.

———. "New Light on Jean Clouet as a Portrait Painter." *Apollo*, 103 (1976), pp. 16–21.

White, John. *Art and Architecture in Italy 1250–1400*. Baltimore, 1966.

Winkler, Friedrich. 1913a. "Gerard David und die Brügger Miniaturmalerei seiner Zeit." *Monatsheft für Kunstwissenschaft*, 6 (1913), pp. 271–80.

———. 1913b. "Miniaturen der Clara de Keysere?" *Mitteilungen der Gesellschaft für vervielfältigende Kunst*. Beilage der *Graphischen Künste*, 2 (1913), pp. 49–53.

———. 1913c. "Simon Marmion als Miniaturmaler." *Jahrbuch der Königlich Preussischen Kunstsammlungen*, 34 (1913), pp. 251–80.

———. "Der Brügger Meister des Dresdener Gebetbuches und seine Werke." *Jahrbuch der Königlich Preussischen Kunstsammlungen*, 35 (1914), pp. 225–44.

———. "Studien zur Geschichte der niederländischen Miniaturmalerei des XV. und XVI. Jahrhunderts." *Jahrbuch der Kunsthistorischen Sammlungen des allerhöchsten Kaiserhauses*, 32 (1915), pp. 279–342.

———. *Der Leipziger Valerius Maximus mit einer Einleitung über die Anfänge des Sittenbildes in den Niederlanden*. Leipzig, 1921.

———. *Die flämische Buchmalerei des XV. und XVI. Jahrhunderts*. Leipzig, 1925.

———. "Neuentdeckte Altniederländer: II, Gerard Horenbout." *Pantheon*, 31 (1943), pp. 55–64.

———. "Das Gebetbuch des Kardinals Albrecht von Brandenburg." *Aachener Kunstblätter des Museumsvereins*, 34–35 (1962–63), pp. 7–107.

———. *Das Werk des Hugo van der Goes*. Berlin, 1964.

Winter, Patrick de. "A Book of Hours of Queen Isabel la Católica." *Bulletin of the Cleveland Museum of Art*, 68 (1981), pp. 342–427.

Wright, Cyril E. *Fontes Harleiani. A Study of the Sources of the Harleian Collection of Manuscripts in the British Museum*. London, 1972.

Wright, Cyril E., and Ruth C. Wright. *The Diary of Humfrey Wanley: 1715–1726*. 2 vols. London, 1966.

Index

Page numbers in **boldface** refer to illustrations.

210   Index

Photo Credits

All photographs have been supplied by the British Library or the authors except in the instances listed below.